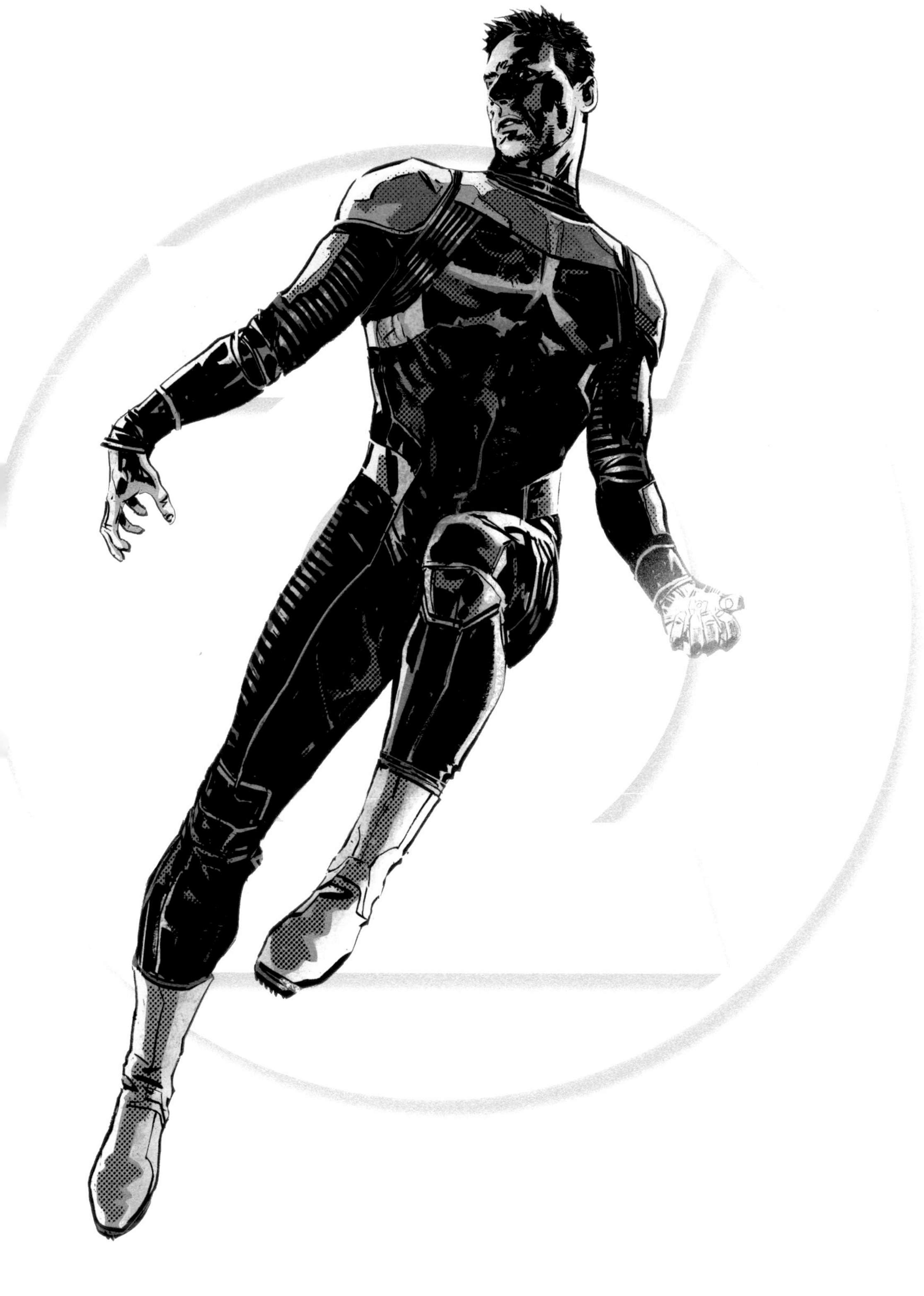

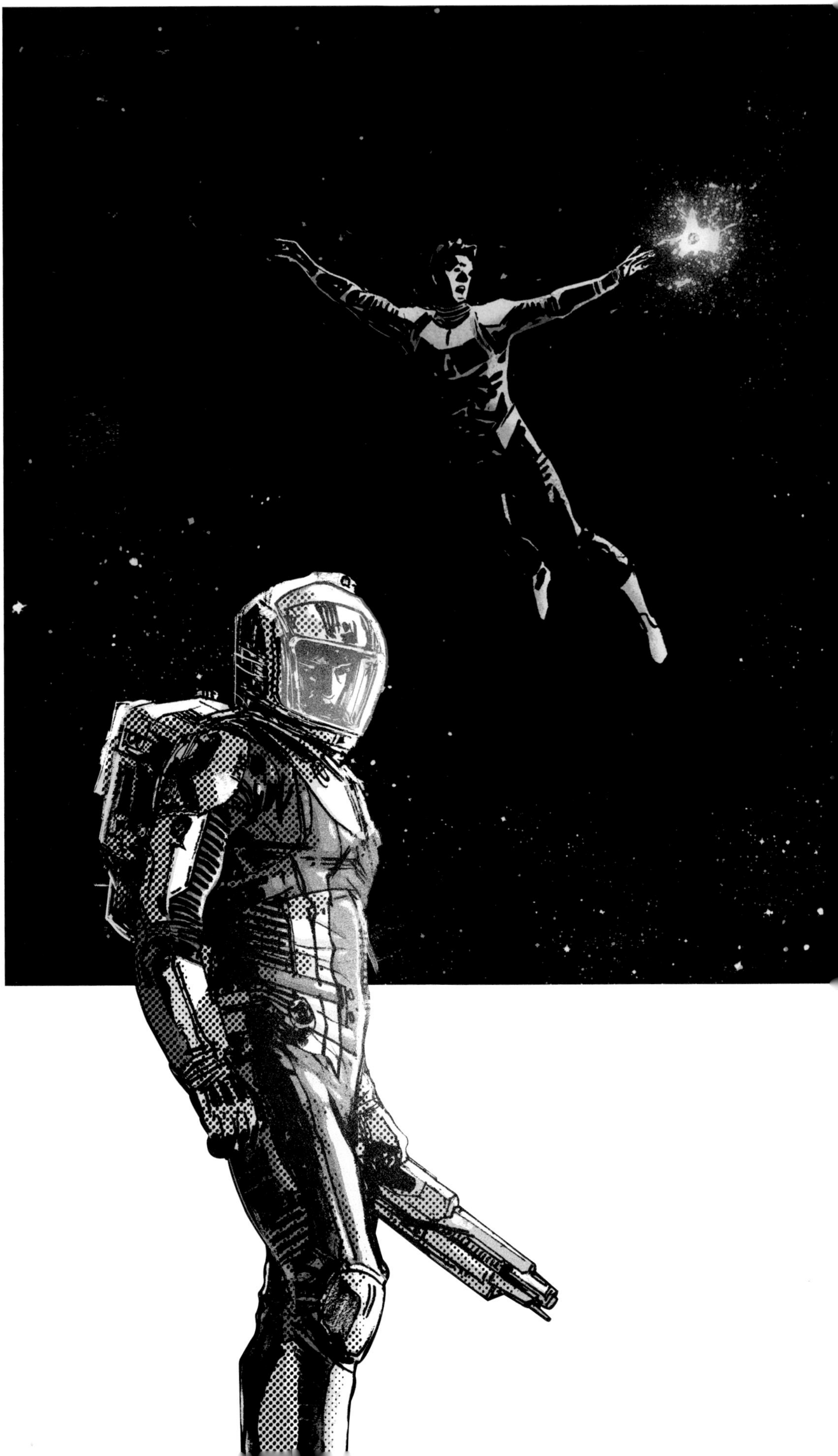

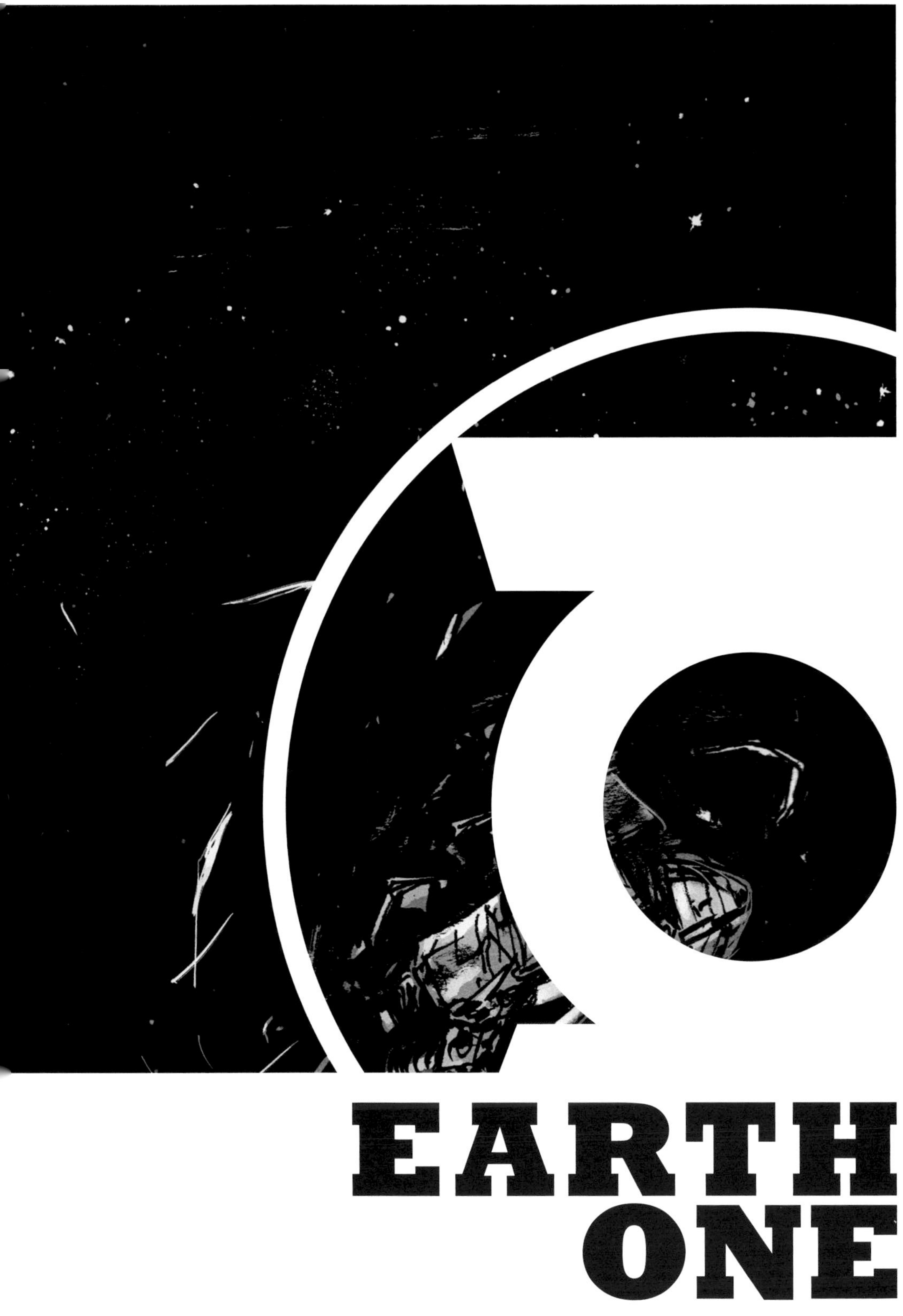

EARTH ONE

Written by Corinna Bechko and Gabriel Hardman

Art by Gabriel Hardman

Colors by Jordan Boyd

Letters by Simon Bowland

Cover by Gabriel Hardman & Jordan Boyd

Kristy Quinn Editor
Steve Cook Design Director – Books
Louis Prandi Publication Design

Bob Harras Senior VP – Editor-in-Chief, DC Comics
Pat McCallum Executive Editor, DC Comics

Diane Nelson President
Dan DiDio Publisher
Jim Lee Publisher
Geoff Johns President & Chief Creative Officer
Amit Desai Executive VP – Business & Marketing Strategy,
Direct to Consumer & Global Franchise Management
Sam Ades Senior VP & General Manager, Digital Services
Bobbie Chase VP & Executive Editor, Young Reader & Talent Development
Mark Chiarello Senior VP – Art, Design & Collected Editions
John Cunningham Senior VP – Sales & Trade Marketing
Anne DePies Senior VP – Business Strategy, Finance & Administration
Don Falletti VP – Manufacturing Operations
Lawrence Ganem VP – Editorial Administration & Talent Relations
Alison Gill Senior VP – Manufacturing & Operations
Hank Kanalz Senior VP – Editorial Strategy & Administration
Jay Kogan VP – Legal Affairs
Jack Mahan VP – Business Affairs
Nick J. Napolitano VP – Manufacturing Administration
Eddie Scannell VP – Consumer Marketing
Courtney Simmons Senior VP – Publicity & Communications
Jim (Ski) Sokolowski VP – Comic Book Specialty Sales & Trade Marketing
Nancy Spears VP – Mass, Book, Digital Sales & Trade Marketing
Michele R. Wells VP – Content Strategy

 GREEN LANTERN: EARTH ONE VOLUME ONE

March, 2018. Published by DC Comics, 2900 W. Alameda Avenue, Burbank, CA 91505. GST # is R125921072. Copyright © 2018 DC Comics. All Rights Reserved. All characters featured in this issue, the distinctive likenesses thereof and related elements are trademarks of DC Comics. The stories, characters and incidents mentioned in this magazine are entirely fictional. DC Comics does not read or accept unsolicited submissions of ideas, stories or artwork. For Advertising and Custom Publishing contact dccomicsadvertising@dccomics. com. For details on DC Comics Ratings, visit dccomics.com/go/ratings.

Printed by LSC Communications, Kendallville, IN, USA. 2/9/18.
First Printing. ISBN: 978-1-4012-4186-5

Library of Congress Cataloging-in-Publication Data

Names: Bechko, Corinna, 1973- writer. | Hardman, Gabriel, writer, artist. | Boyd, Jordan, colourist, artist. | Bowland, Simon, letterer.
Title: Green Lantern : earth one / written by Corinna Bechko and Gabriel Hardman ; art by Gabriel Hardman ; colors by Jordan Boyd ; letters by Simon Bowland ; cover by Gabriel Hardman & Jordan Boyd.
Description: Burbank, CA : DC Comics, 2018-
Identifiers: LCCN 2017060572 | ISBN 9781401241865 (v. 1 : hardback)
Subjects: LCSH: Comic books, strips, etc. | BISAC: COMICS & GRAPHIC NOVELS /
Superheroes.
Classification: LCC PN6728.G74 B27 2018 | DDC 741.5/973--dc23
LC record available at https://lccn.loc.gov/2017060572

PEFC Certified
Printed on paper from sustainably managed forests, controlled sources
PEFC/29-31-337
www.pefc.org

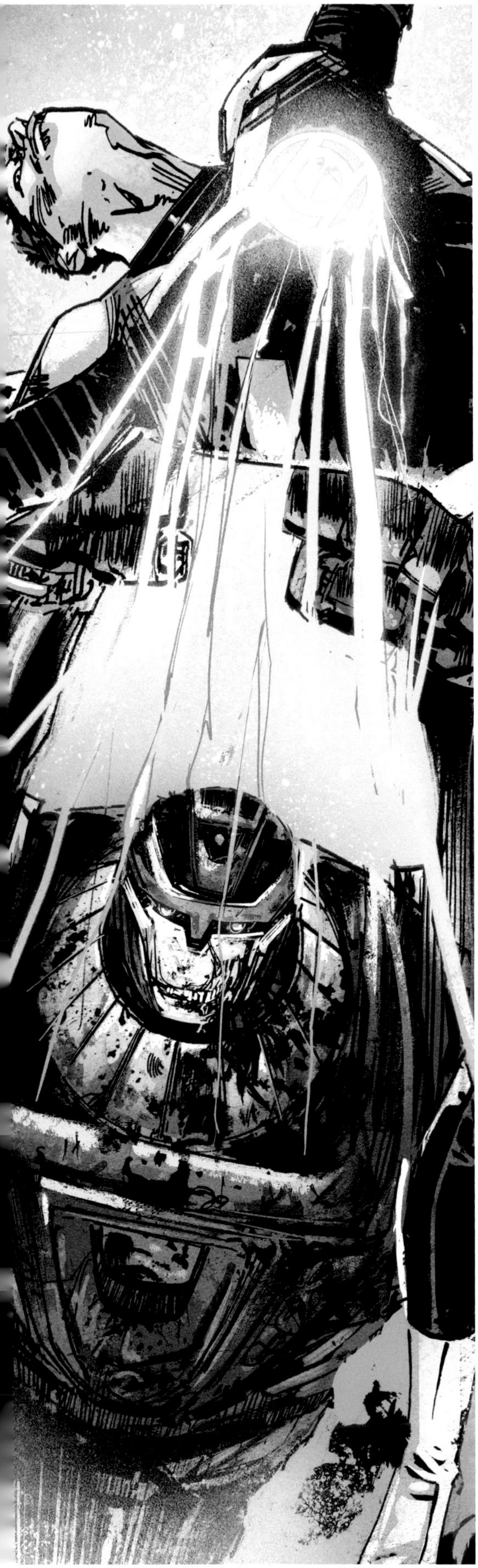

DEDICATIONS

For my one algebra teacher who embraced the fact that everyone learns differently. Thanks to him, I will always associate calculations with music, and never forget that space exploration is impossible without the equivalent of long drum solos.

And for everyone else who shares his vision that we can find the solution to any problem if we just think about it the right way.

— Corinna

For Camila, my best pal.

— Gabriel

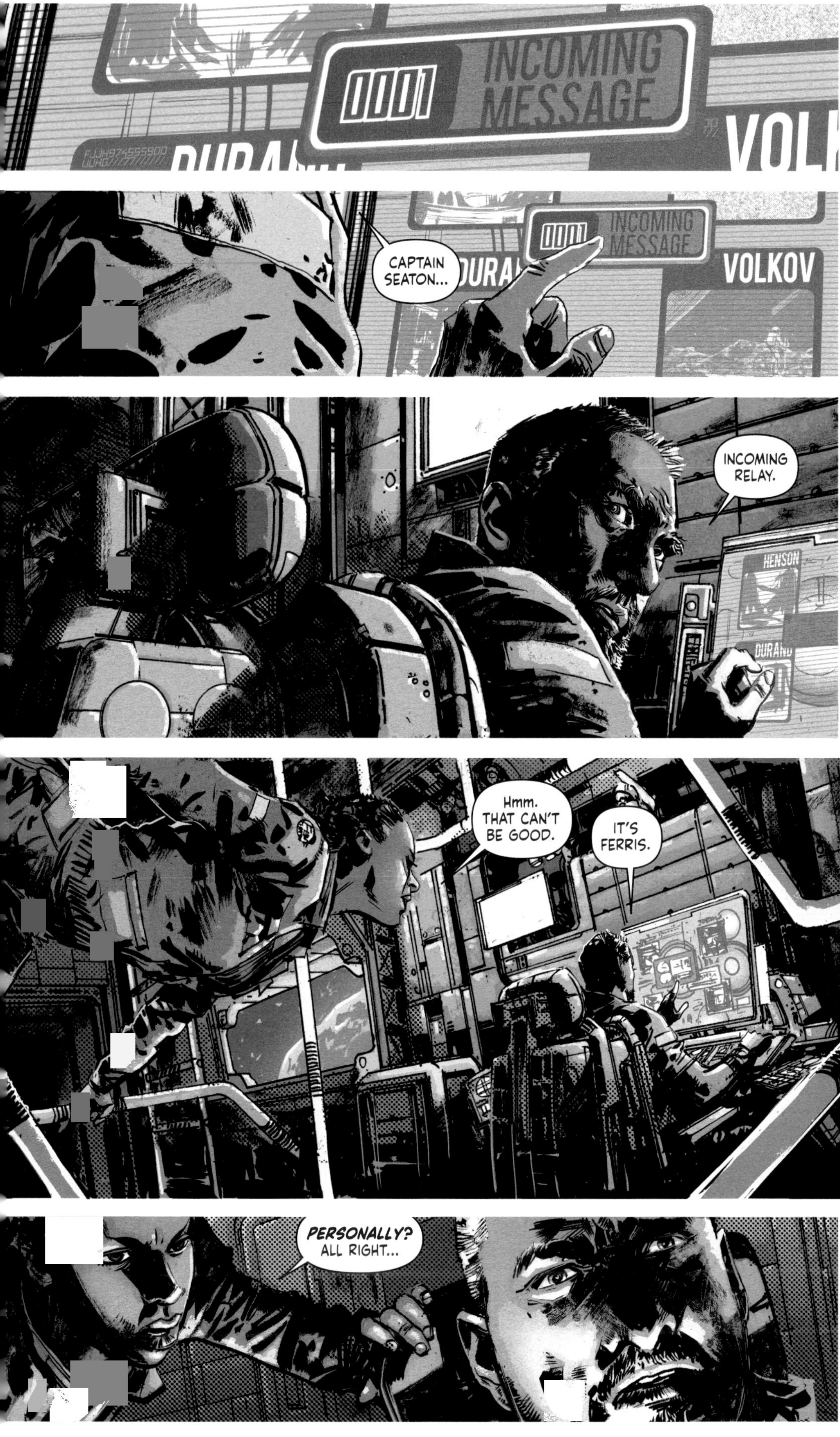
0001
INCOMING MESSAGE
DURAND
VOLK
CAPTAIN SEATON...
0001
INCOMING MESSAGE
VOLKOV
INCOMING RELAY.
HENSON
DURAND
Hmm. THAT CAN'T BE GOOD.
IT'S FERRIS.
PERSONALLY? ALL RIGHT...

FERRIS 6
MONARCHA ENERGY
PALLADIUM MINING
EXPEDITION OPERATED
BY FERRIS GALACTIC

...LET'S SEE IT.

ASTEROID BELT
BETWEEN MARS
AND JUPITER

UNCLAIMED
ASTEROID 89

METALLIC CONTENT BELOW VIABLE THRESHOLD

DAMN.

EIGHT-NINE-FIVE, THIS IS SIX, ROGER.

LISTEN UP, EVERYBODY.

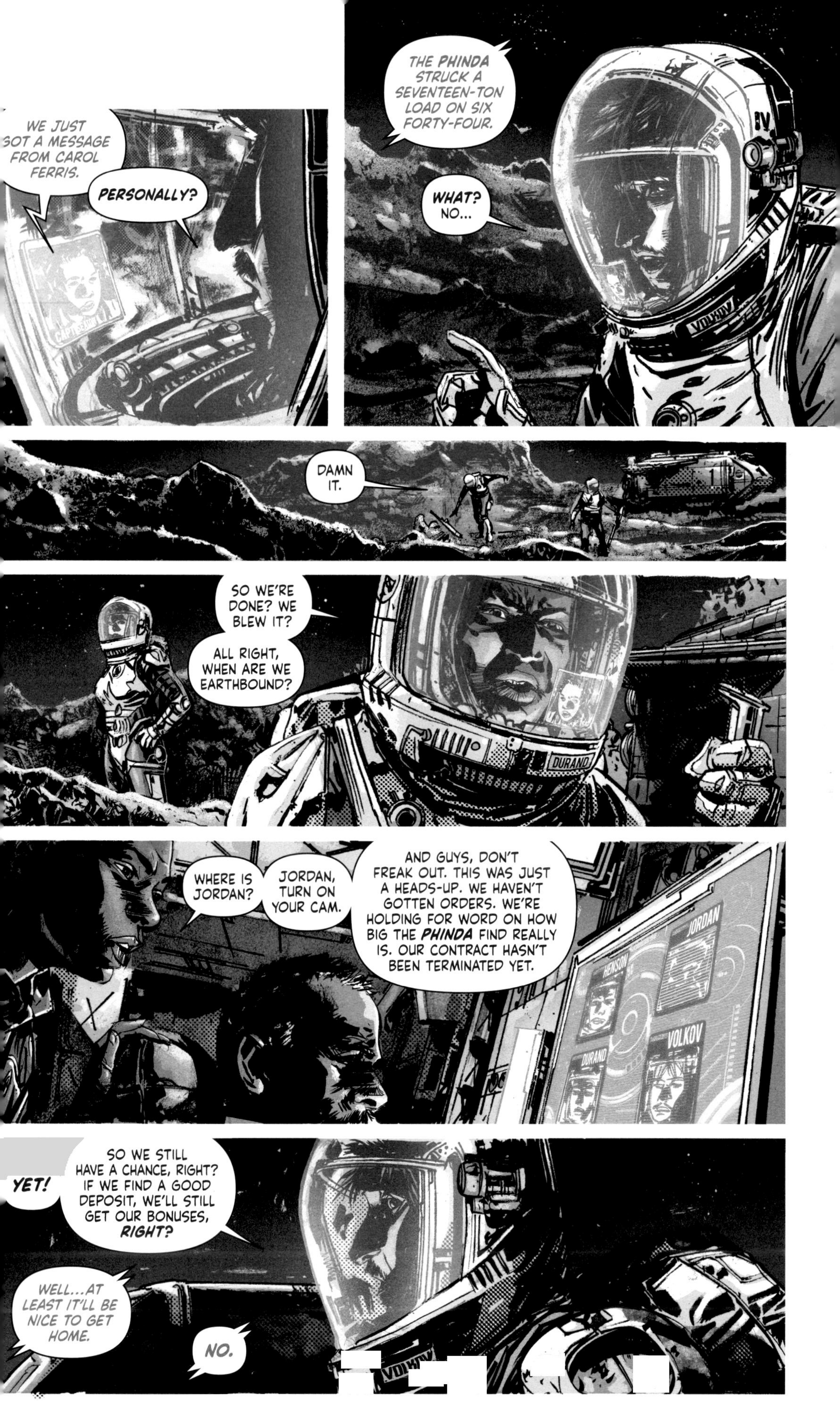

WE JUST GOT A MESSAGE FROM CAROL FERRIS.
PERSONALLY?
THE PHINDA STRUCK A SEVENTEEN-TON LOAD ON SIX FORTY-FOUR.
WHAT? NO...
VOLKOV
DAMN IT.
SO WE'RE DONE? WE BLEW IT?
ALL RIGHT, WHEN ARE WE EARTHBOUND?
DURAND
WHERE IS JORDAN?
JORDAN, TURN ON YOUR CAM.
AND GUYS, DON'T FREAK OUT. THIS WAS JUST A HEADS-UP. WE HAVEN'T GOTTEN ORDERS. WE'RE HOLDING FOR WORD ON HOW BIG THE PHINDA FIND REALLY IS. OUR CONTRACT HASN'T BEEN TERMINATED YET.
HENSON
JORDAN
DURAND
VOLKOV
YET!
SO WE STILL HAVE A CHANCE, RIGHT? IF WE FIND A GOOD DEPOSIT, WE'LL STILL GET OUR BONUSES, RIGHT?
WELL...AT LEAST IT'LL BE NICE TO GET HOME.
NO.

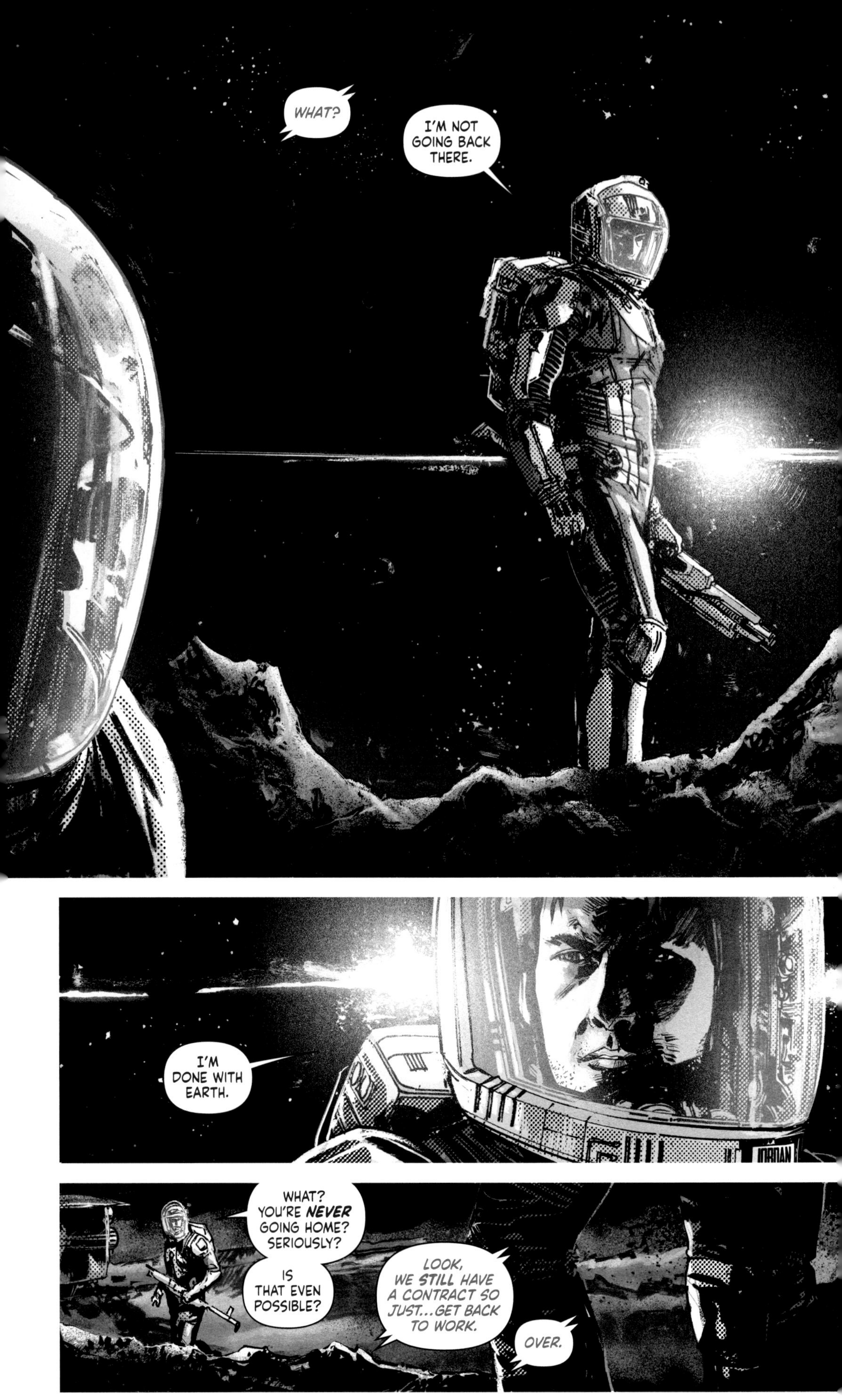
WHAT?
I'M NOT GOING BACK THERE.
I'M DONE WITH EARTH.
WHAT? YOU'RE NEVER GOING HOME? SERIOUSLY?
IS THAT EVEN POSSIBLE?
LOOK, WE STILL HAVE A CONTRACT SO JUST...GET BACK TO WORK.
OVER.

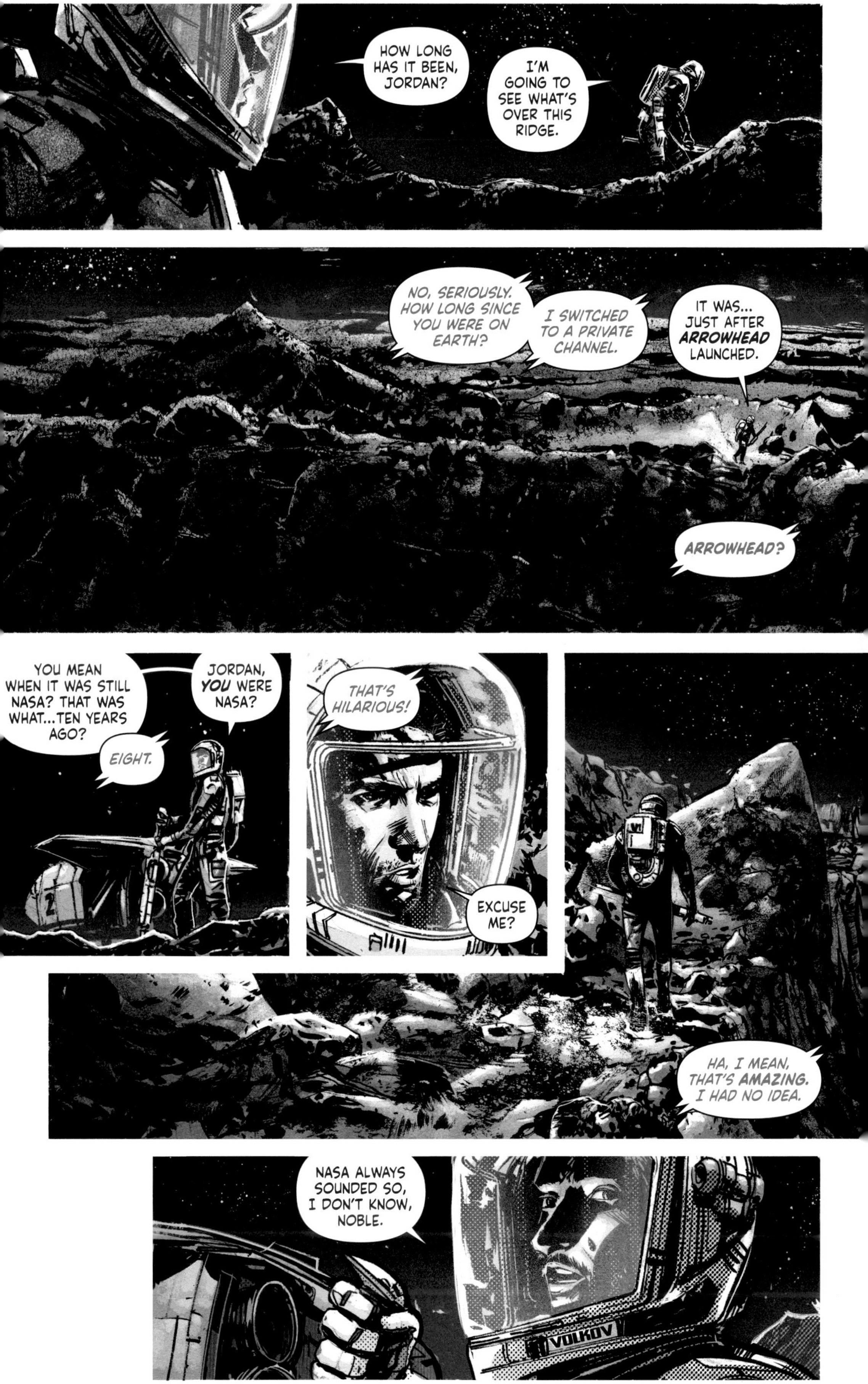
HOW LONG HAS IT BEEN, JORDAN?
I'M GOING TO SEE WHAT'S OVER THIS RIDGE.
NO, SERIOUSLY. HOW LONG SINCE YOU WERE ON EARTH?
I SWITCHED TO A PRIVATE CHANNEL.
IT WAS... JUST AFTER ARROWHEAD LAUNCHED.
ARROWHEAD?
YOU MEAN WHEN IT WAS STILL NASA? THAT WAS WHAT...TEN YEARS AGO?
JORDAN, YOU WERE NASA?
EIGHT.
THAT'S HILARIOUS!
EXCUSE ME?
HA, I MEAN, THAT'S AMAZING. I HAD NO IDEA.
NASA ALWAYS SOUNDED SO, I DON'T KNOW, NOBLE.
VOLKOV

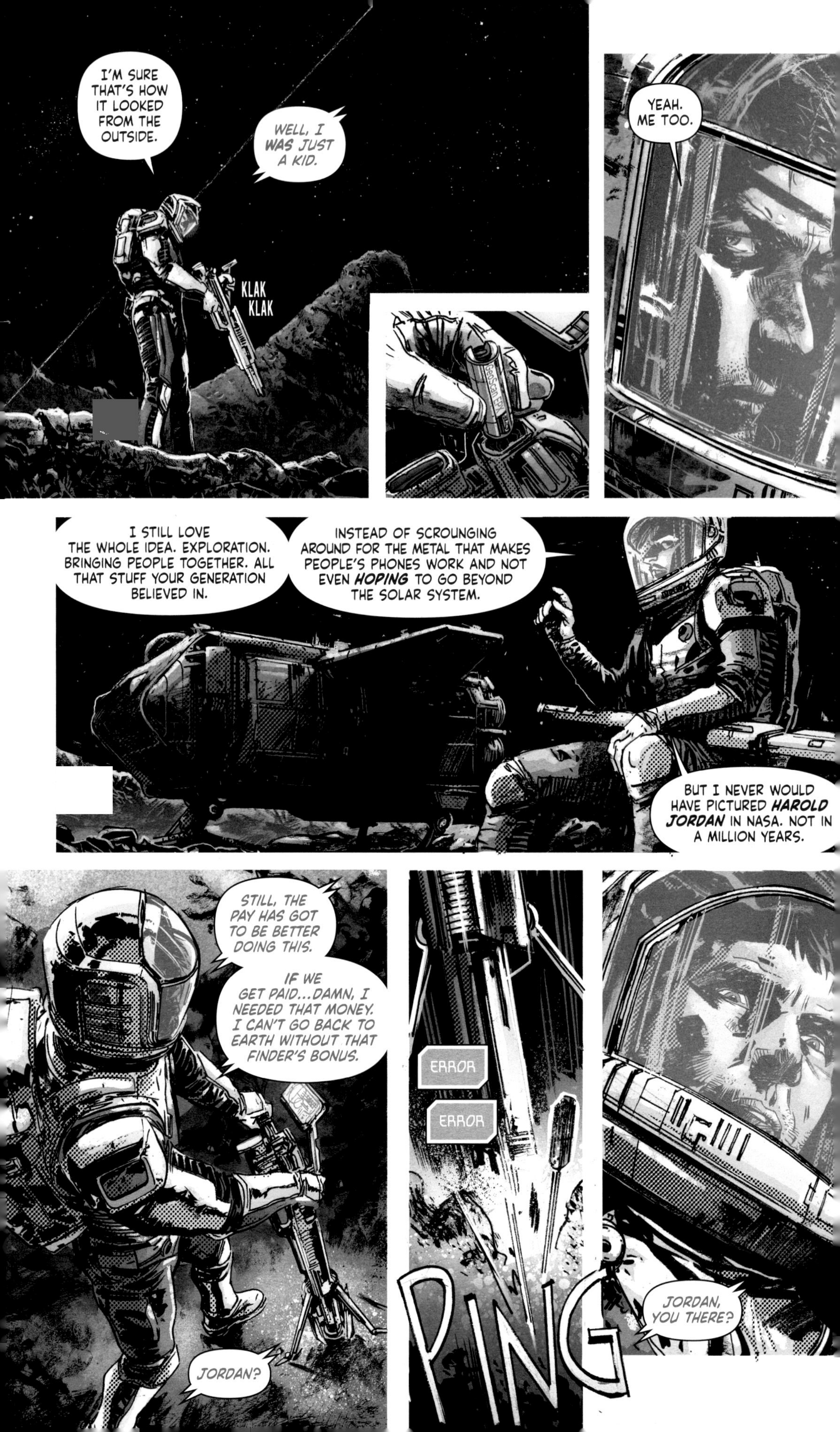
I'M SURE THAT'S HOW IT LOOKED FROM THE OUTSIDE.
WELL, I WAS JUST A KID.
KLAK KLAK
YEAH. ME TOO.
I STILL LOVE THE WHOLE IDEA. EXPLORATION. BRINGING PEOPLE TOGETHER. ALL THAT STUFF YOUR GENERATION BELIEVED IN.
INSTEAD OF SCROUNGING AROUND FOR THE METAL THAT MAKES PEOPLE'S PHONES WORK AND NOT EVEN HOPING TO GO BEYOND THE SOLAR SYSTEM.
BUT I NEVER WOULD HAVE PICTURED HAROLD JORDAN IN NASA. NOT IN A MILLION YEARS.
STILL, THE PAY HAS GOT TO BE BETTER DOING THIS.
IF WE GET PAID...DAMN, I NEEDED THAT MONEY. I CAN'T GO BACK TO EARTH WITHOUT THAT FINDER'S BONUS.
JORDAN?
ERROR
ERROR
PING
JORDAN, YOU THERE?

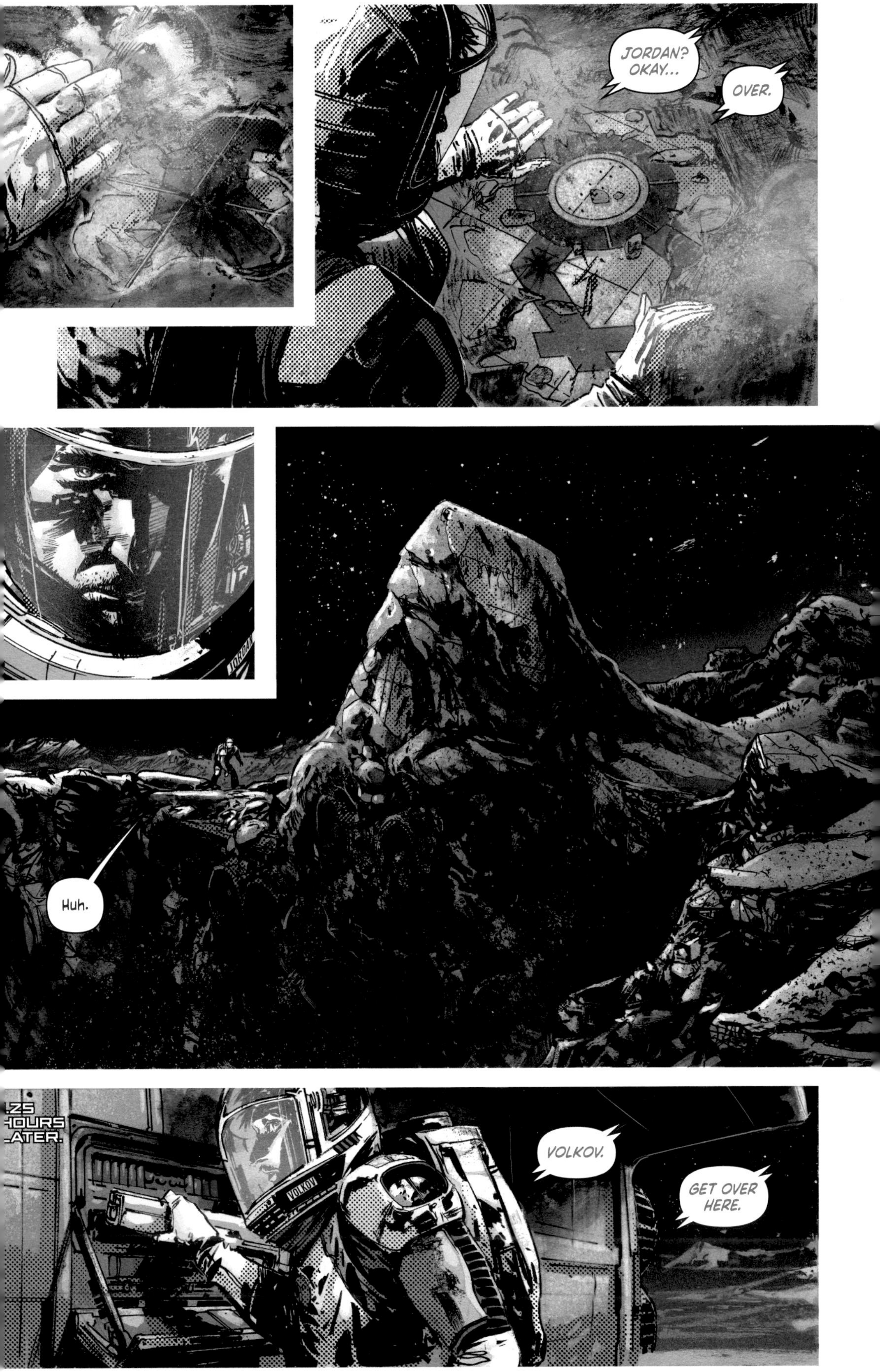
JORDAN? OKAY...
OVER.
Huh.
.25 HOURS LATER.
VOLKOV.
GET OVER HERE.

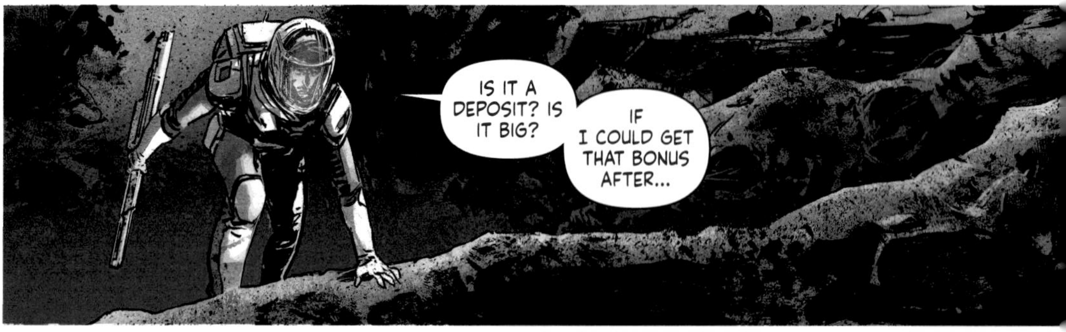
IS IT A DEPOSIT? IS IT BIG?
IF I COULD GET THAT BONUS AFTER...

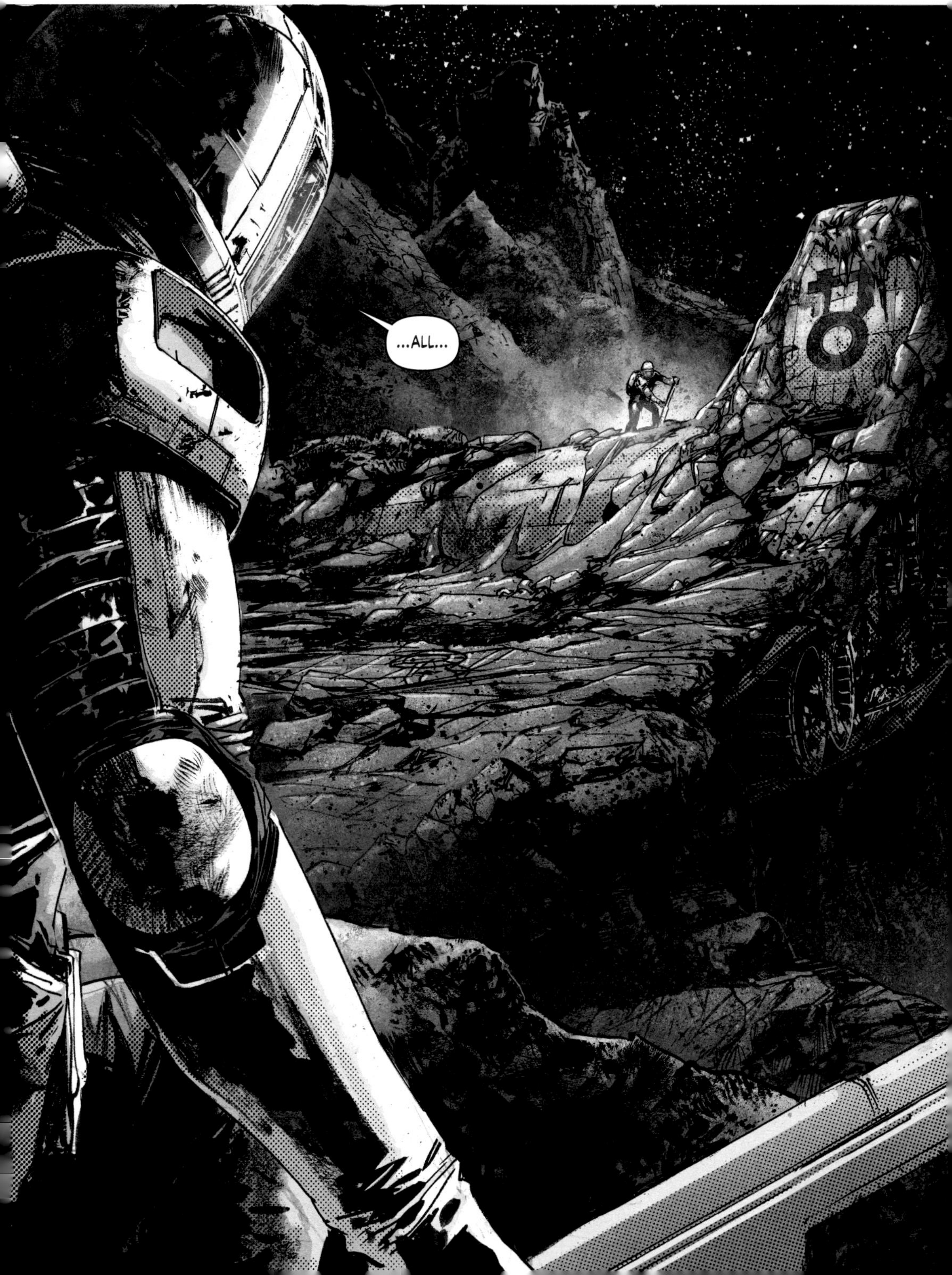
...ALL...

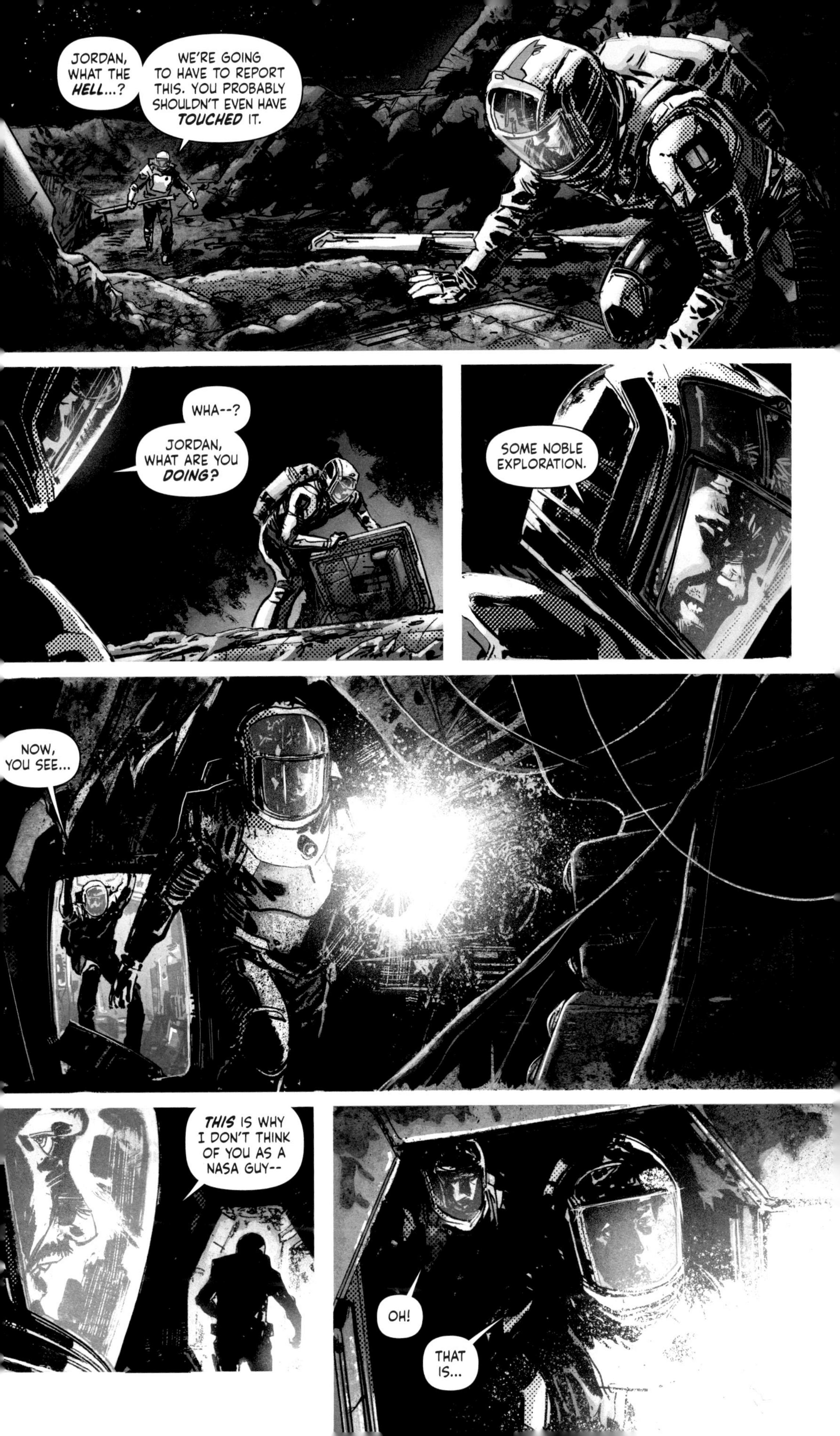
JORDAN, WHAT THE *HELL*...?
WE'RE GOING TO HAVE TO REPORT THIS. YOU PROBABLY SHOULDN'T EVEN HAVE *TOUCHED* IT.
WHA--?
JORDAN, WHAT ARE YOU *DOING?*
SOME NOBLE EXPLORATION.
NOW, YOU SEE...
THIS IS WHY I DON'T THINK OF YOU AS A NASA GUY--
OH!
THAT IS...

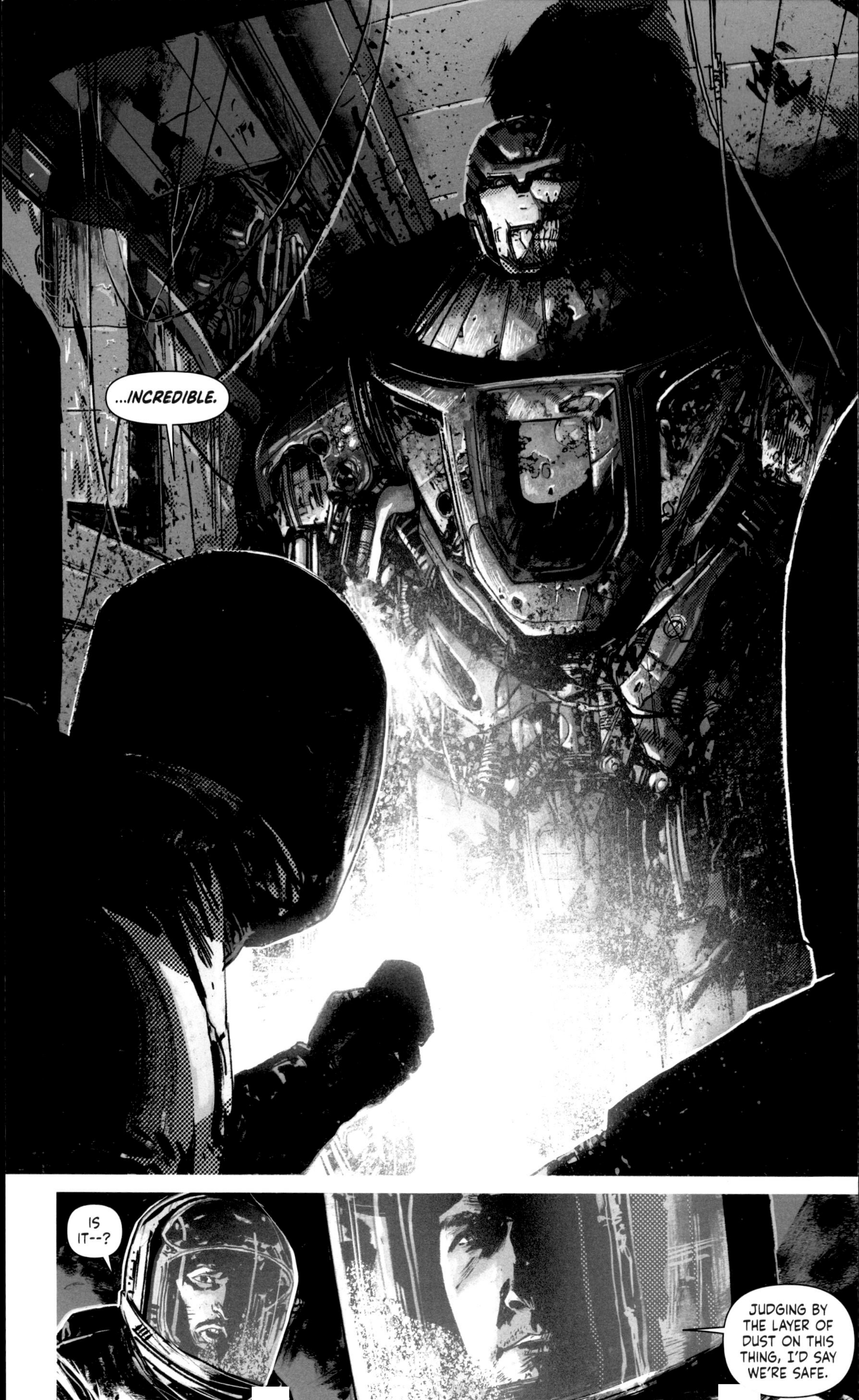
...INCREDIBLE.
IS IT--?
JUDGING BY THE LAYER OF DUST ON THIS THING, I'D SAY WE'RE SAFE.

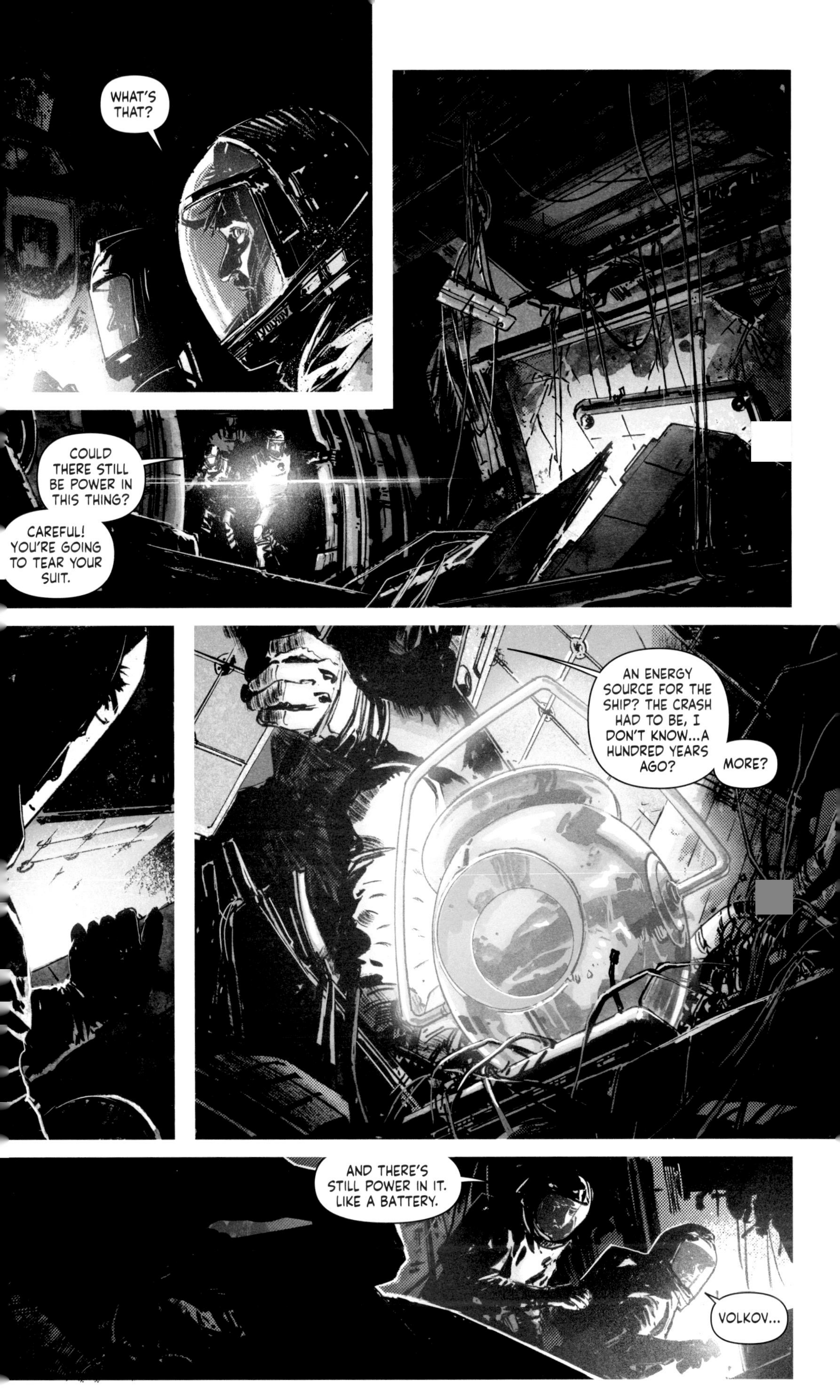
WHAT'S THAT?
COULD THERE STILL BE POWER IN THIS THING?
CAREFUL! YOU'RE GOING TO TEAR YOUR SUIT.
AN ENERGY SOURCE FOR THE SHIP? THE CRASH HAD TO BE, I DON'T KNOW...A HUNDRED YEARS AGO?
MORE?
AND THERE'S STILL POWER IN IT. LIKE A BATTERY.
VOLKOV...

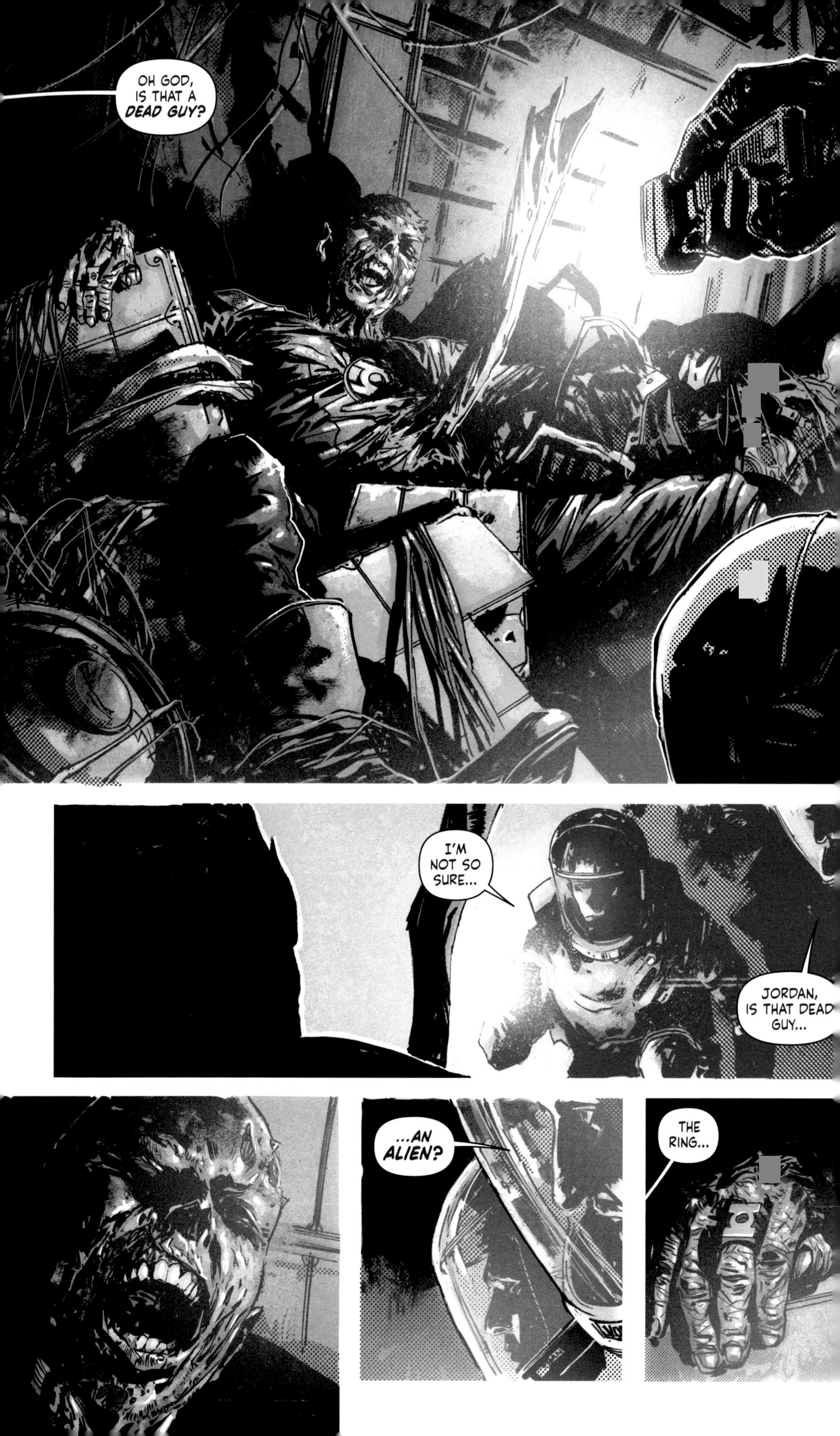
OH GOD, IS THAT A DEAD GUY?
I'M NOT SO SURE...
JORDAN, IS THAT DEAD GUY...
...AN ALIEN?
THE RING...

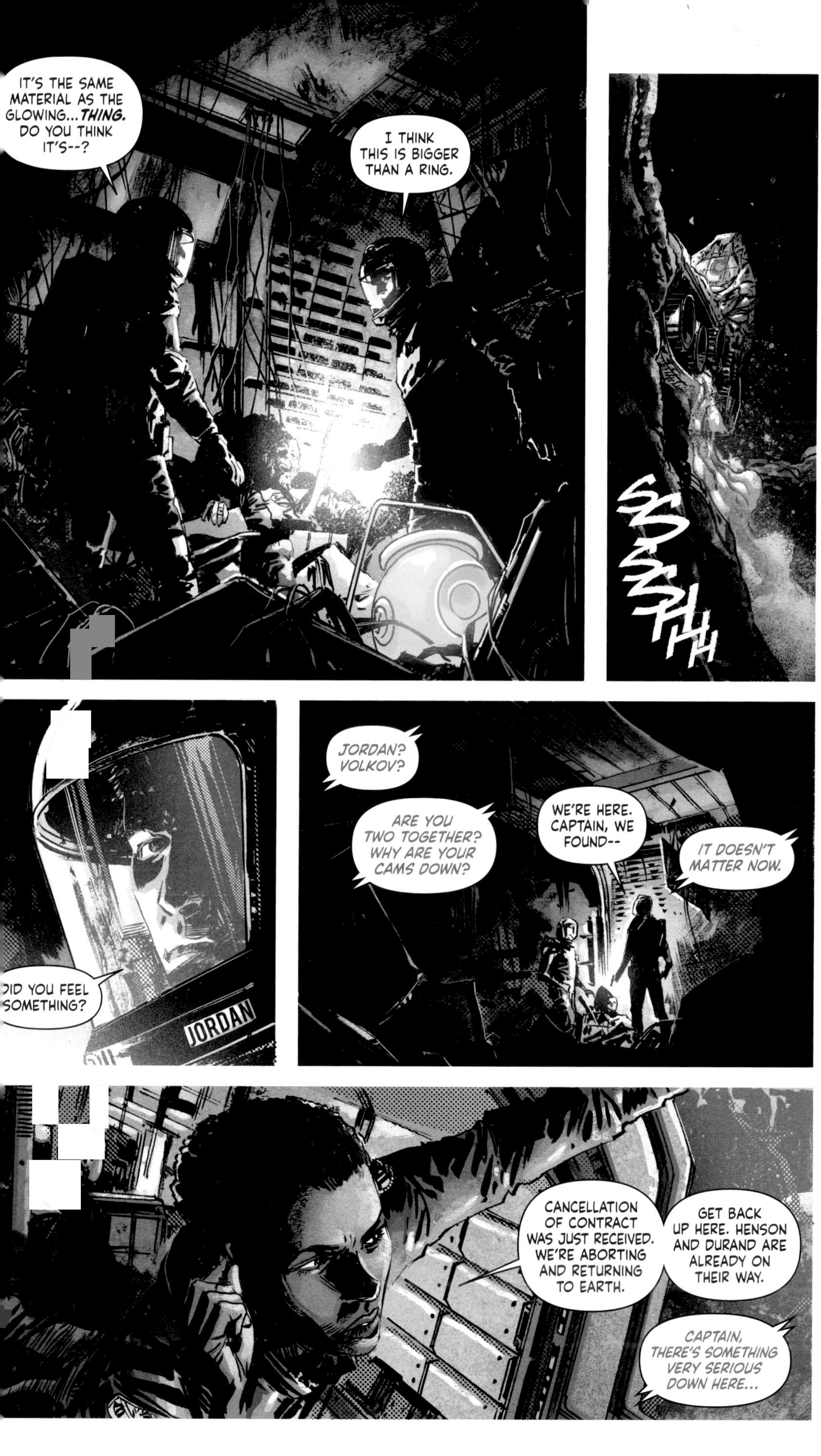

IT'S THE SAME MATERIAL AS THE GLOWING...THING. DO YOU THINK IT'S--?
I THINK THIS IS BIGGER THAN A RING.
SSSSHHH
DID YOU FEEL SOMETHING?
JORDAN
JORDAN? VOLKOV?
ARE YOU TWO TOGETHER? WHY ARE YOUR CAMS DOWN?
WE'RE HERE. CAPTAIN, WE FOUND--
IT DOESN'T MATTER NOW.
CANCELLATION OF CONTRACT WAS JUST RECEIVED. WE'RE ABORTING AND RETURNING TO EARTH.
GET BACK UP HERE. HENSON AND DURAND ARE ALREADY ON THEIR WAY.
CAPTAIN, THERE'S SOMETHING VERY SERIOUS DOWN HERE...

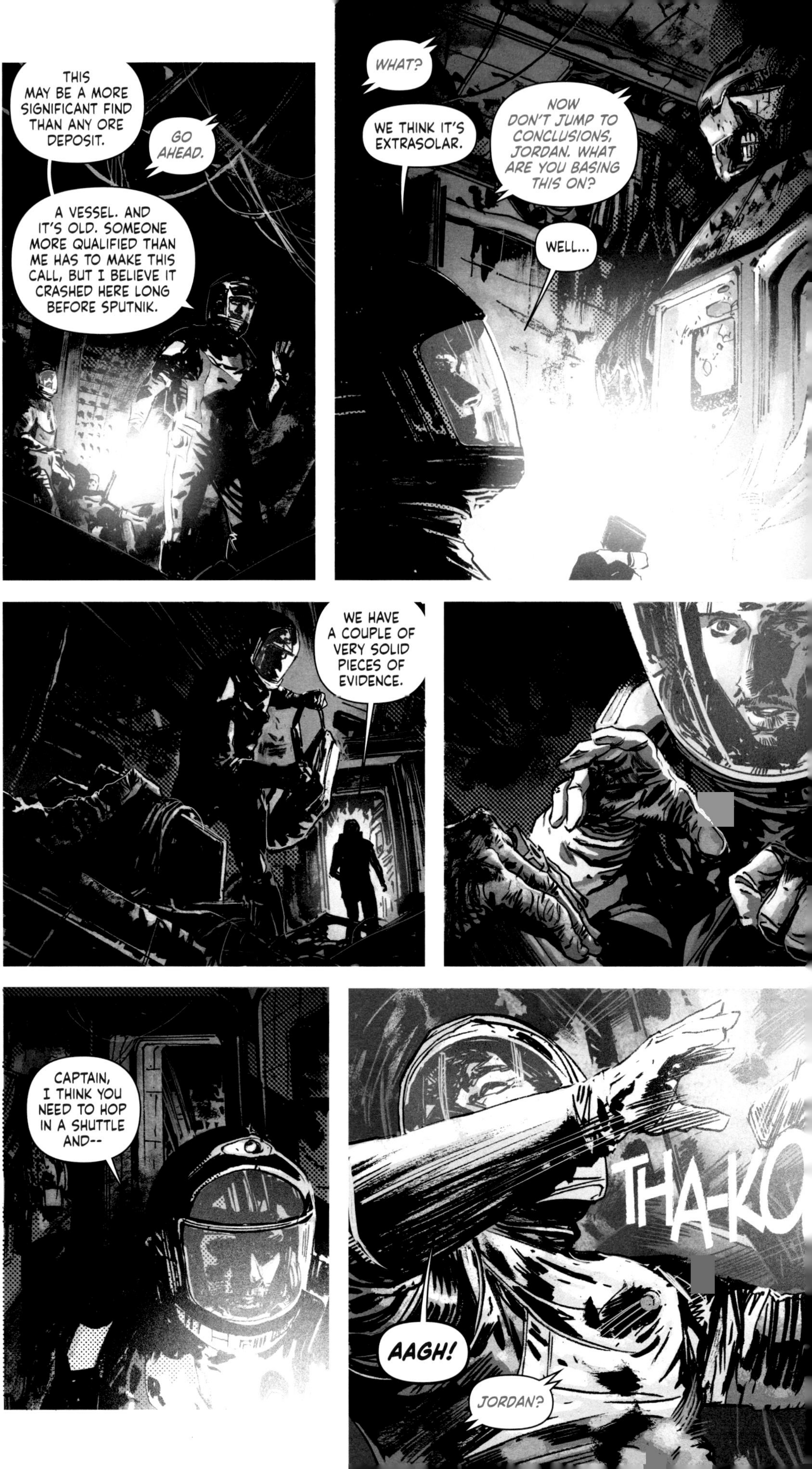
THIS MAY BE A MORE SIGNIFICANT FIND THAN ANY ORE DEPOSIT.
GO AHEAD.
A VESSEL. AND IT'S OLD. SOMEONE MORE QUALIFIED THAN ME HAS TO MAKE THIS CALL, BUT I BELIEVE IT CRASHED HERE LONG BEFORE SPUTNIK.
WHAT?
WE THINK IT'S EXTRASOLAR.
NOW DON'T JUMP TO CONCLUSIONS, JORDAN. WHAT ARE YOU BASING THIS ON?
WELL...
WE HAVE A COUPLE OF VERY SOLID PIECES OF EVIDENCE.
CAPTAIN, I THINK YOU NEED TO HOP IN A SHUTTLE AND--
THA-KO
AAGH!
JORDAN?

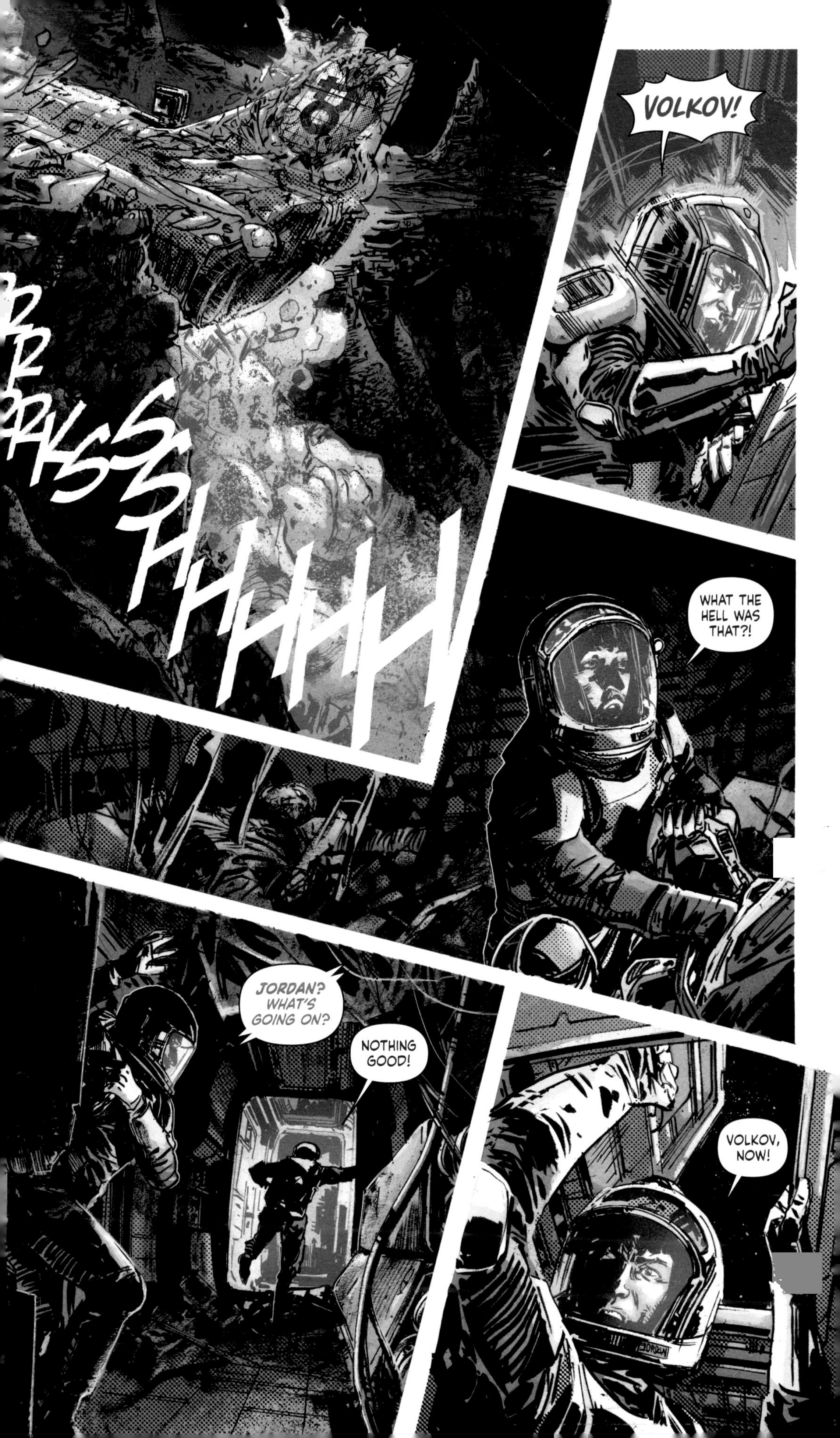
VOLKOV!
WHAT THE HELL WAS THAT?!
JORDAN? WHAT'S GOING ON?
NOTHING GOOD!
VOLKOV, NOW!

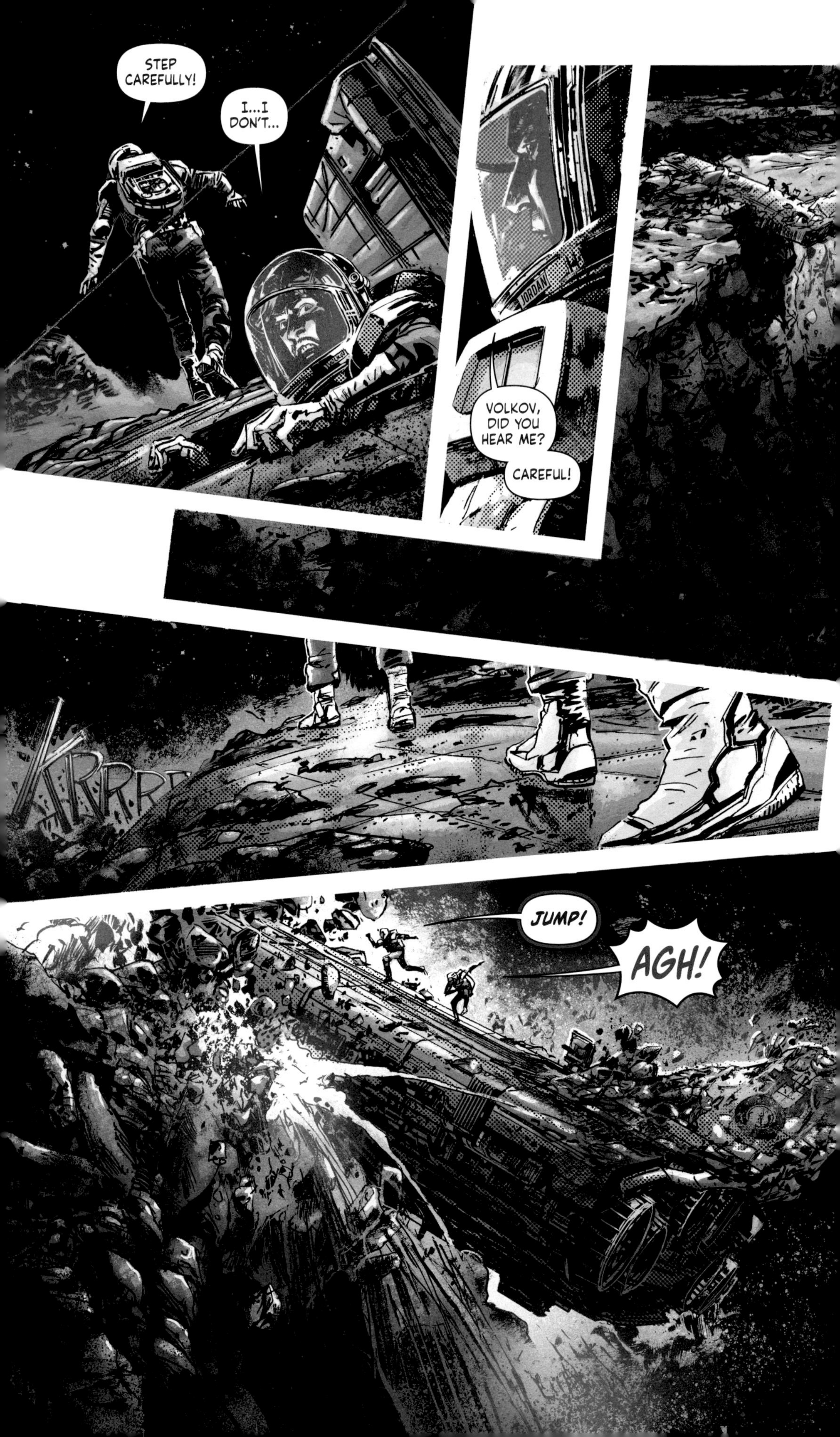
STEP CAREFULLY!
I...I DON'T...
JORDAN
VOLKOV, DID YOU HEAR ME?
CAREFUL!
KRRRR
JUMP!
AGH!

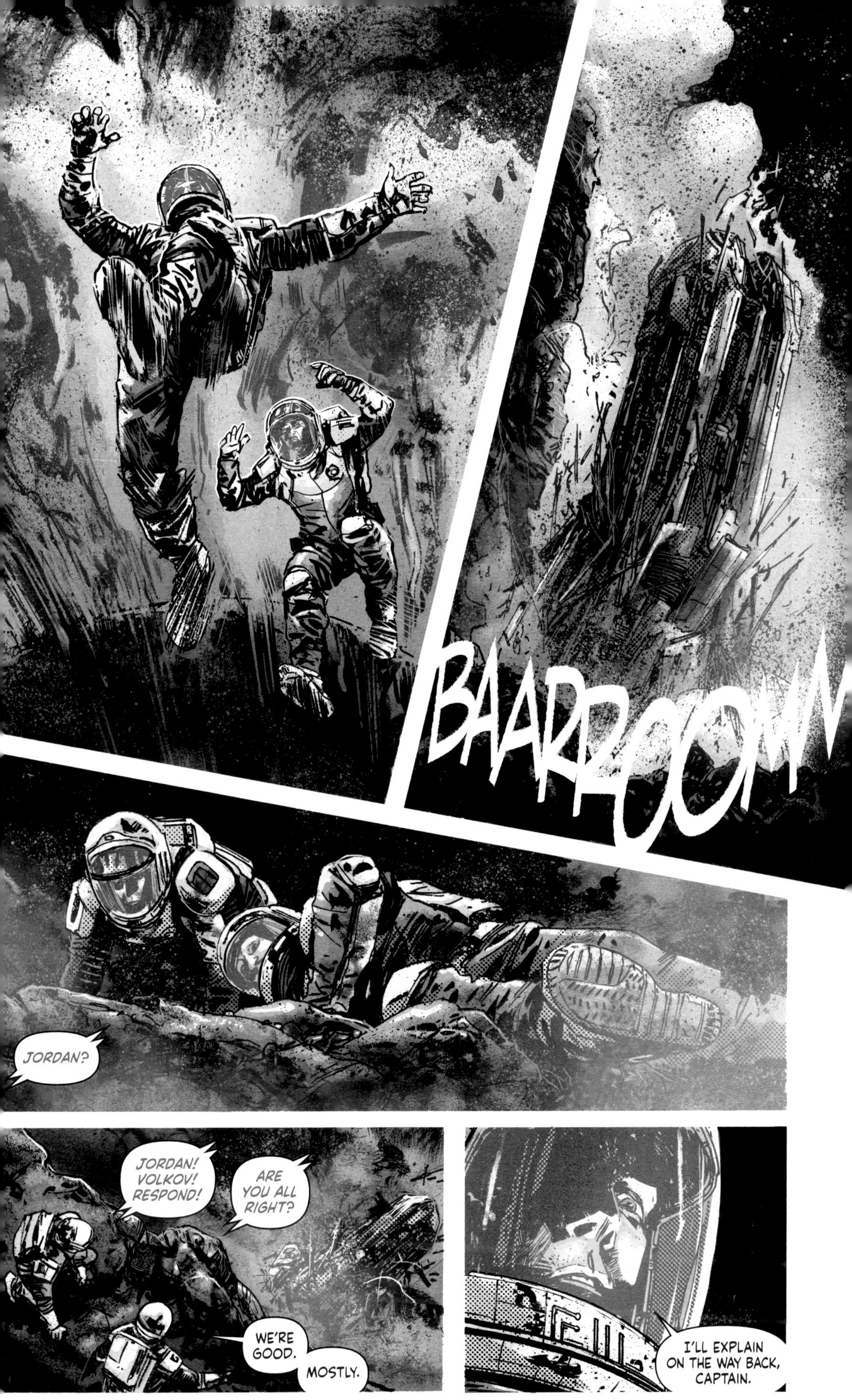
BAARROOM
JORDAN?
JORDAN! VOLKOV! RESPOND!
ARE YOU ALL RIGHT?
WE'RE GOOD.
MOSTLY.
I'LL EXPLAIN ON THE WAY BACK, CAPTAIN.

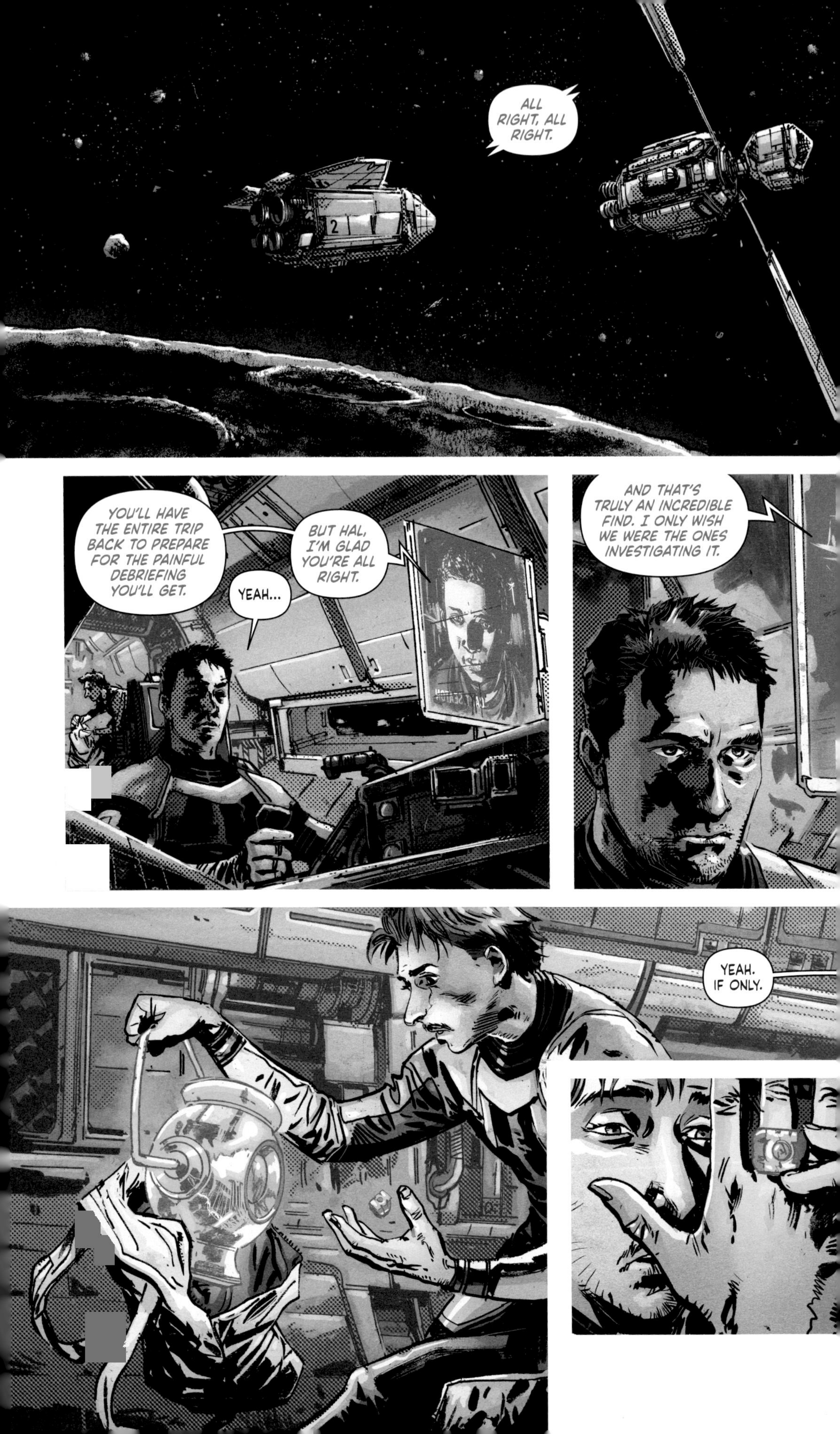
ALL RIGHT, ALL RIGHT.
YOU'LL HAVE THE ENTIRE TRIP BACK TO PREPARE FOR THE PAINFUL DEBRIEFING YOU'LL GET.
YEAH...
BUT HAL, I'M GLAD YOU'RE ALL RIGHT.
AND THAT'S TRULY AN INCREDIBLE FIND. I ONLY WISH WE WERE THE ONES INVESTIGATING IT.
YEAH. IF ONLY.

HOLY--

AHHHH!

WRA-SHH!

AHHH!

FFSS SSHH

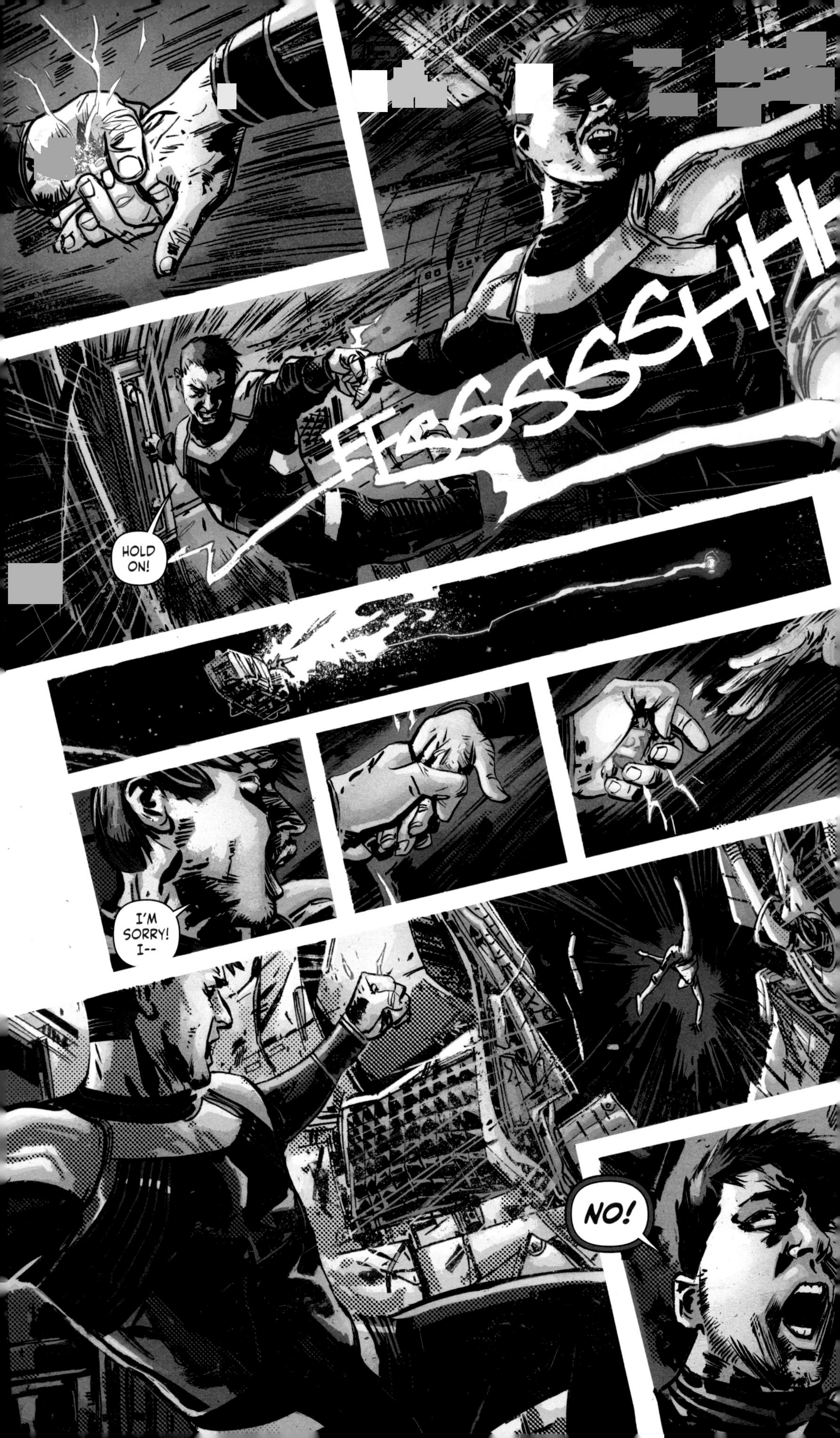
HOLD ON!
I'M SORRY! I--
NO!

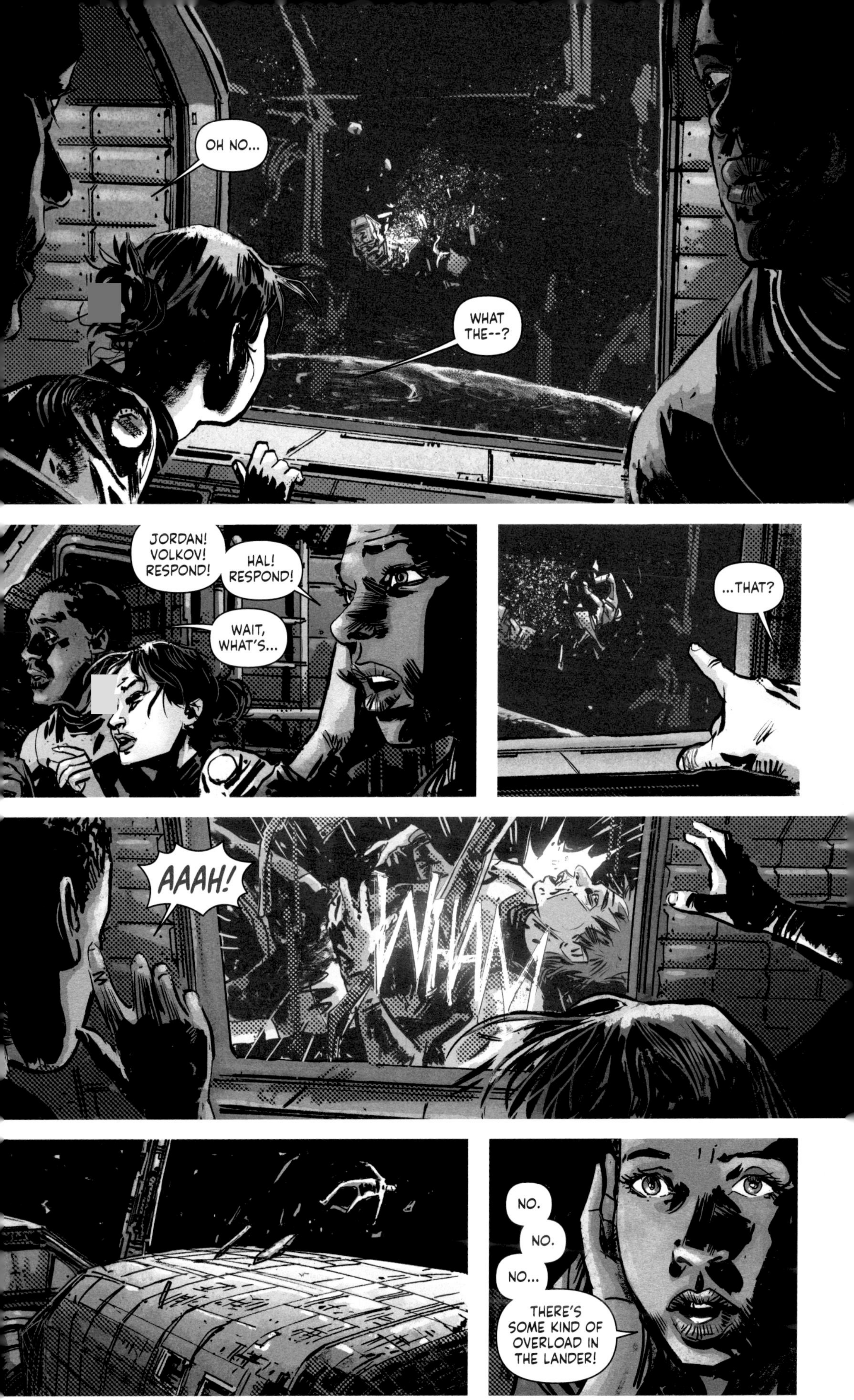
OH NO...
WHAT THE--?
JORDAN! VOLKOV! RESPOND!
HAL! RESPOND!
WAIT, WHAT'S...
...THAT?
AAAH!
WHAM
NO.
NO.
NO...
THERE'S SOME KIND OF OVERLOAD IN THE LANDER!

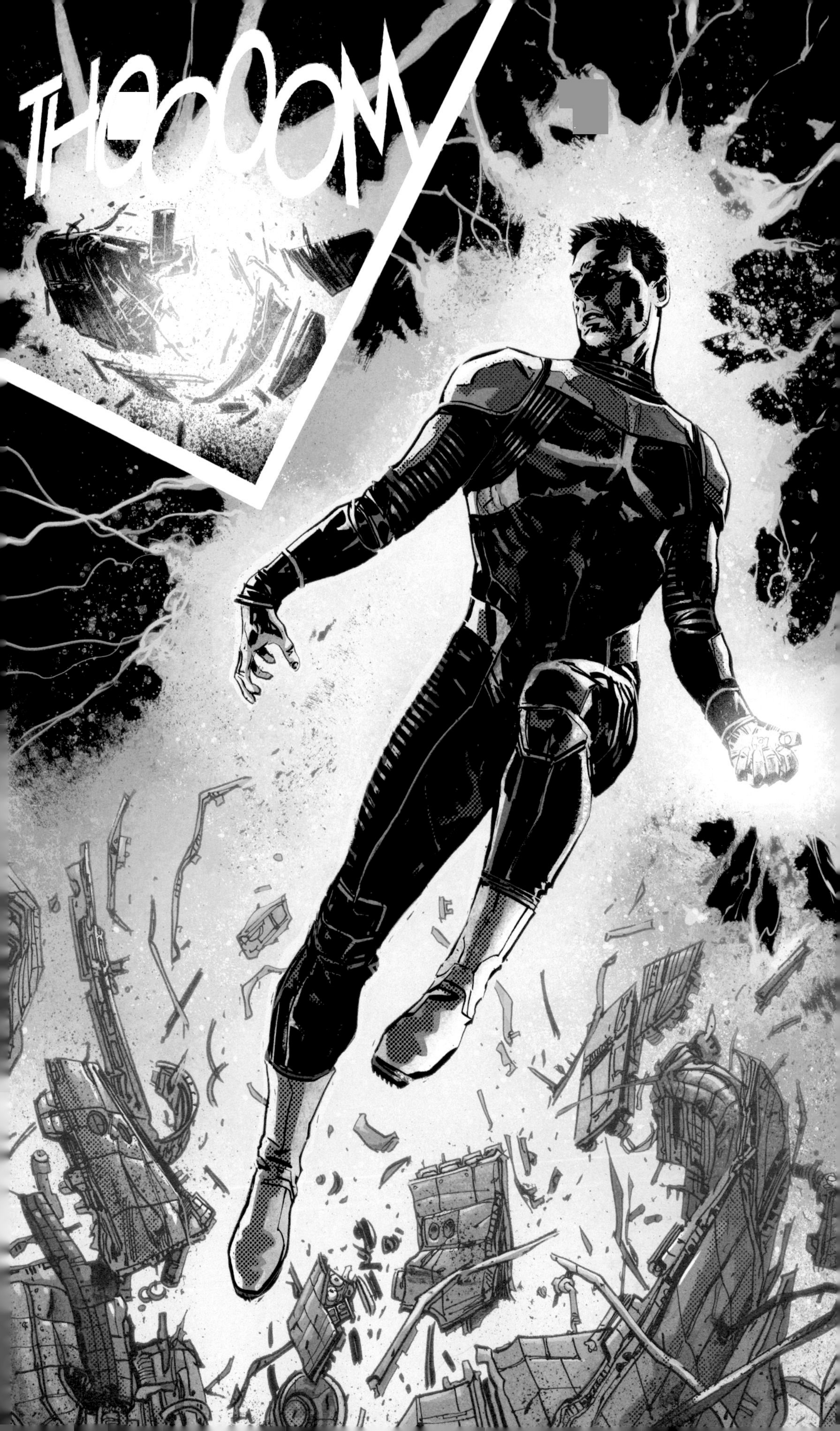
THOOOOM

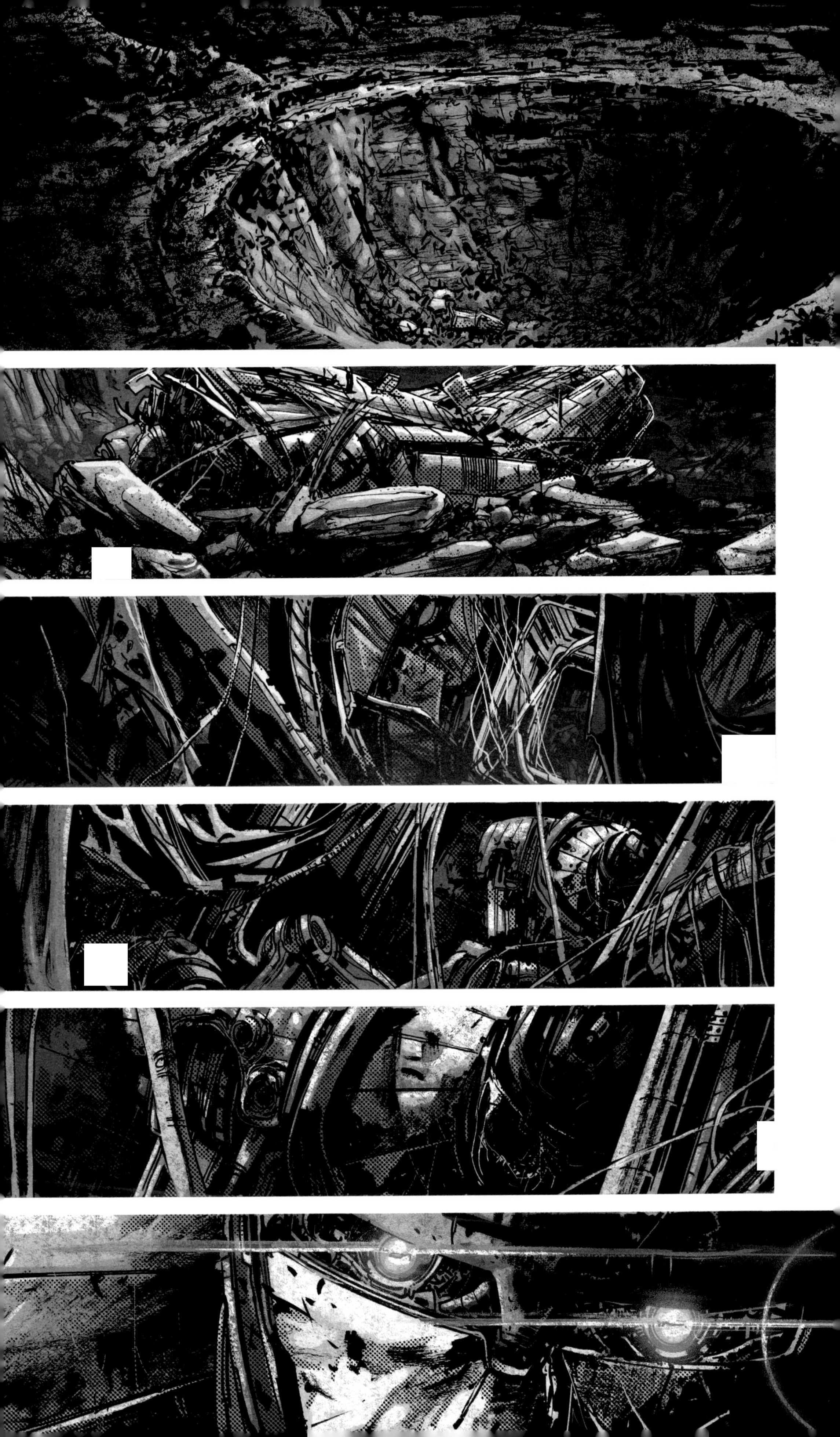

WAIT, DID HE JUST MOVE? IS HE ACTUALLY *ALIVE* OUT THERE?

JORDAN, COME IN!

JORDAN, CAN YOU HEAR ME?

IMPOSSIBLE.

OH MY GOD, HE *IS!*

JORDAN, CAN YOU ANSWER US?

IT MUST-- I...*I DON'T UNDERSTAND.*

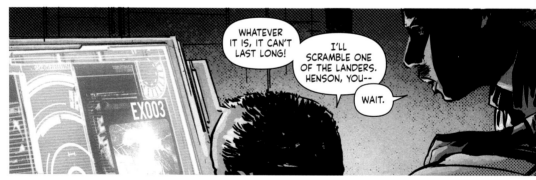

WHATEVER IT IS, IT CAN'T LAST LONG!

I'LL SCRAMBLE ONE OF THE LANDERS. HENSON, YOU--

WAIT.

EX003

BUT CAPTAIN, WE'VE GOT TO DO SOMETHING...

AND *FAST!*

FJJFE-08878900// HY0753684///////

EX003

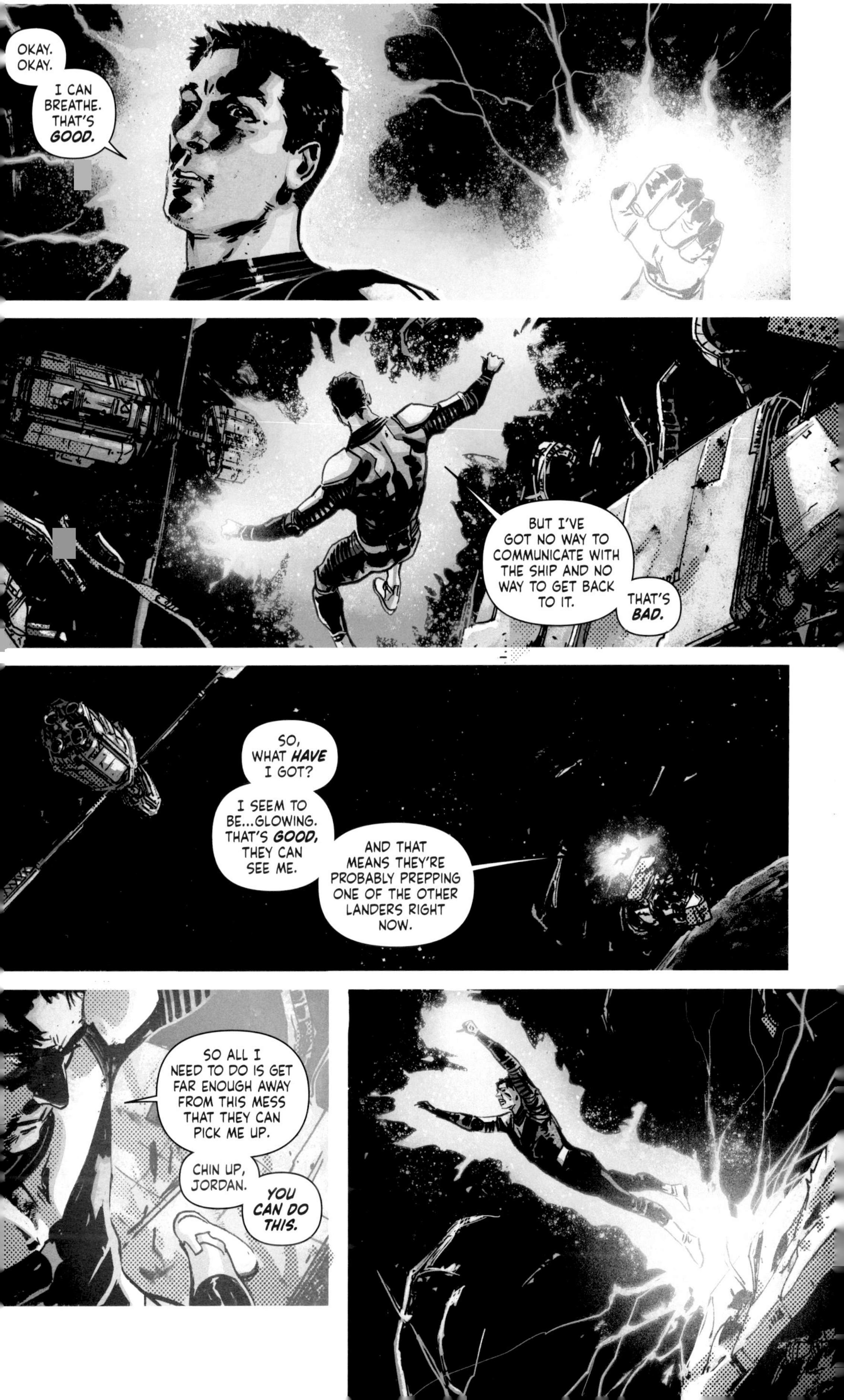
OKAY. OKAY.
I CAN BREATHE. THAT'S *GOOD.*
BUT I'VE GOT NO WAY TO COMMUNICATE WITH THE SHIP AND NO WAY TO GET BACK TO IT.
THAT'S *BAD.*
SO, WHAT *HAVE* I GOT?
I SEEM TO BE...GLOWING. THAT'S *GOOD,* THEY CAN SEE ME.
AND THAT MEANS THEY'RE PROBABLY PREPPING ONE OF THE OTHER LANDERS RIGHT NOW.
SO ALL I NEED TO DO IS GET FAR ENOUGH AWAY FROM THIS MESS THAT THEY CAN PICK ME UP.
CHIN UP, JORDAN.
YOU CAN DO THIS.

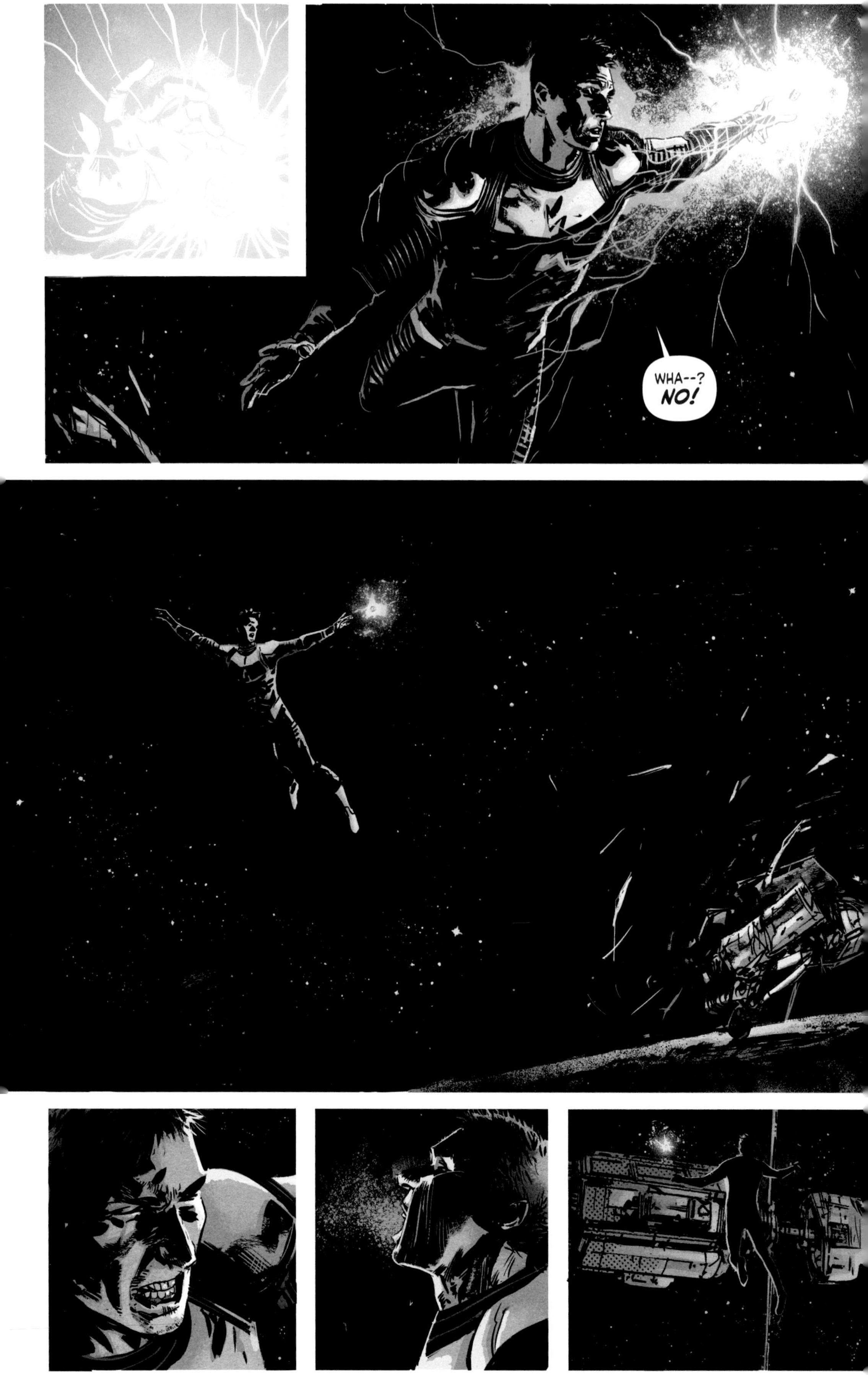
WHA--? NO!

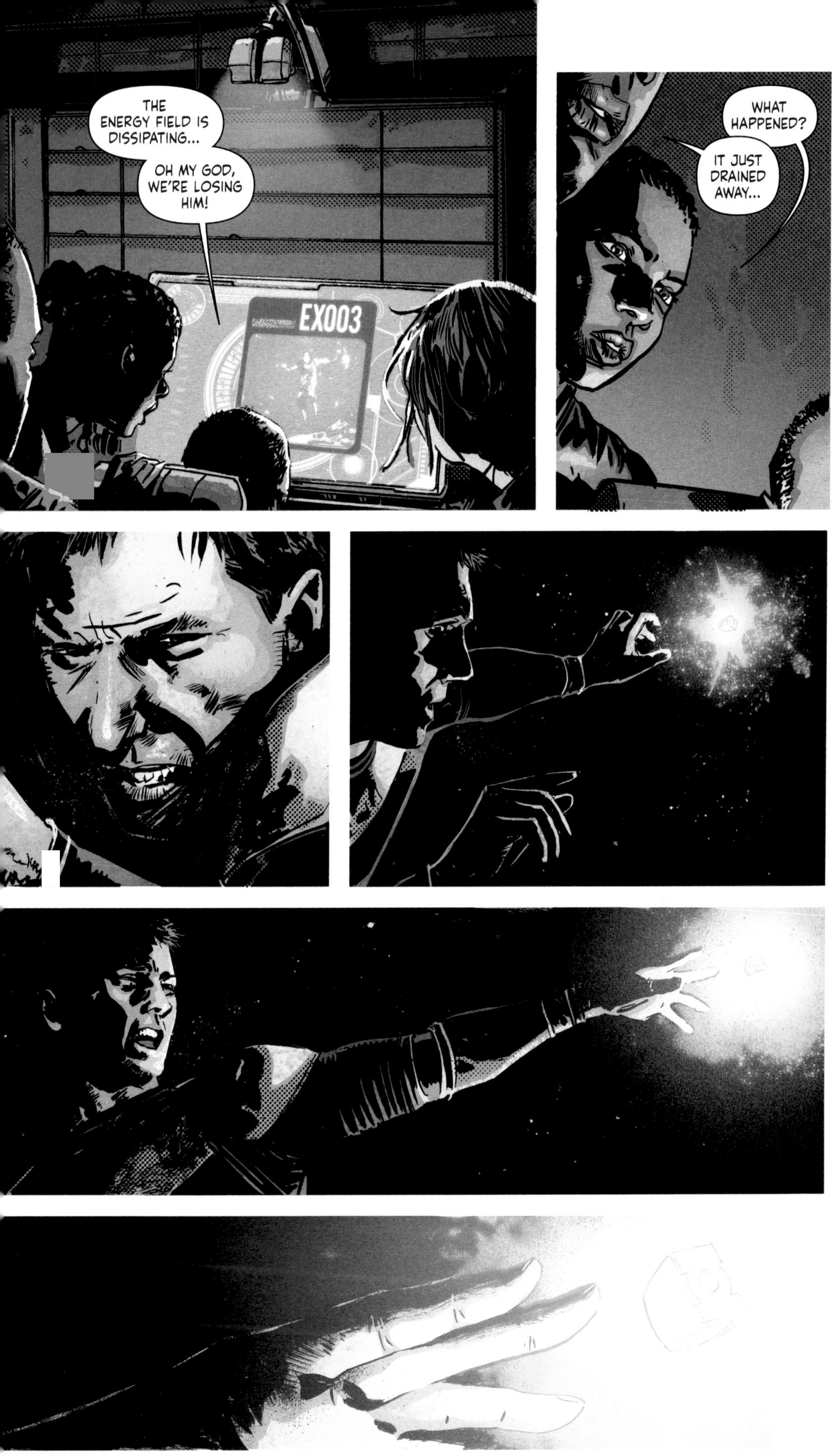
THE ENERGY FIELD IS DISSIPATING...
OH MY GOD, WE'RE LOSING HIM!
EX003
WHAT HAPPENED?
IT JUST DRAINED AWAY...

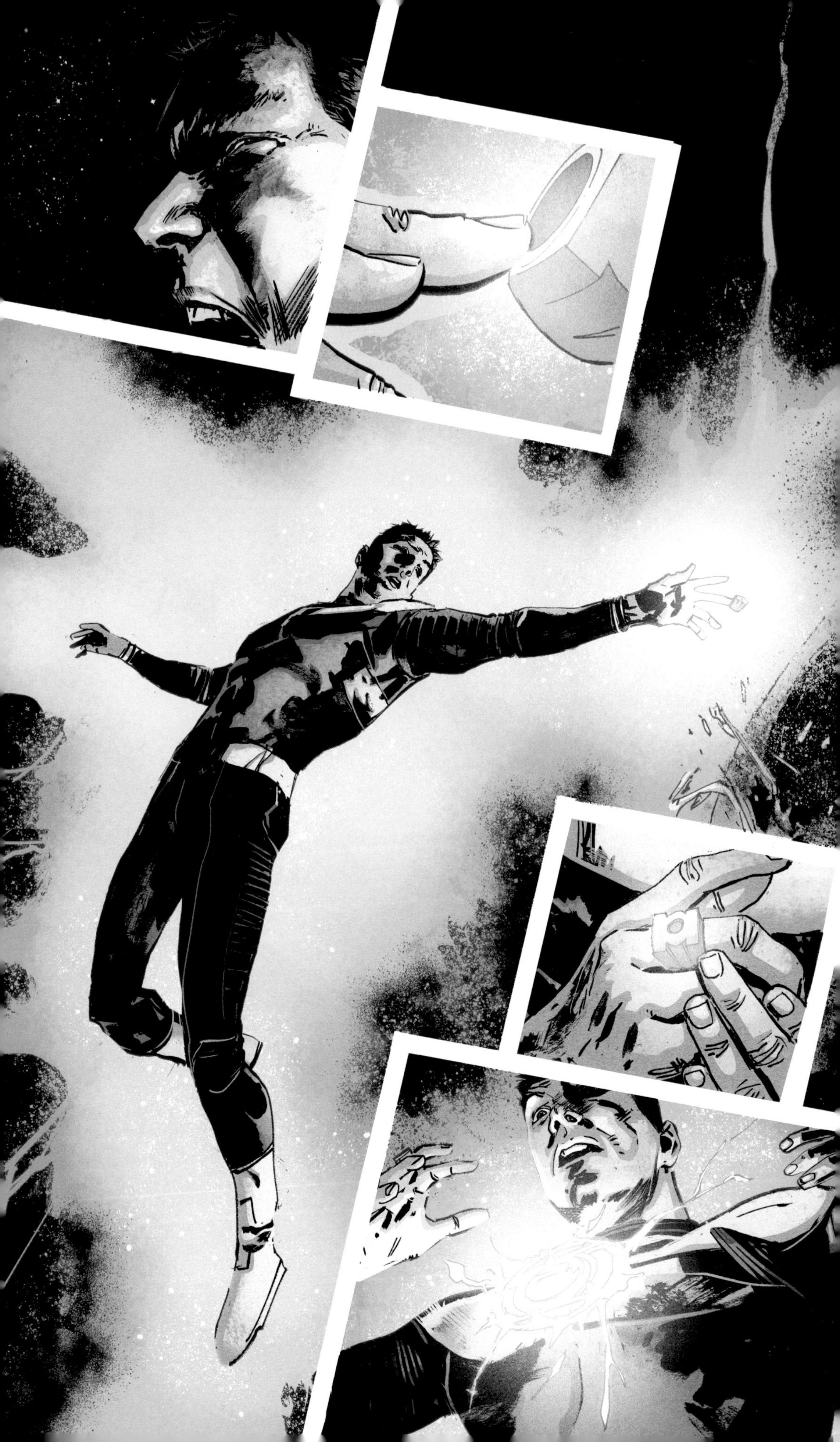

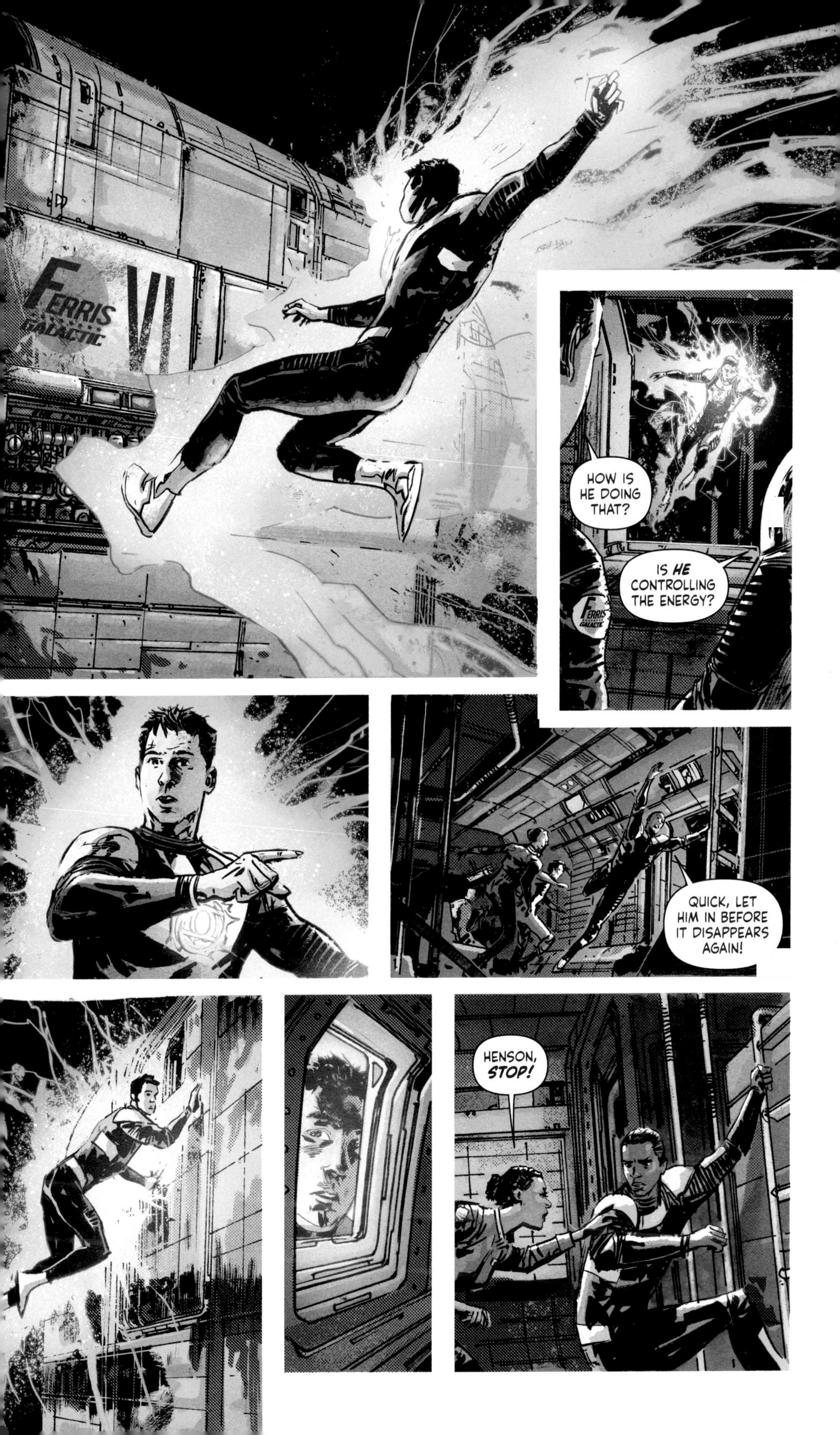
FERRIS GALACTIC
VI
HOW IS HE DOING THAT?
IS HE CONTROLLING THE ENERGY?
FERRIS GALACTIC
QUICK, LET HIM IN BEFORE IT DISAPPEARS AGAIN!
HENSON, STOP!

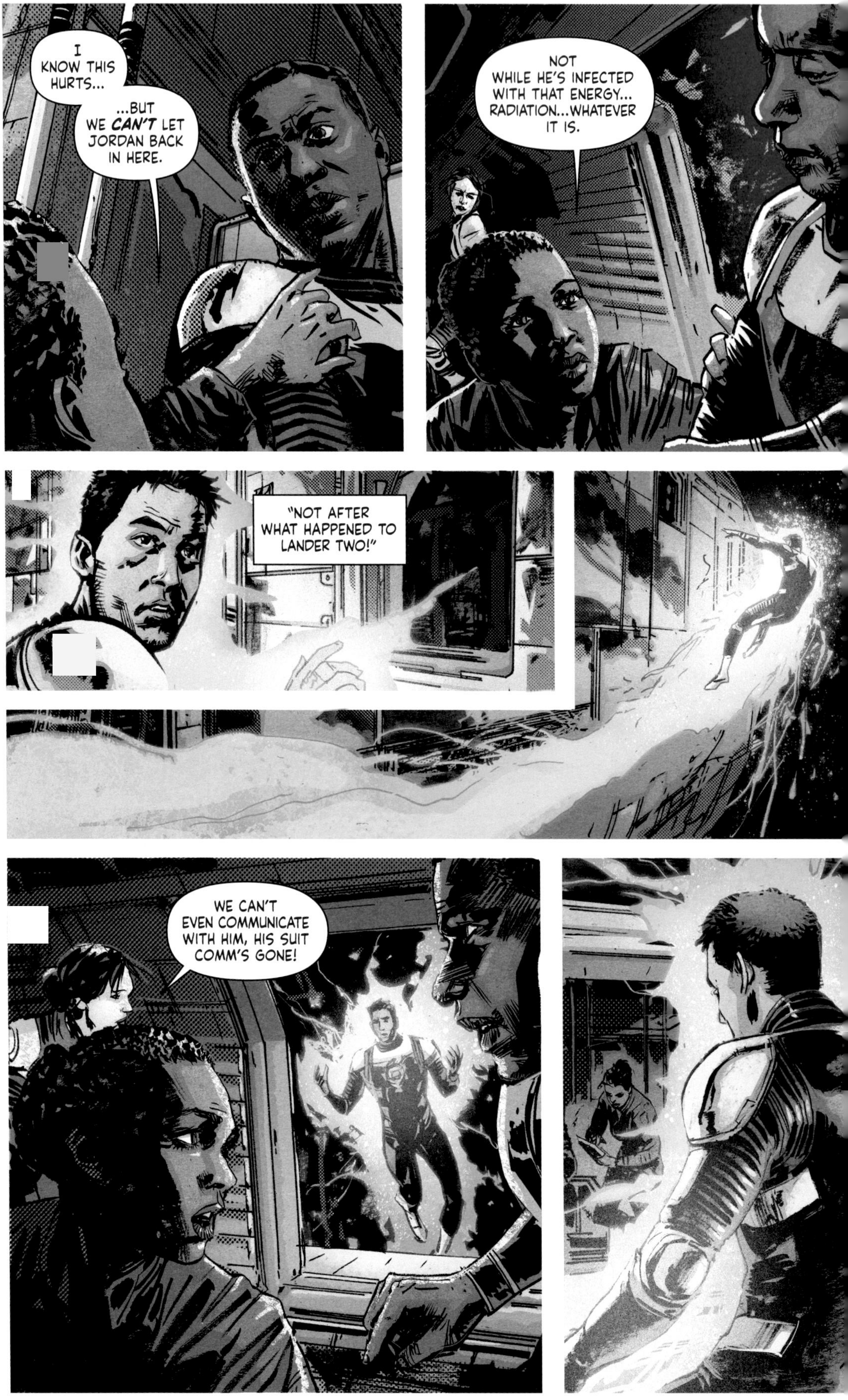

I KNOW THIS HURTS...
...BUT WE CAN'T LET JORDAN BACK IN HERE.
NOT WHILE HE'S INFECTED WITH THAT ENERGY... RADIATION...WHATEVER IT IS.
"NOT AFTER WHAT HAPPENED TO LANDER TWO!"
WE CAN'T EVEN COMMUNICATE WITH HIM, HIS SUIT COMM'S GONE!

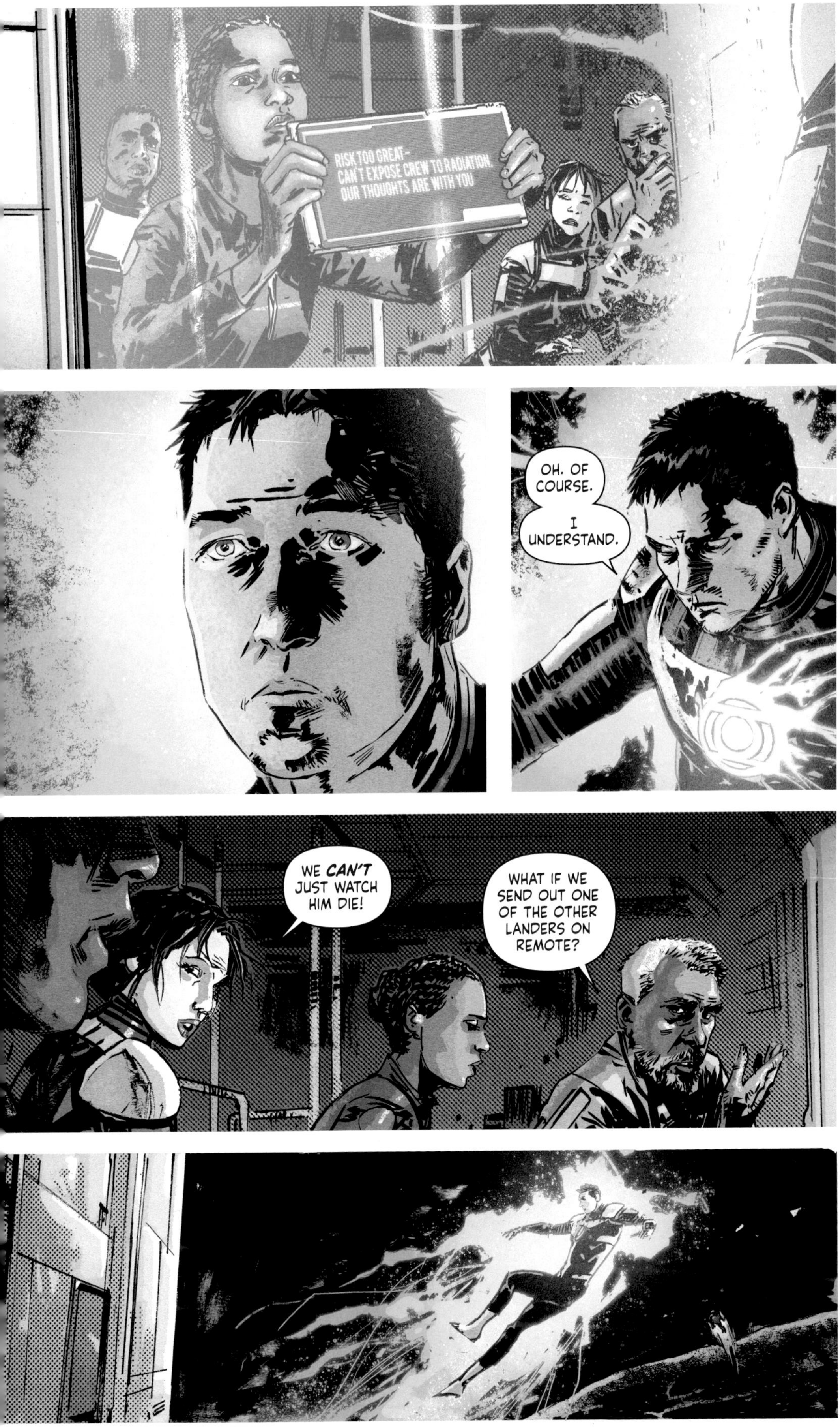
RISK TOO GREAT–
CAN'T EXPOSE CREW TO RADIATION.
OUR THOUGHTS ARE WITH YOU
OH. OF COURSE.
I UNDERSTAND.
WE ***CAN'T*** JUST WATCH HIM DIE!
WHAT IF WE SEND OUT ONE OF THE OTHER LANDERS ON REMOTE?

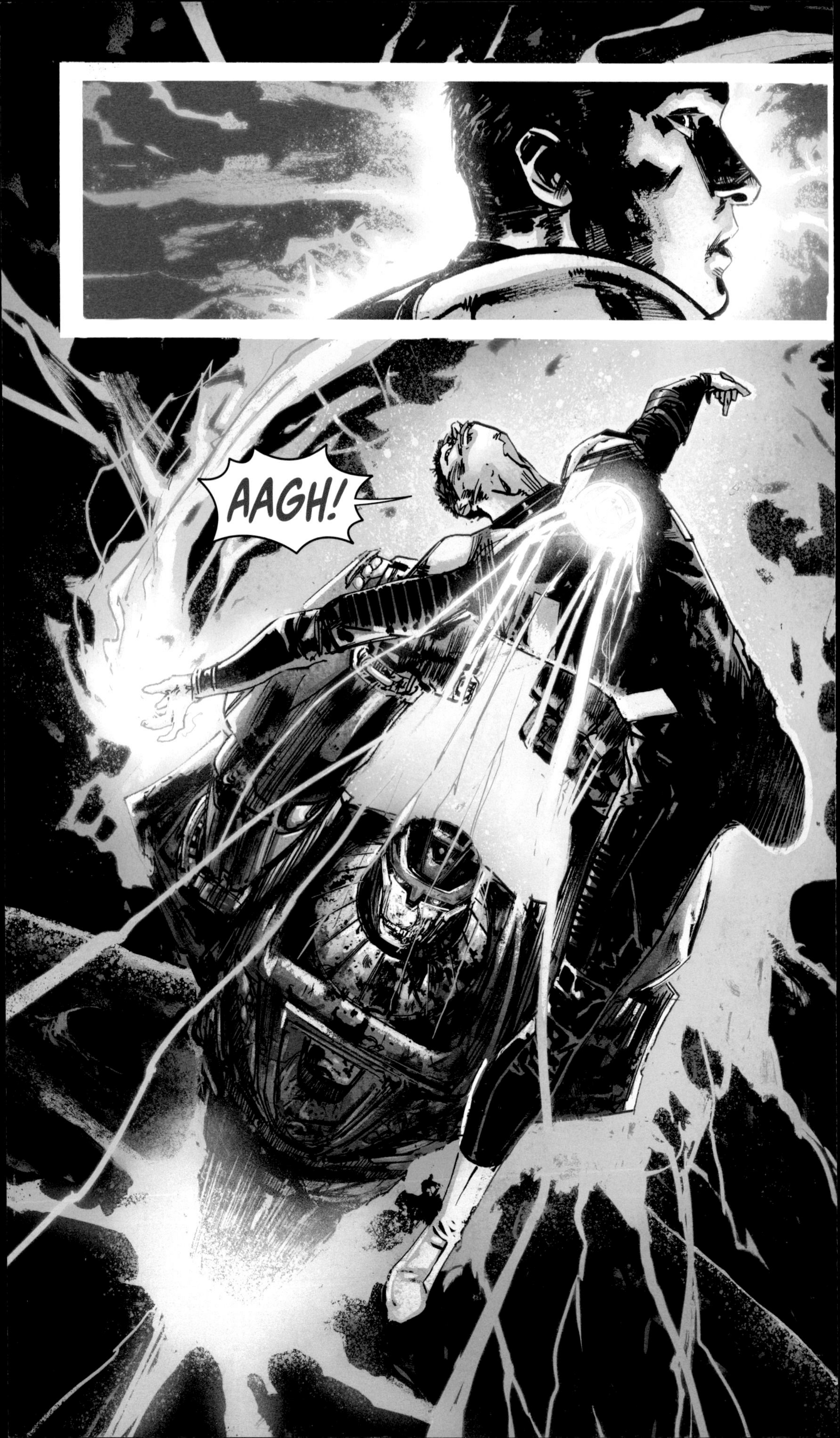
AAGH!

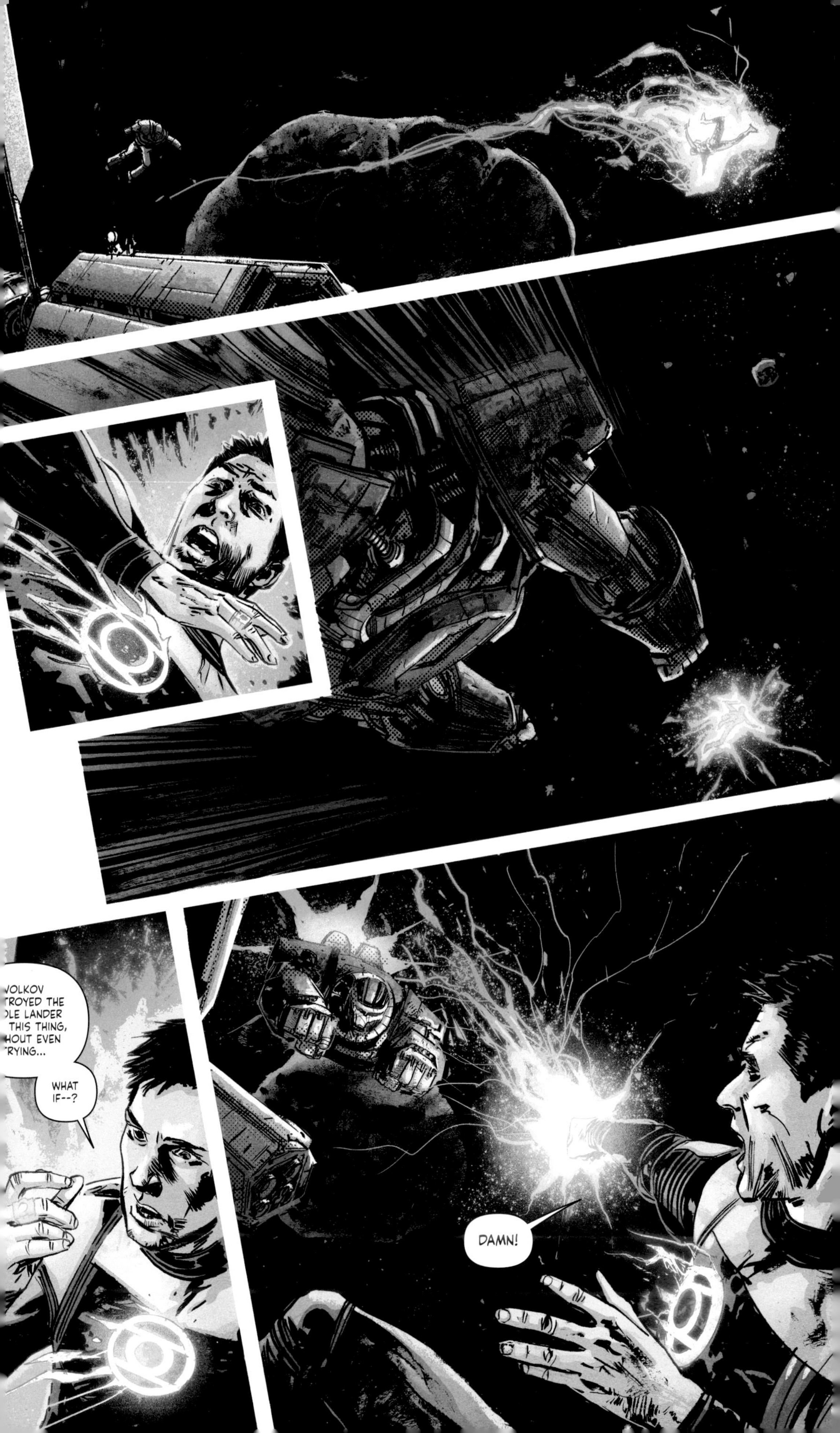
VOLKOV
TROYED THE
OLE LANDER
THIS THING,
HOUT EVEN
TRYING...
WHAT
IF--?
DAMN!

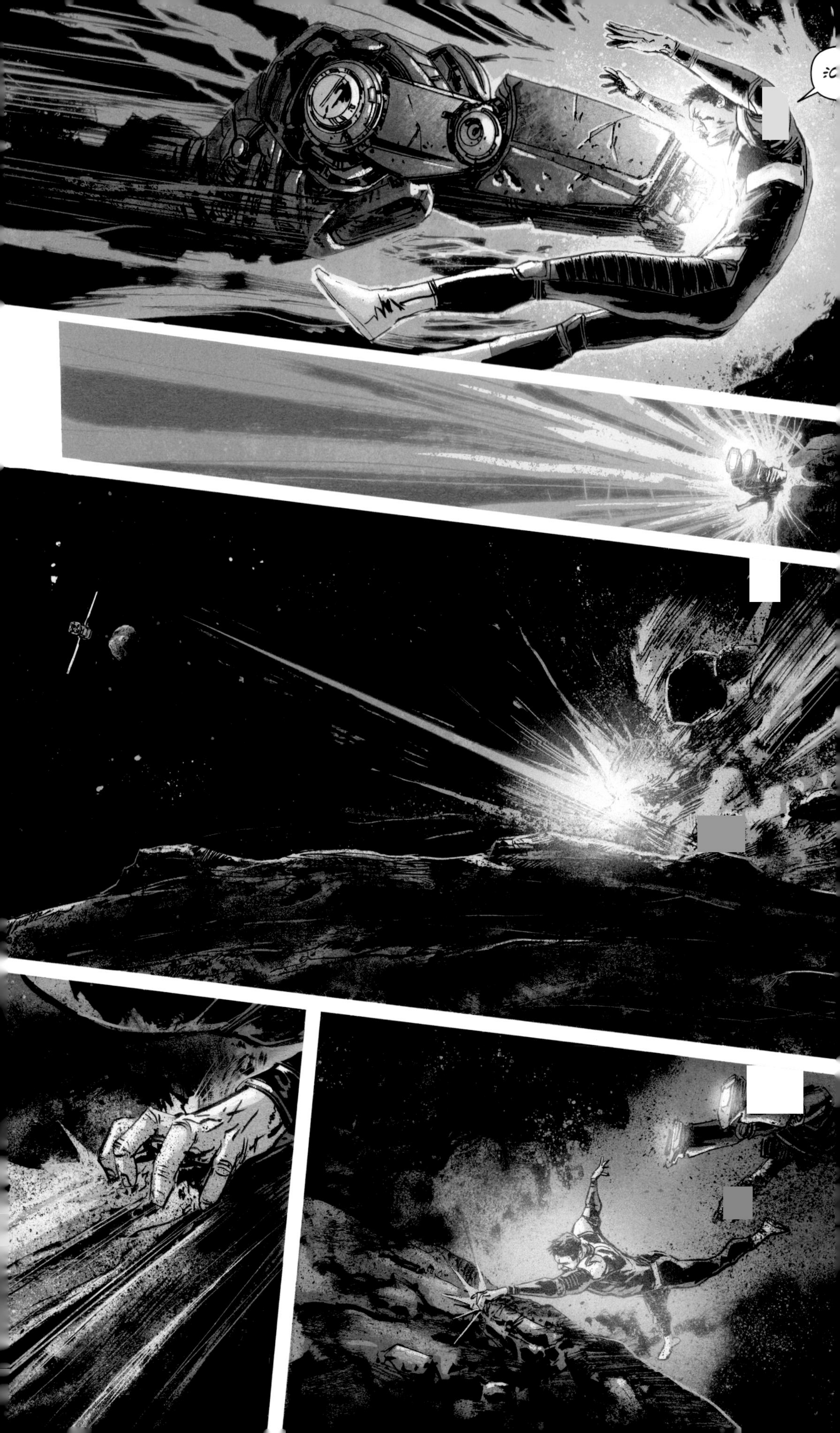

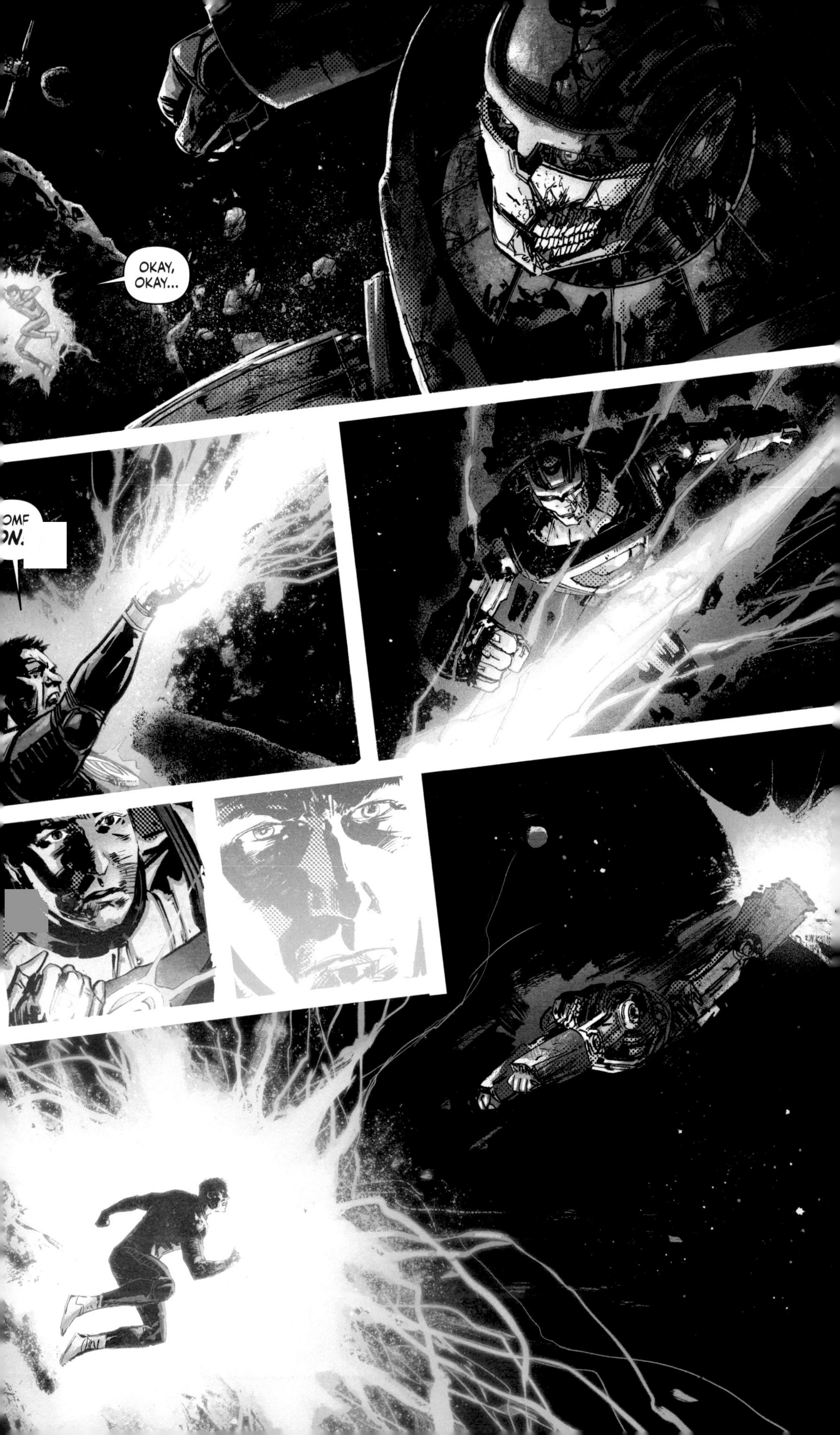
OKAY, OKAY...

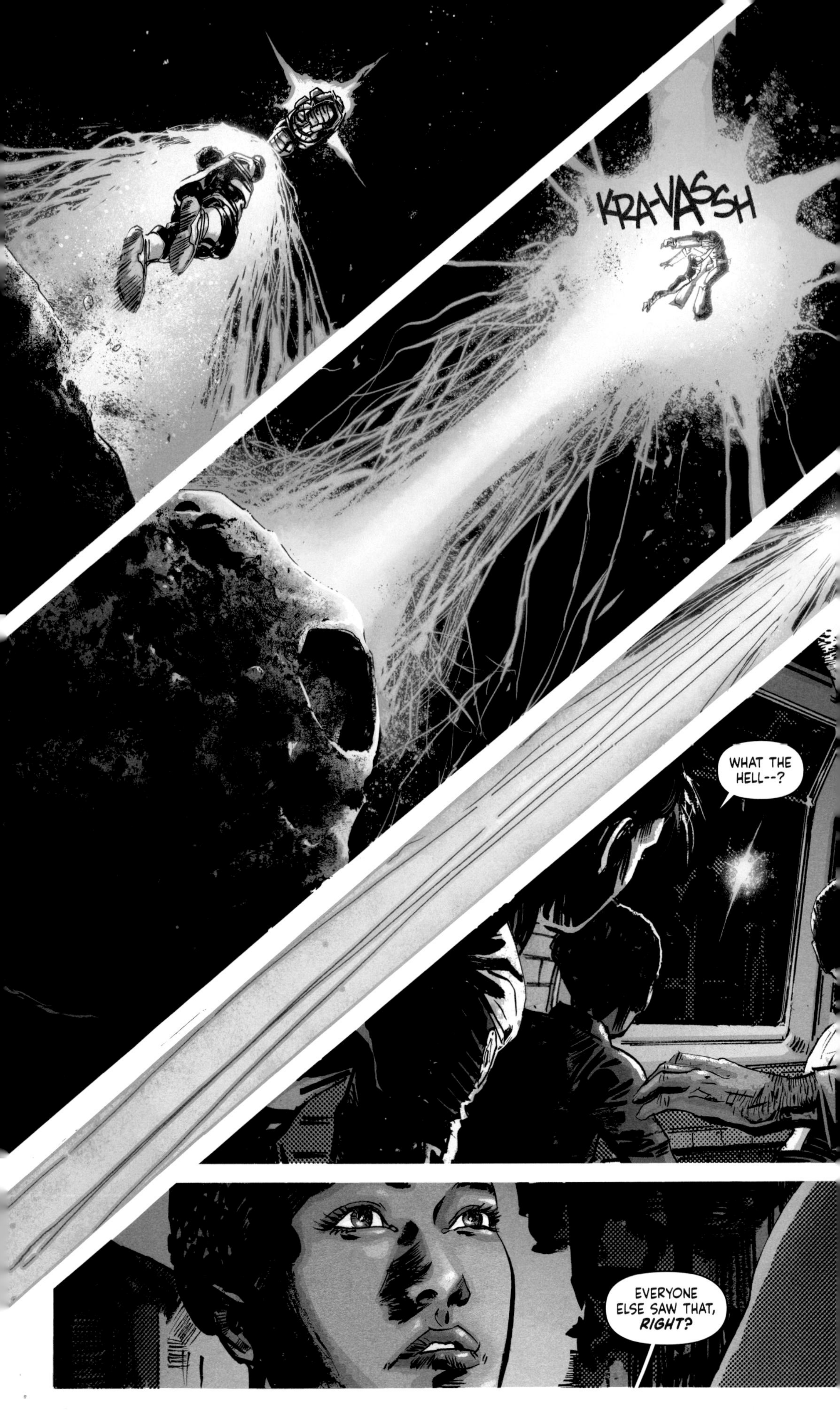
KRA-VASSH
WHAT THE HELL--?
EVERYONE ELSE SAW THAT, *RIGHT?*

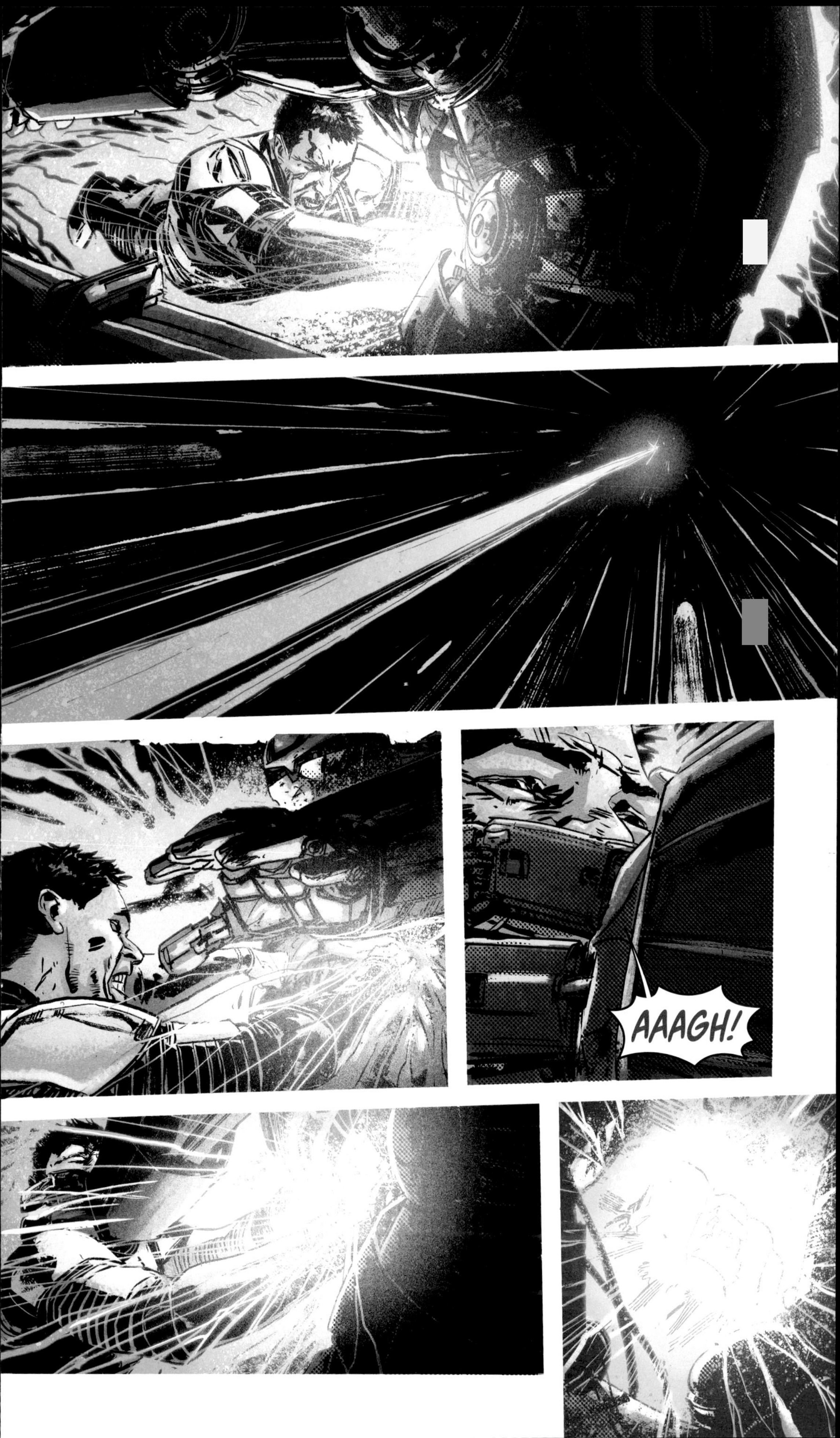
AAAGH!

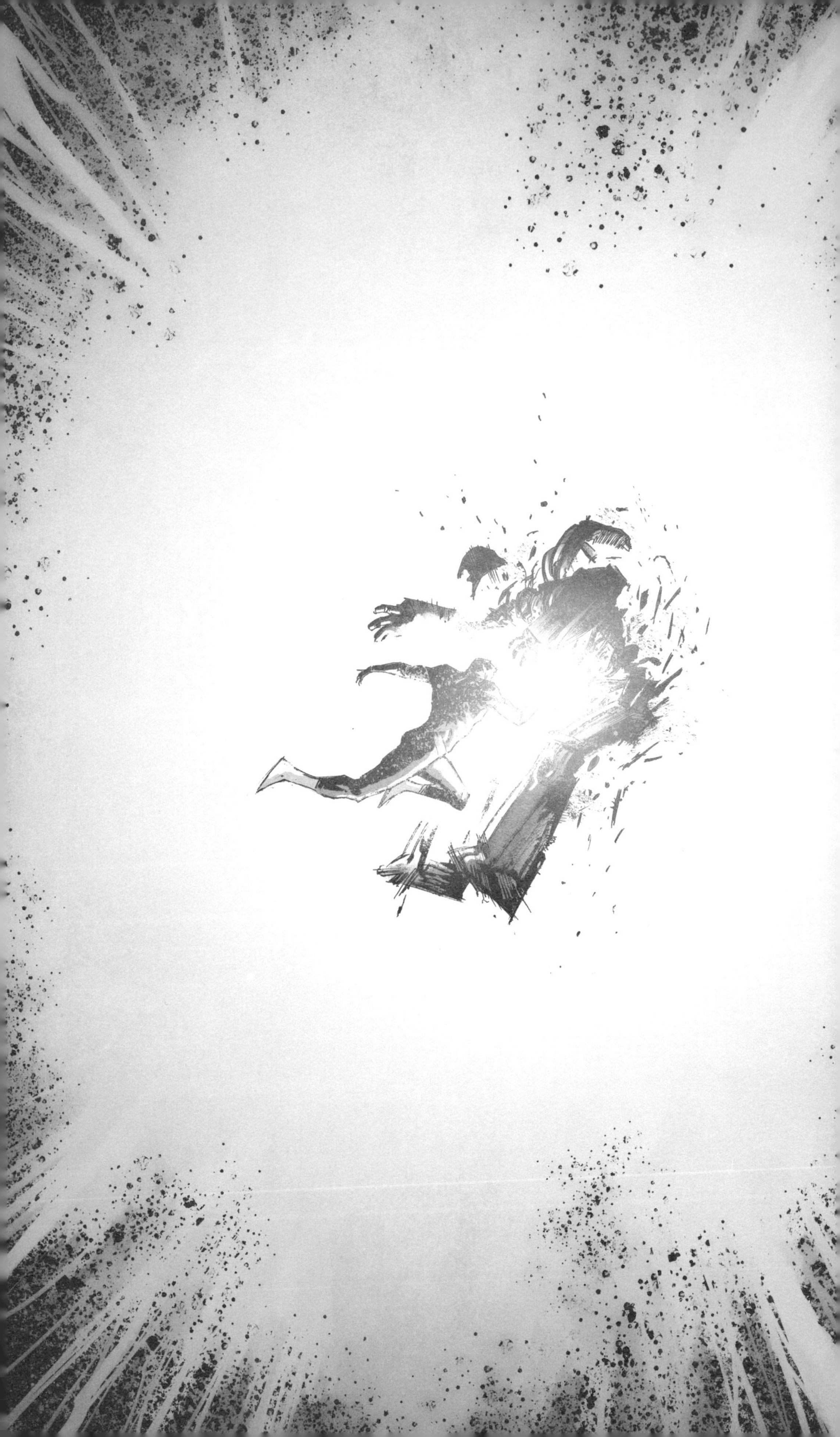

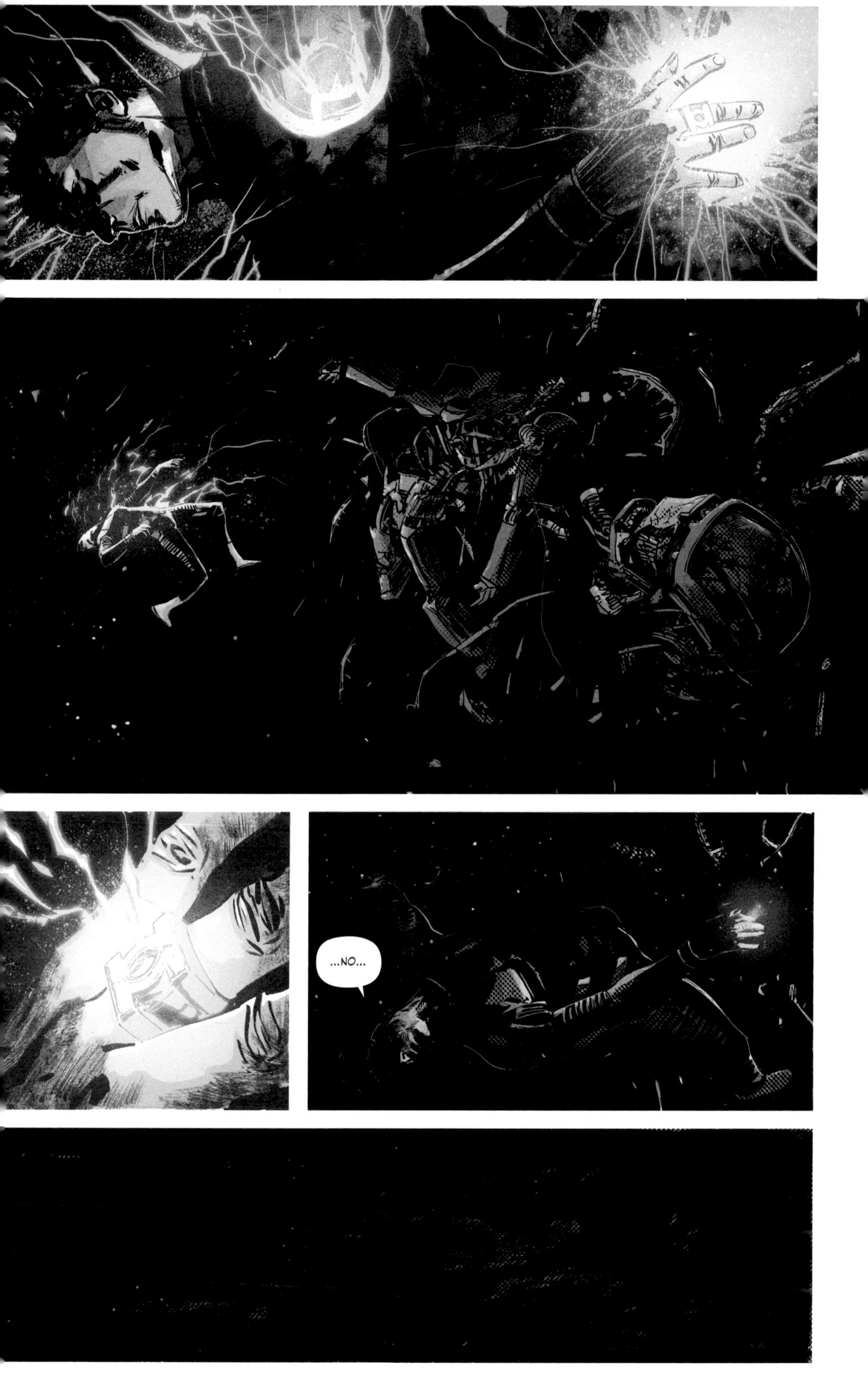
...NO...

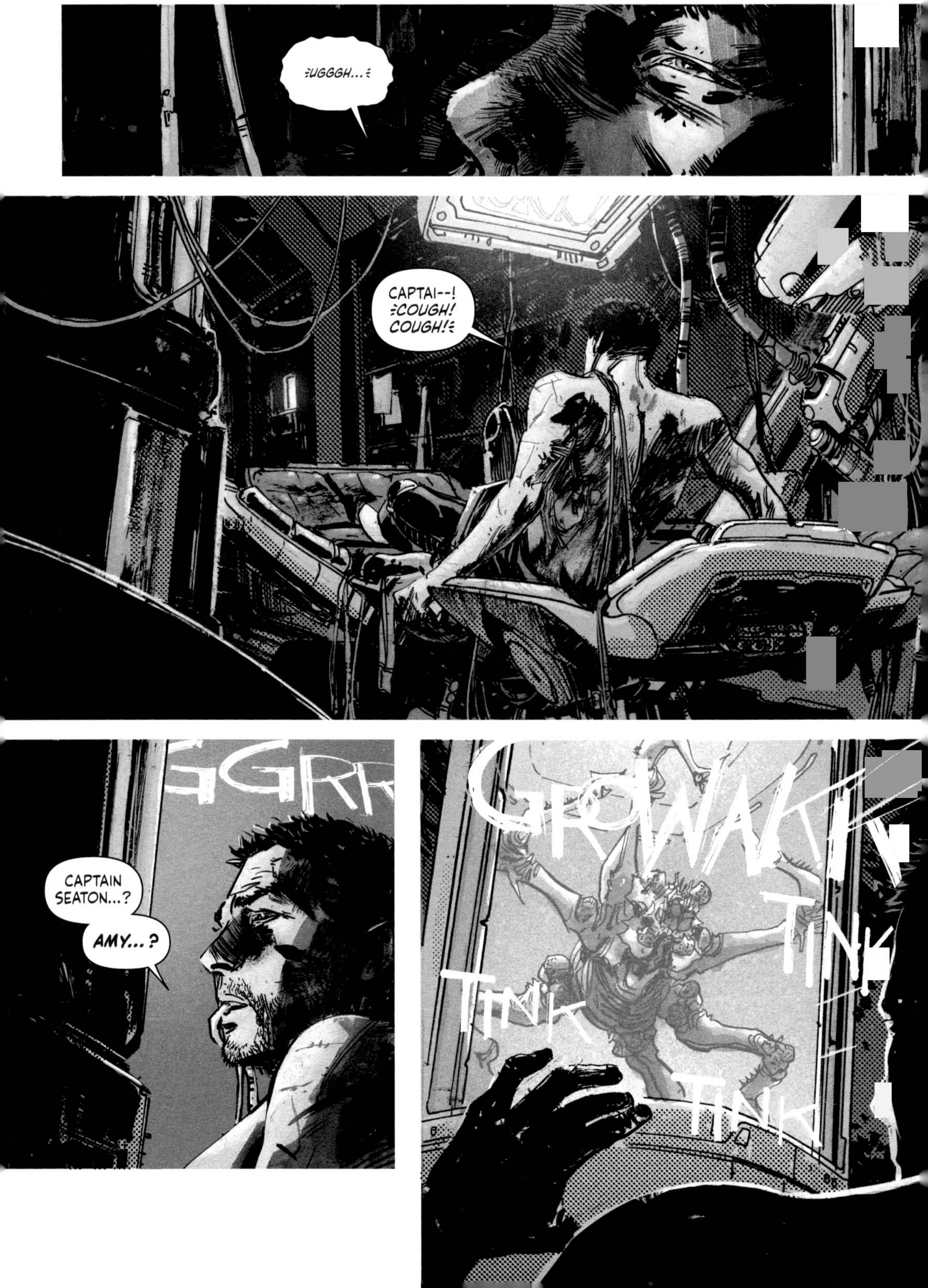
UGGGH...
CAPTAI--! COUGH! COUGH!
GRR
CAPTAIN SEATON...?
AMY...?
GROWAK!
TINK
TINK
TINK

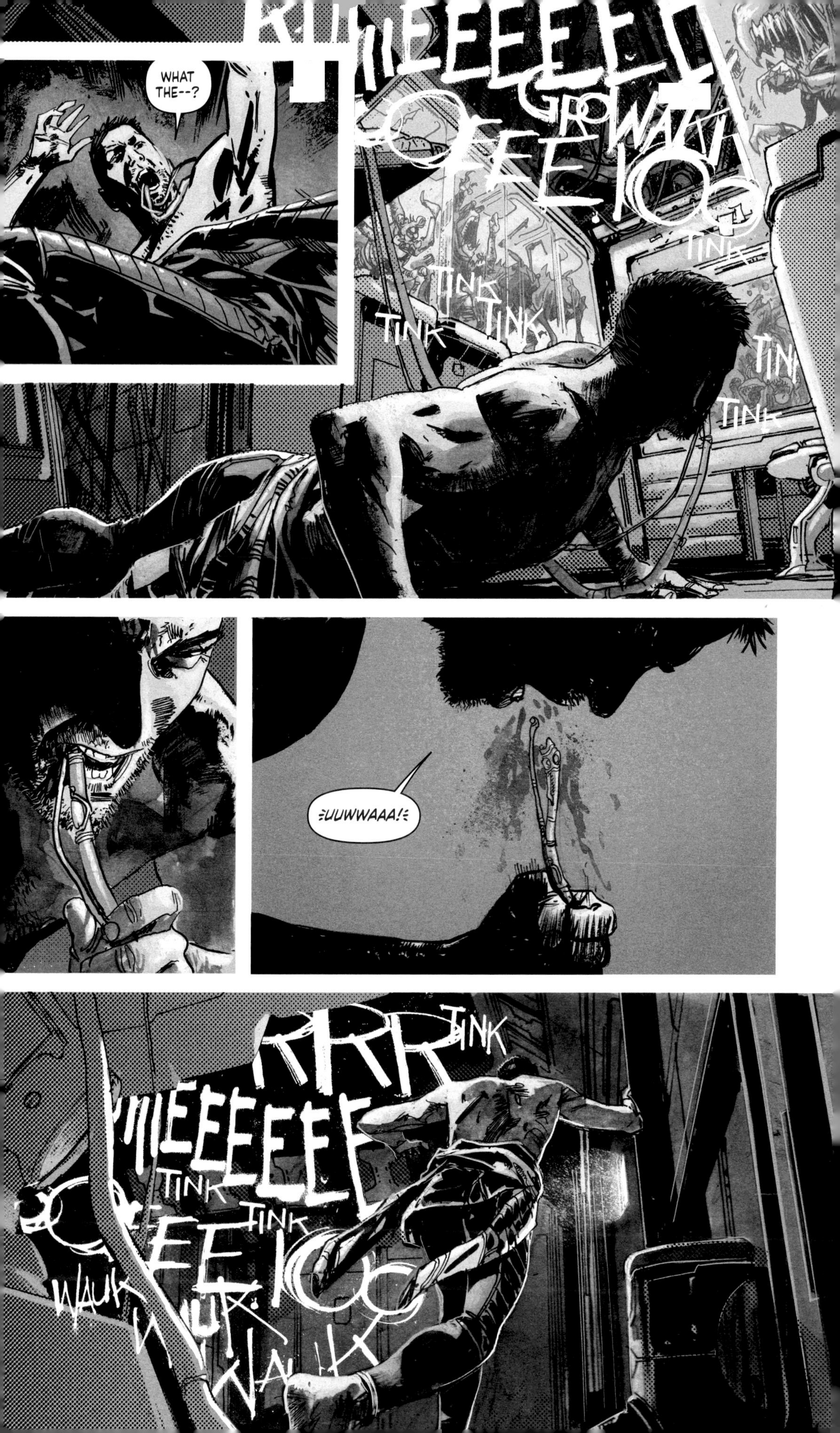

WHAT THE--?
TINK
TINK
TINK
TINK
TINK
TINK
UUWWAAA!
TINK
TINK
TINK

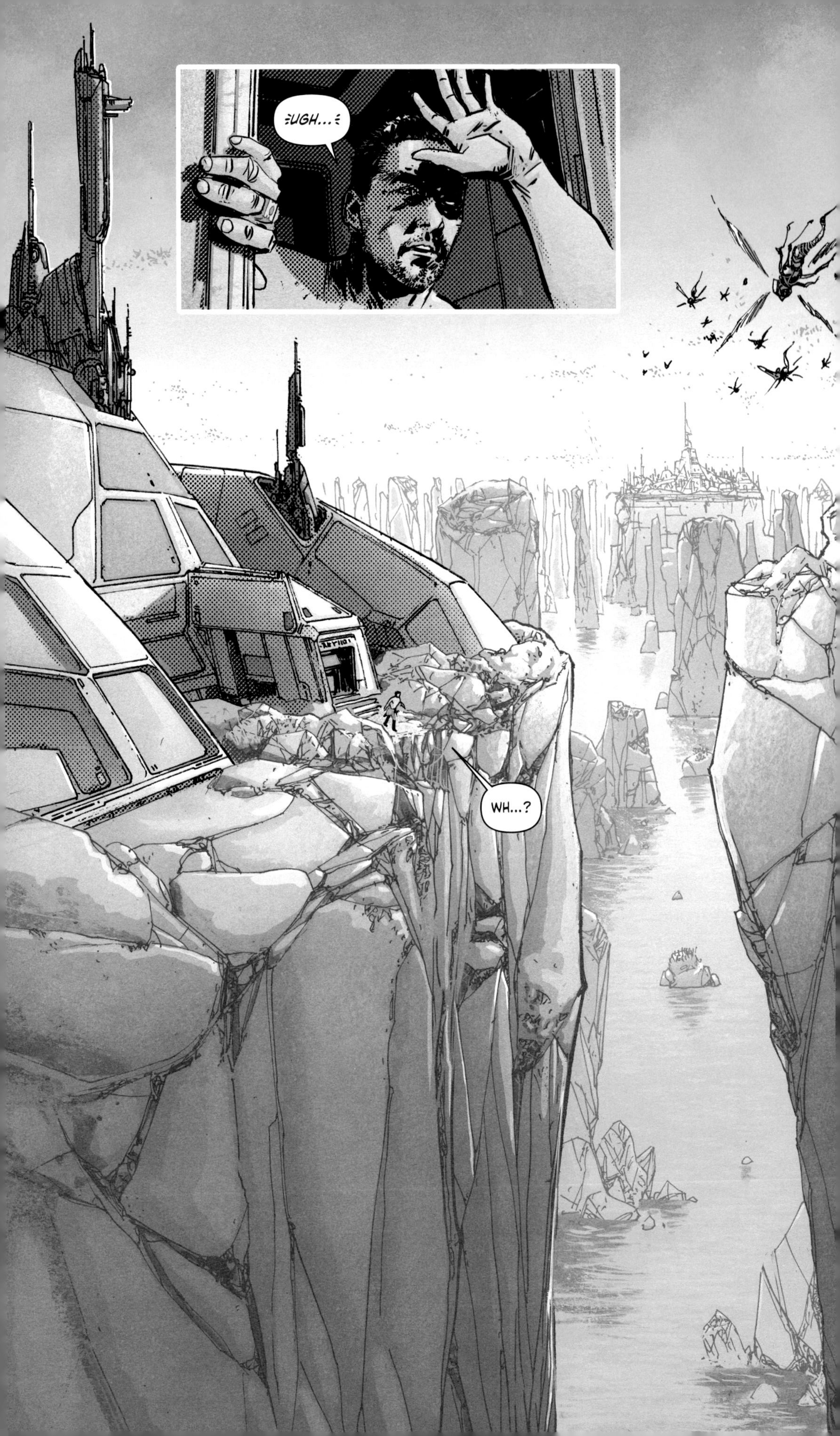
UGH...
WH...?

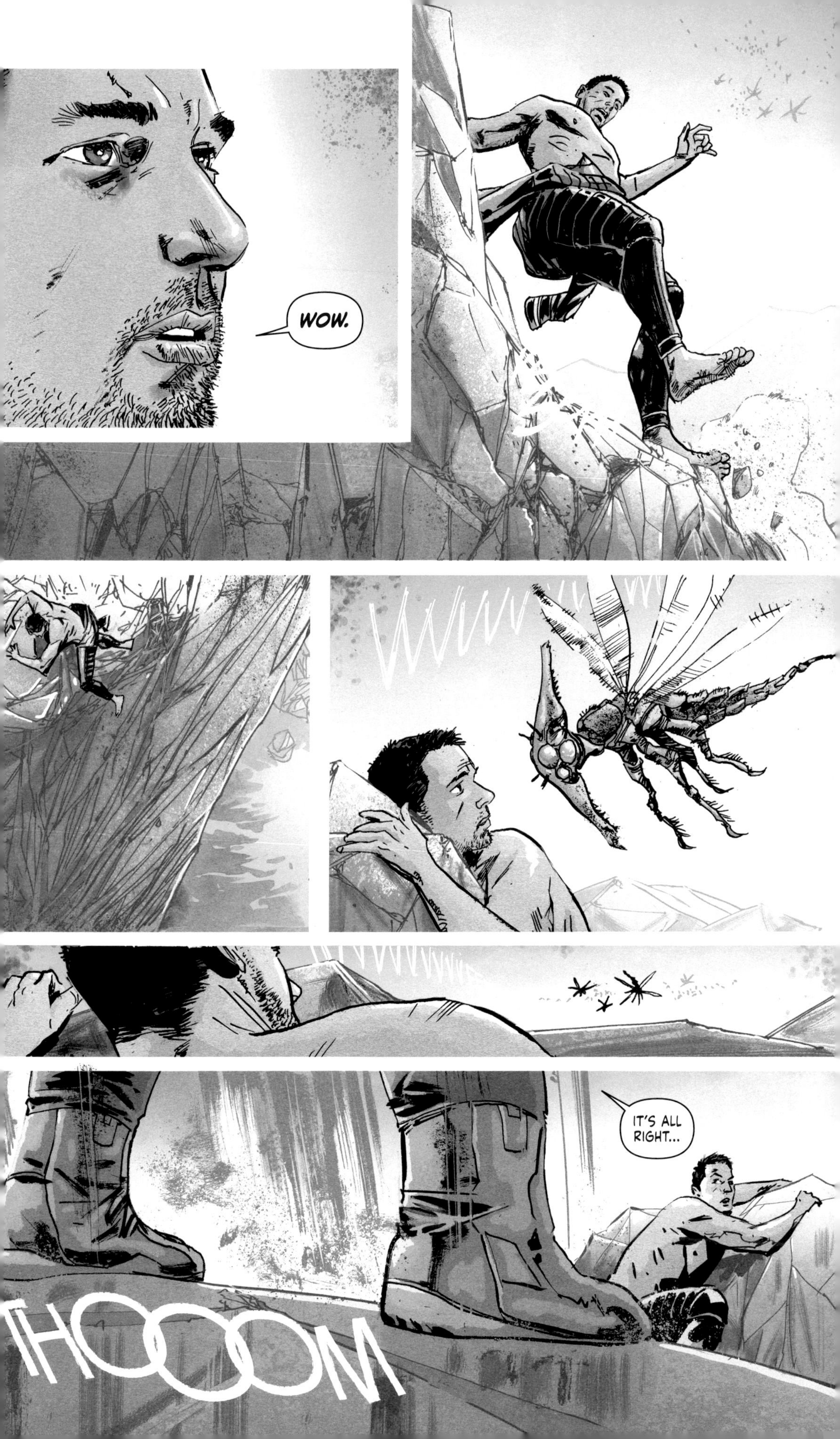
WOW.
IT'S ALL RIGHT...
THOOOM

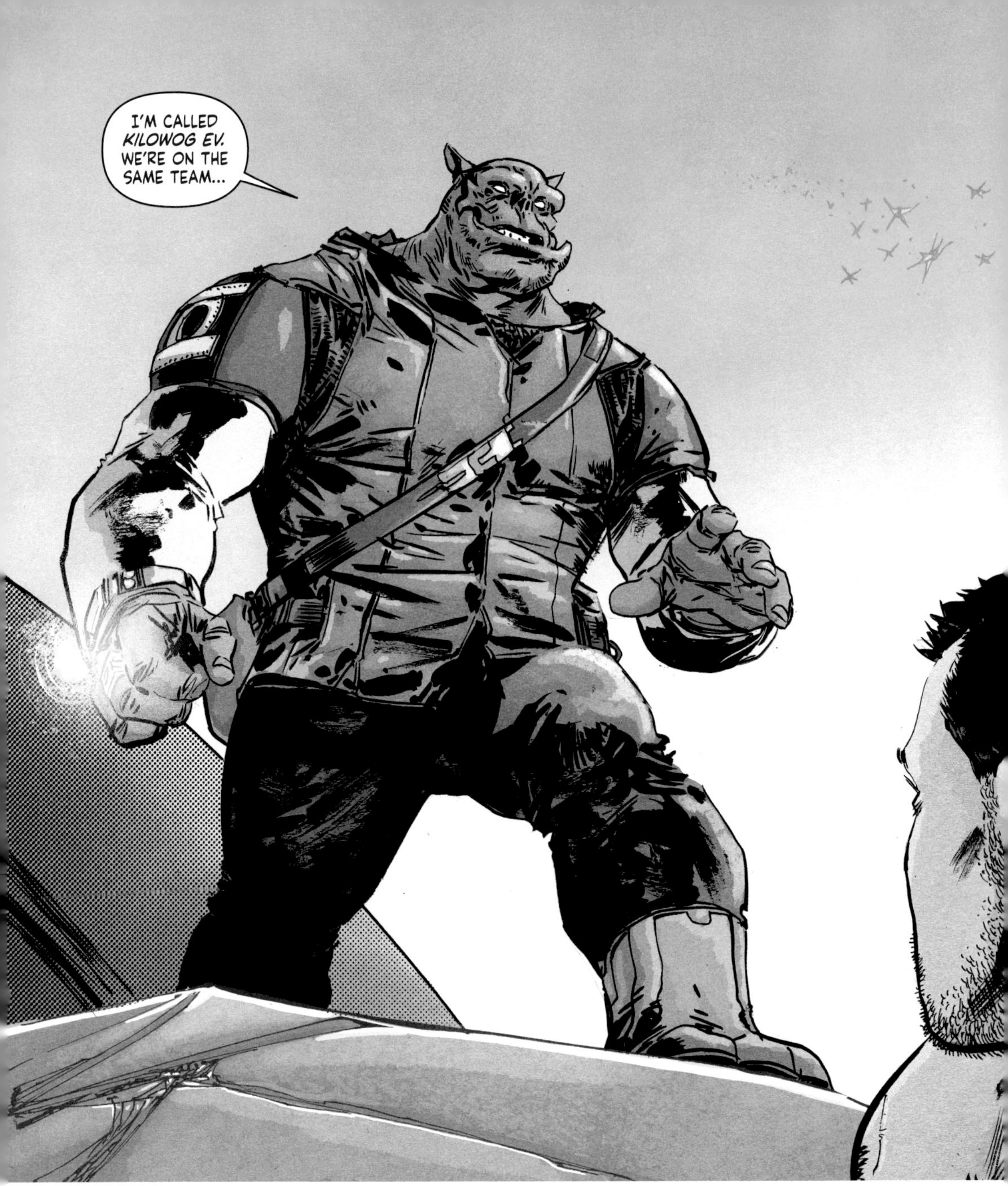
I'M CALLED KILOWOG EV. WE'RE ON THE SAME TEAM...

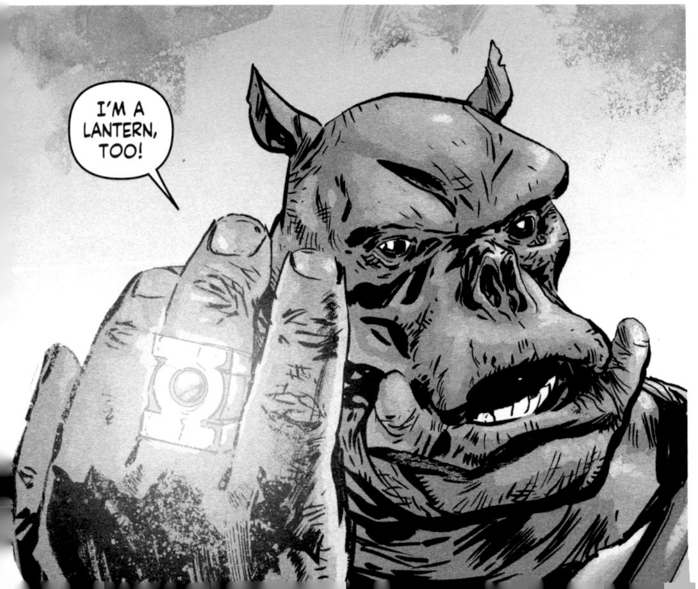
I'M A LANTERN, TOO!

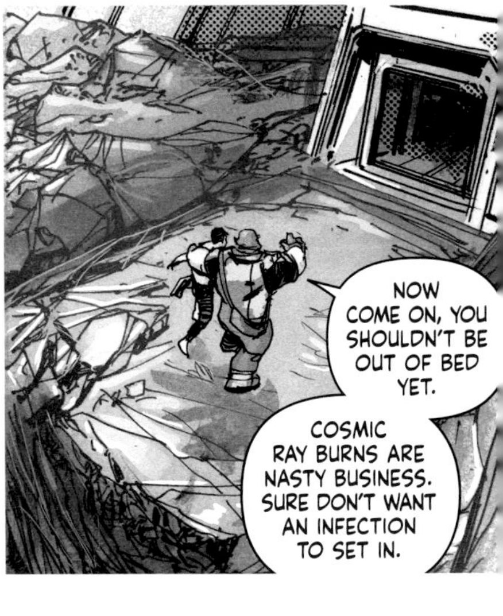
NOW COME ON, YOU SHOULDN'T BE OUT OF BED YET.
COSMIC RAY BURNS ARE NASTY BUSINESS. SURE DON'T WANT AN INFECTION TO SET IN.

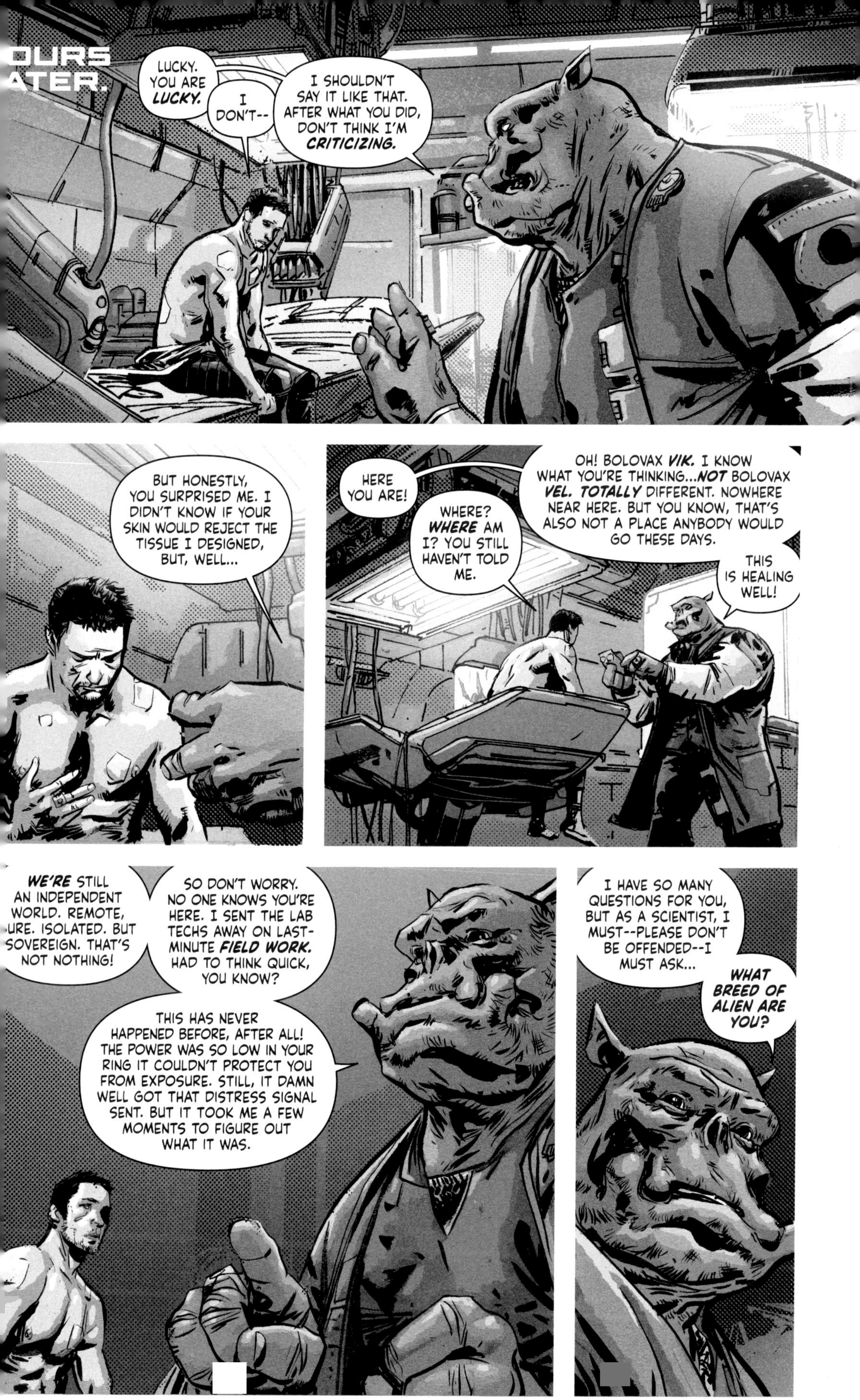
OURS
ATER.
LUCKY. YOU ARE LUCKY.
I DON'T--
I SHOULDN'T SAY IT LIKE THAT. AFTER WHAT YOU DID, DON'T THINK I'M CRITICIZING.
BUT HONESTLY, YOU SURPRISED ME. I DIDN'T KNOW IF YOUR SKIN WOULD REJECT THE TISSUE I DESIGNED, BUT, WELL...
HERE YOU ARE!
WHERE? WHERE AM I? YOU STILL HAVEN'T TOLD ME.
OH! BOLOVAX VIK. I KNOW WHAT YOU'RE THINKING...NOT BOLOVAX VEL. TOTALLY DIFFERENT. NOWHERE NEAR HERE. BUT YOU KNOW, THAT'S ALSO NOT A PLACE ANYBODY WOULD GO THESE DAYS.
THIS IS HEALING WELL!
WE'RE STILL AN INDEPENDENT WORLD. REMOTE, URE. ISOLATED. BUT SOVEREIGN. THAT'S NOT NOTHING!
SO DON'T WORRY. NO ONE KNOWS YOU'RE HERE. I SENT THE LAB TECHS AWAY ON LAST-MINUTE FIELD WORK. HAD TO THINK QUICK, YOU KNOW?
THIS HAS NEVER HAPPENED BEFORE, AFTER ALL! THE POWER WAS SO LOW IN YOUR RING IT COULDN'T PROTECT YOU FROM EXPOSURE. STILL, IT DAMN WELL GOT THAT DISTRESS SIGNAL SENT. BUT IT TOOK ME A FEW MOMENTS TO FIGURE OUT WHAT IT WAS.
I HAVE SO MANY QUESTIONS FOR YOU, BUT AS A SCIENTIST, I MUST--PLEASE DON'T BE OFFENDED--I MUST ASK...
WHAT BREED OF ALIEN ARE YOU?

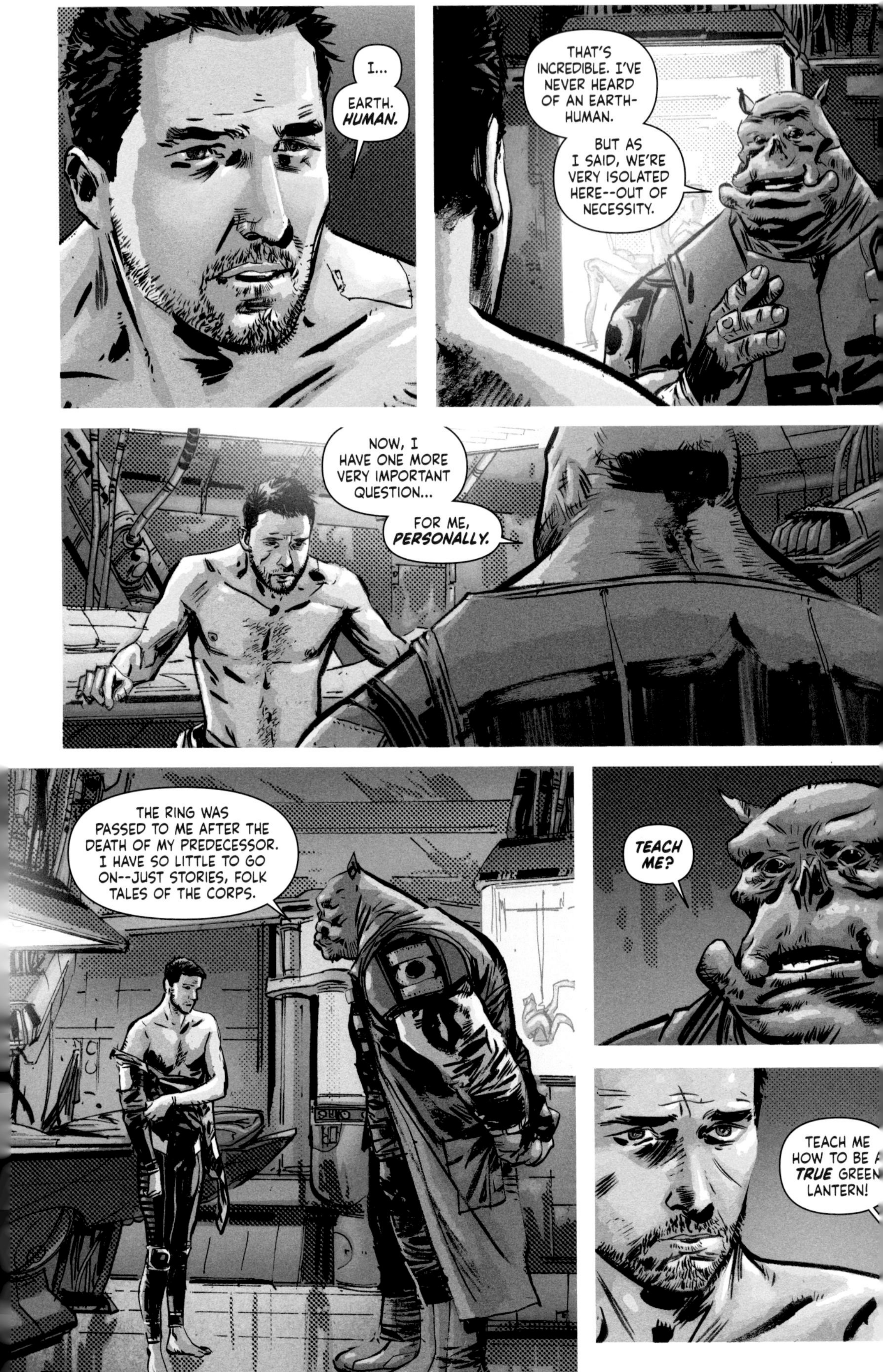
I...
EARTH. *HUMAN.*
THAT'S INCREDIBLE. I'VE NEVER HEARD OF AN EARTH-HUMAN.
BUT AS I SAID, WE'RE VERY ISOLATED HERE--OUT OF NECESSITY.
NOW, I HAVE ONE MORE VERY IMPORTANT QUESTION...
FOR ME, *PERSONALLY.*
THE RING WAS PASSED TO ME AFTER THE DEATH OF MY PREDECESSOR. I HAVE SO LITTLE TO GO ON--JUST STORIES, FOLK TALES OF THE CORPS.
TEACH ME?
TEACH ME HOW TO BE A *TRUE* GREEN LANTERN!

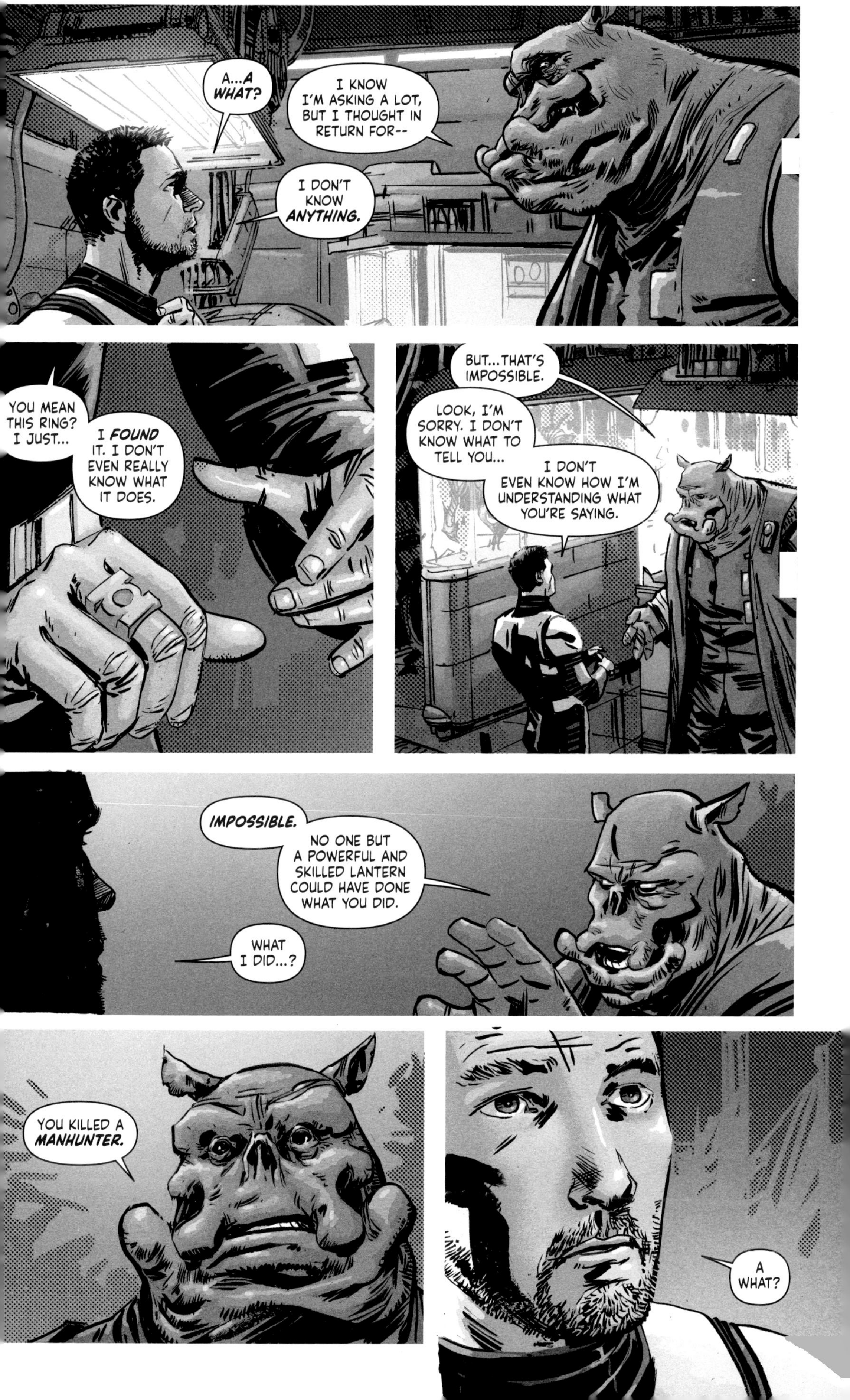
A...A *WHAT?*
I KNOW I'M ASKING A LOT, BUT I THOUGHT IN RETURN FOR--
I DON'T KNOW *ANYTHING.*
YOU MEAN THIS RING? I JUST...
I *FOUND* IT. I DON'T EVEN REALLY KNOW WHAT IT DOES.
BUT...THAT'S IMPOSSIBLE.
LOOK, I'M SORRY. I DON'T KNOW WHAT TO TELL YOU...
I DON'T EVEN KNOW HOW I'M UNDERSTANDING WHAT YOU'RE SAYING.
IMPOSSIBLE.
NO ONE BUT A POWERFUL AND SKILLED LANTERN COULD HAVE DONE WHAT YOU DID.
WHAT I DID...?
YOU KILLED A *MANHUNTER.*
A WHAT?

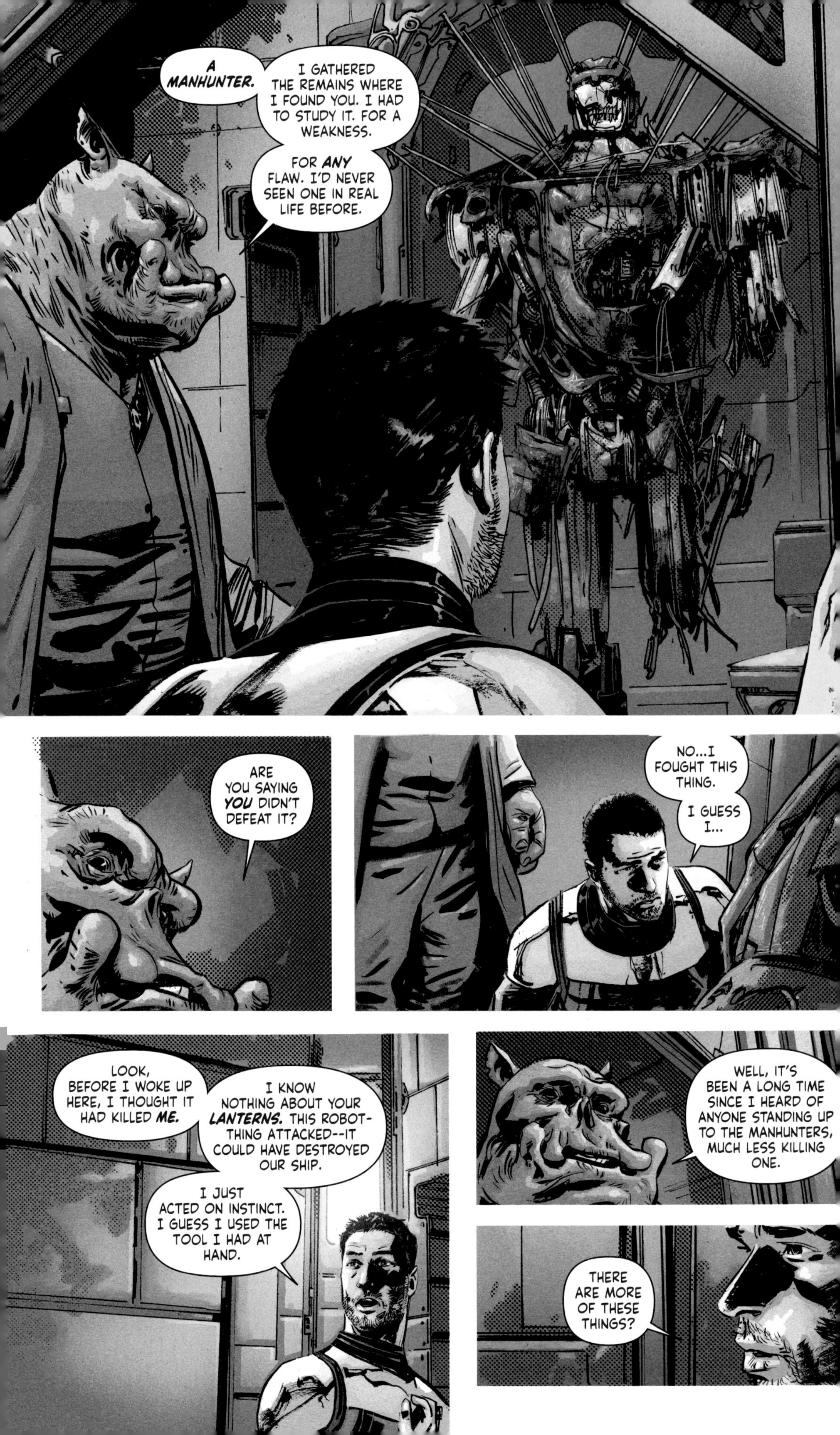
A MANHUNTER.
I GATHERED THE REMAINS WHERE I FOUND YOU. I HAD TO STUDY IT. FOR A WEAKNESS.
FOR ANY FLAW. I'D NEVER SEEN ONE IN REAL LIFE BEFORE.
ARE YOU SAYING YOU DIDN'T DEFEAT IT?
NO...I FOUGHT THIS THING.
I GUESS I...
LOOK, BEFORE I WOKE UP HERE, I THOUGHT IT HAD KILLED ME.
I KNOW NOTHING ABOUT YOUR LANTERNS. THIS ROBOT-THING ATTACKED--IT COULD HAVE DESTROYED OUR SHIP.
I JUST ACTED ON INSTINCT. I GUESS I USED THE TOOL I HAD AT HAND.
WELL, IT'S BEEN A LONG TIME SINCE I HEARD OF ANYONE STANDING UP TO THE MANHUNTERS, MUCH LESS KILLING ONE.
THERE ARE MORE OF THESE THINGS?

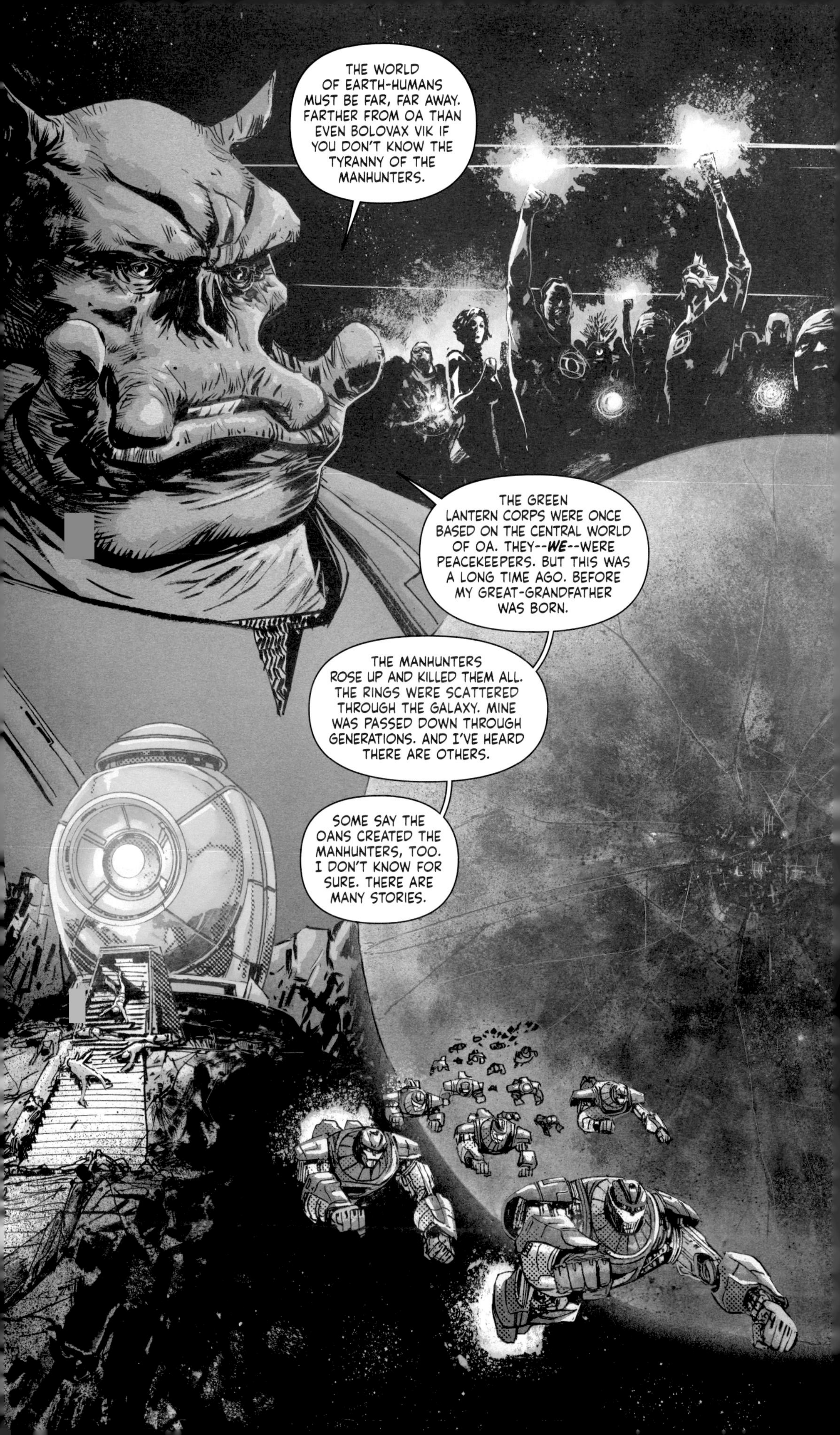
THE WORLD OF EARTH-HUMANS MUST BE FAR, FAR AWAY. FARTHER FROM OA THAN EVEN BOLOVAX VIK IF YOU DON'T KNOW THE TYRANNY OF THE MANHUNTERS.
THE GREEN LANTERN CORPS WERE ONCE BASED ON THE CENTRAL WORLD OF OA. THEY--*WE*--WERE PEACEKEEPERS. BUT THIS WAS A LONG TIME AGO. BEFORE MY GREAT-GRANDFATHER WAS BORN.
THE MANHUNTERS ROSE UP AND KILLED THEM ALL. THE RINGS WERE SCATTERED THROUGH THE GALAXY. MINE WAS PASSED DOWN THROUGH GENERATIONS. AND I'VE HEARD THERE ARE OTHERS.
SOME SAY THE OANS CREATED THE MANHUNTERS, TOO. I DON'T KNOW FOR SURE. THERE ARE MANY STORIES.

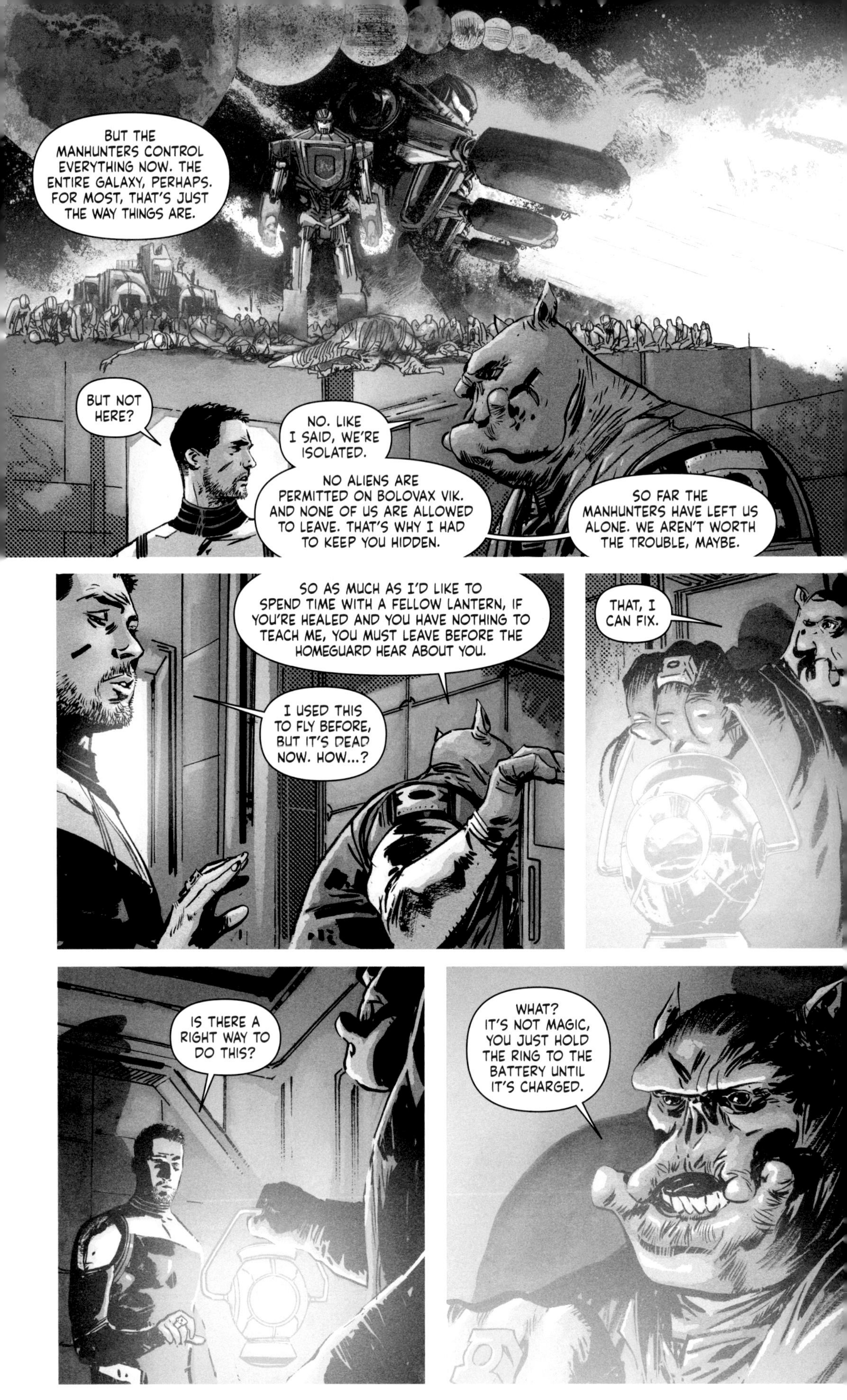
BUT THE MANHUNTERS CONTROL EVERYTHING NOW. THE ENTIRE GALAXY, PERHAPS. FOR MOST, THAT'S JUST THE WAY THINGS ARE.
BUT NOT HERE?
NO. LIKE I SAID, WE'RE ISOLATED.
NO ALIENS ARE PERMITTED ON BOLOVAX VIK. AND NONE OF US ARE ALLOWED TO LEAVE. THAT'S WHY I HAD TO KEEP YOU HIDDEN.
SO FAR THE MANHUNTERS HAVE LEFT US ALONE. WE AREN'T WORTH THE TROUBLE, MAYBE.
SO AS MUCH AS I'D LIKE TO SPEND TIME WITH A FELLOW LANTERN, IF YOU'RE HEALED AND YOU HAVE NOTHING TO TEACH ME, YOU MUST LEAVE BEFORE THE HOMEGUARD HEAR ABOUT YOU.
I USED THIS TO FLY BEFORE, BUT IT'S DEAD NOW. HOW...?
THAT, I CAN FIX.
IS THERE A RIGHT WAY TO DO THIS?
WHAT? IT'S NOT MAGIC, YOU JUST HOLD THE RING TO THE BATTERY UNTIL IT'S CHARGED.

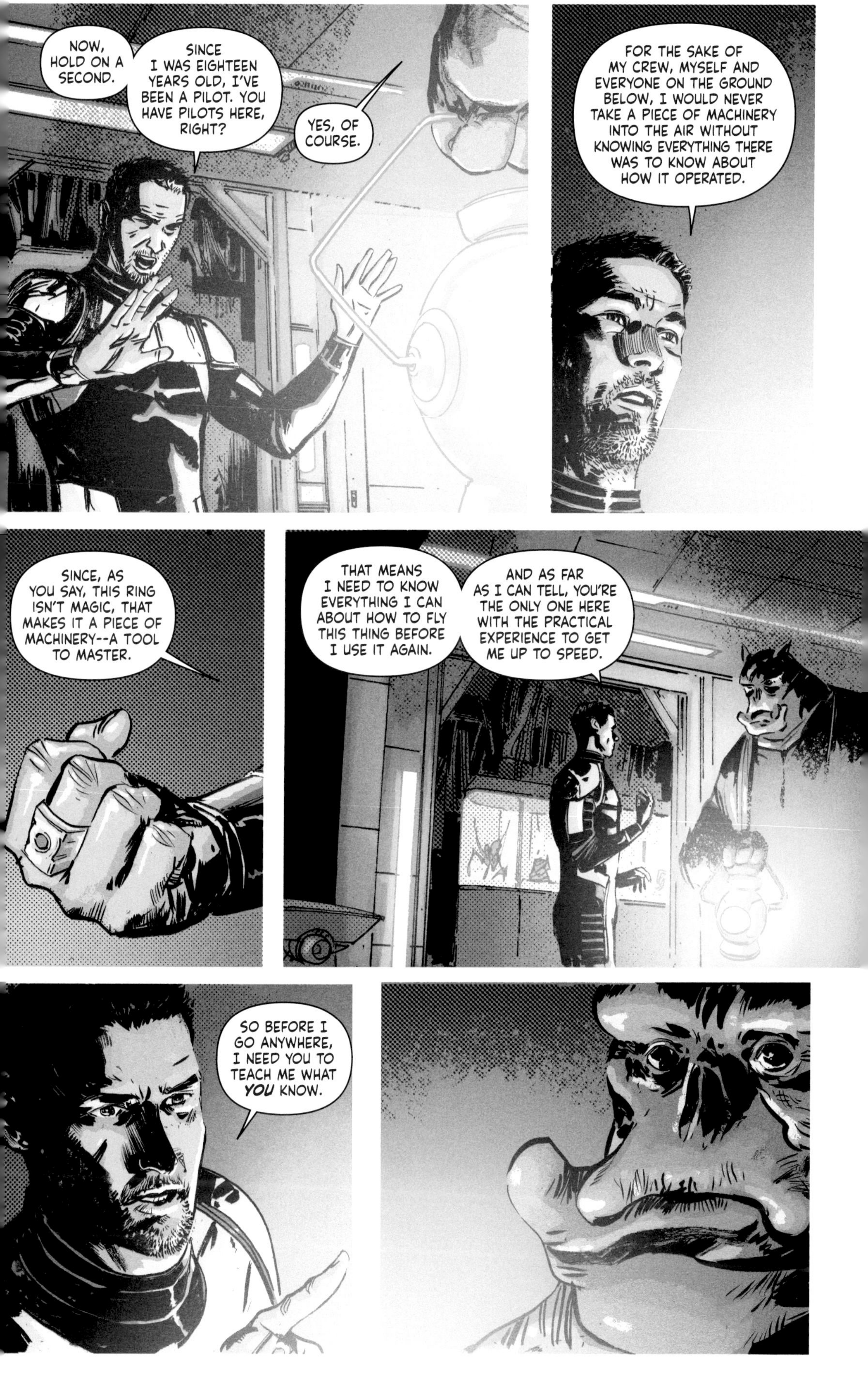

NOW, HOLD ON A SECOND.
SINCE I WAS EIGHTEEN YEARS OLD, I'VE BEEN A PILOT. YOU HAVE PILOTS HERE, RIGHT?
YES, OF COURSE.
FOR THE SAKE OF MY CREW, MYSELF AND EVERYONE ON THE GROUND BELOW, I WOULD NEVER TAKE A PIECE OF MACHINERY INTO THE AIR WITHOUT KNOWING EVERYTHING THERE WAS TO KNOW ABOUT HOW IT OPERATED.
SINCE, AS YOU SAY, THIS RING ISN'T MAGIC, THAT MAKES IT A PIECE OF MACHINERY--A TOOL TO MASTER.
THAT MEANS I NEED TO KNOW EVERYTHING I CAN ABOUT HOW TO FLY THIS THING BEFORE I USE IT AGAIN.
AND AS FAR AS I CAN TELL, YOU'RE THE ONLY ONE HERE WITH THE PRACTICAL EXPERIENCE TO GET ME UP TO SPEED.
SO BEFORE I GO ANYWHERE, I NEED YOU TO TEACH ME WHAT *YOU* KNOW.

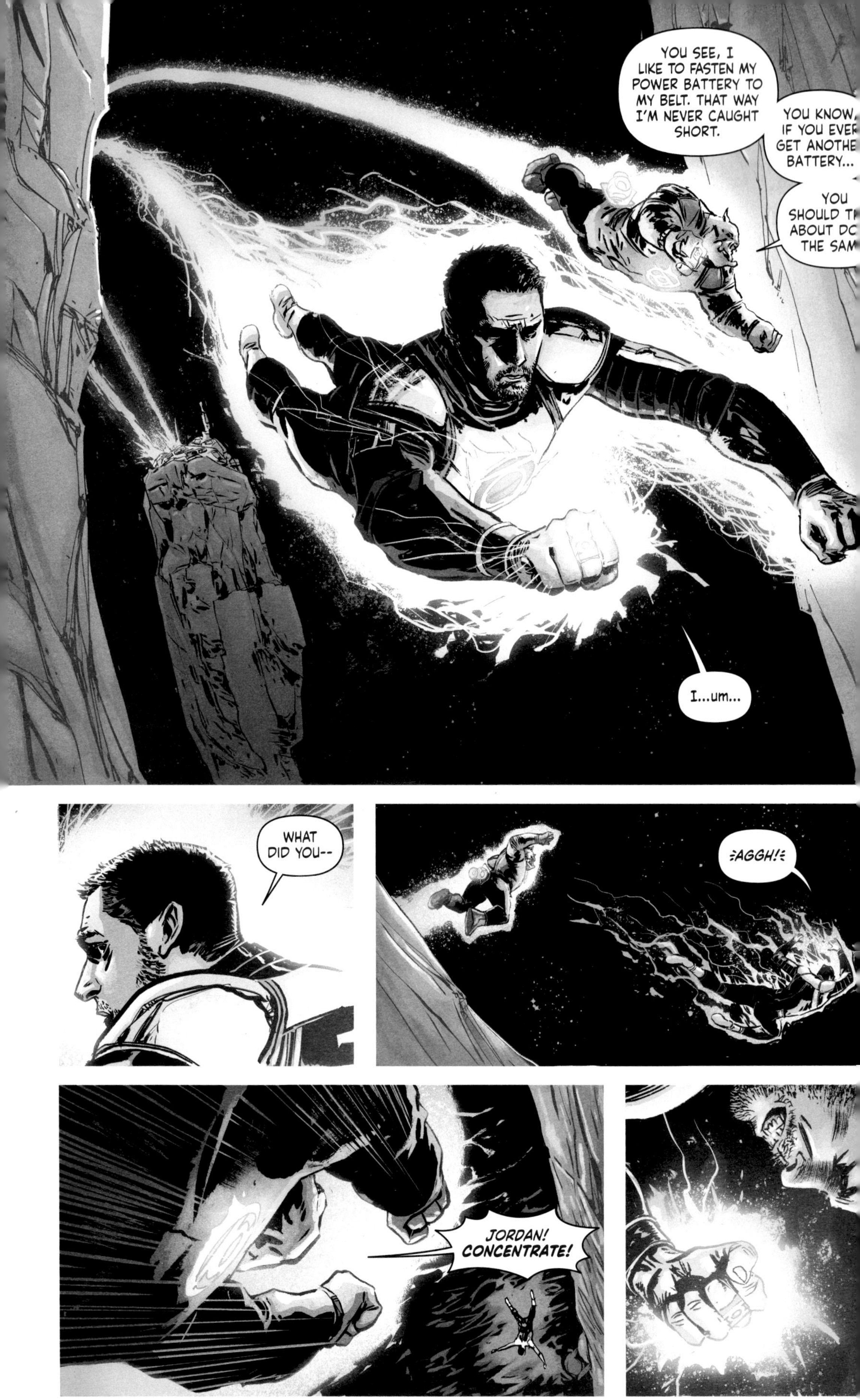
YOU SEE, I LIKE TO FASTEN MY POWER BATTERY TO MY BELT. THAT WAY I'M NEVER CAUGHT SHORT.
YOU KNOW, IF YOU EVER GET ANOTHE BATTERY...
YOU SHOULD T ABOUT DO THE SAM
I...um...
WHAT DID YOU--
AGGH!
JORDAN! CONCENTRATE!

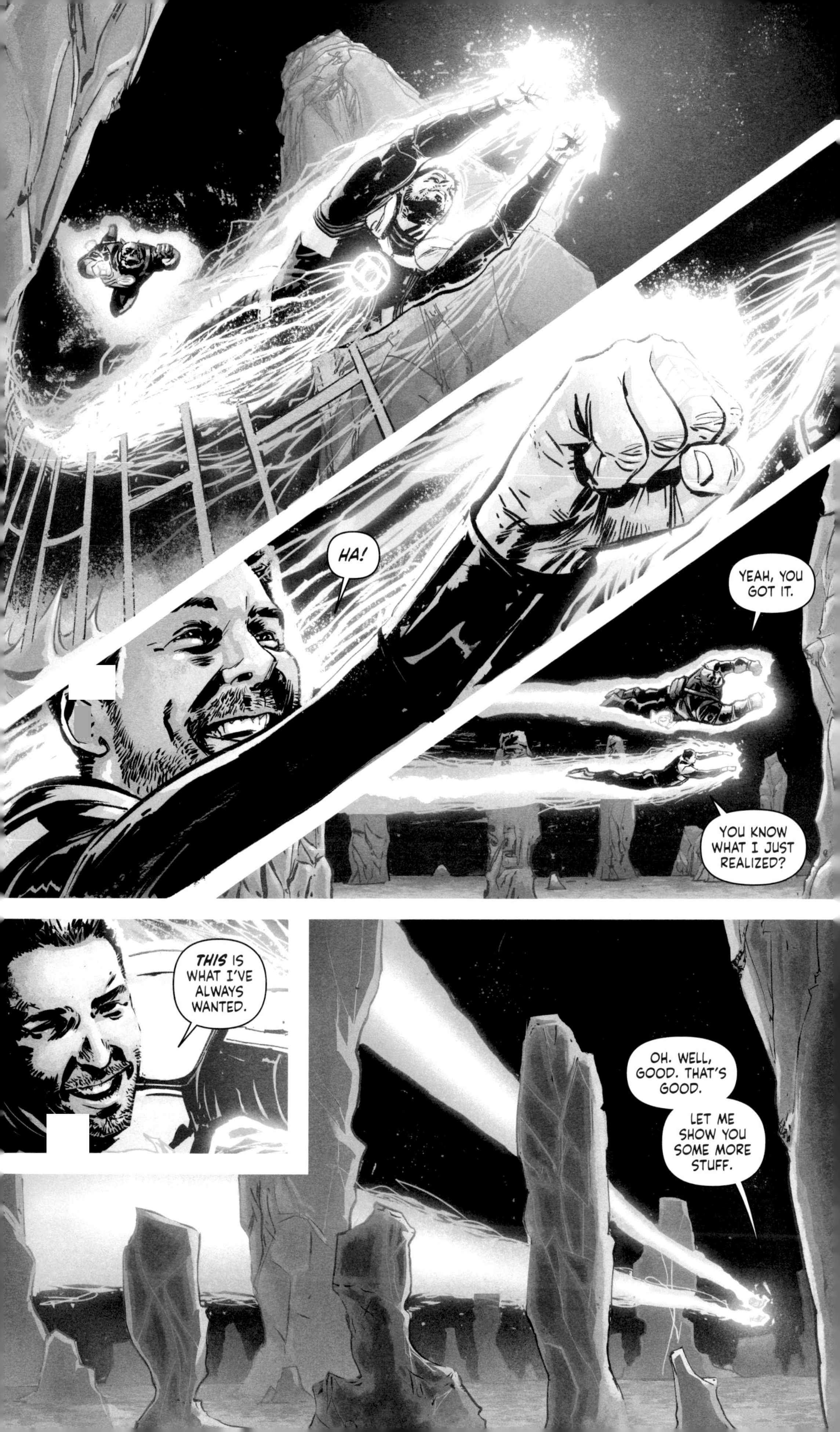

HA!
YEAH, YOU GOT IT.
YOU KNOW WHAT I JUST REALIZED?
THIS IS WHAT I'VE ALWAYS WANTED.
OH. WELL, GOOD. THAT'S GOOD.
LET ME SHOW YOU SOME MORE STUFF.

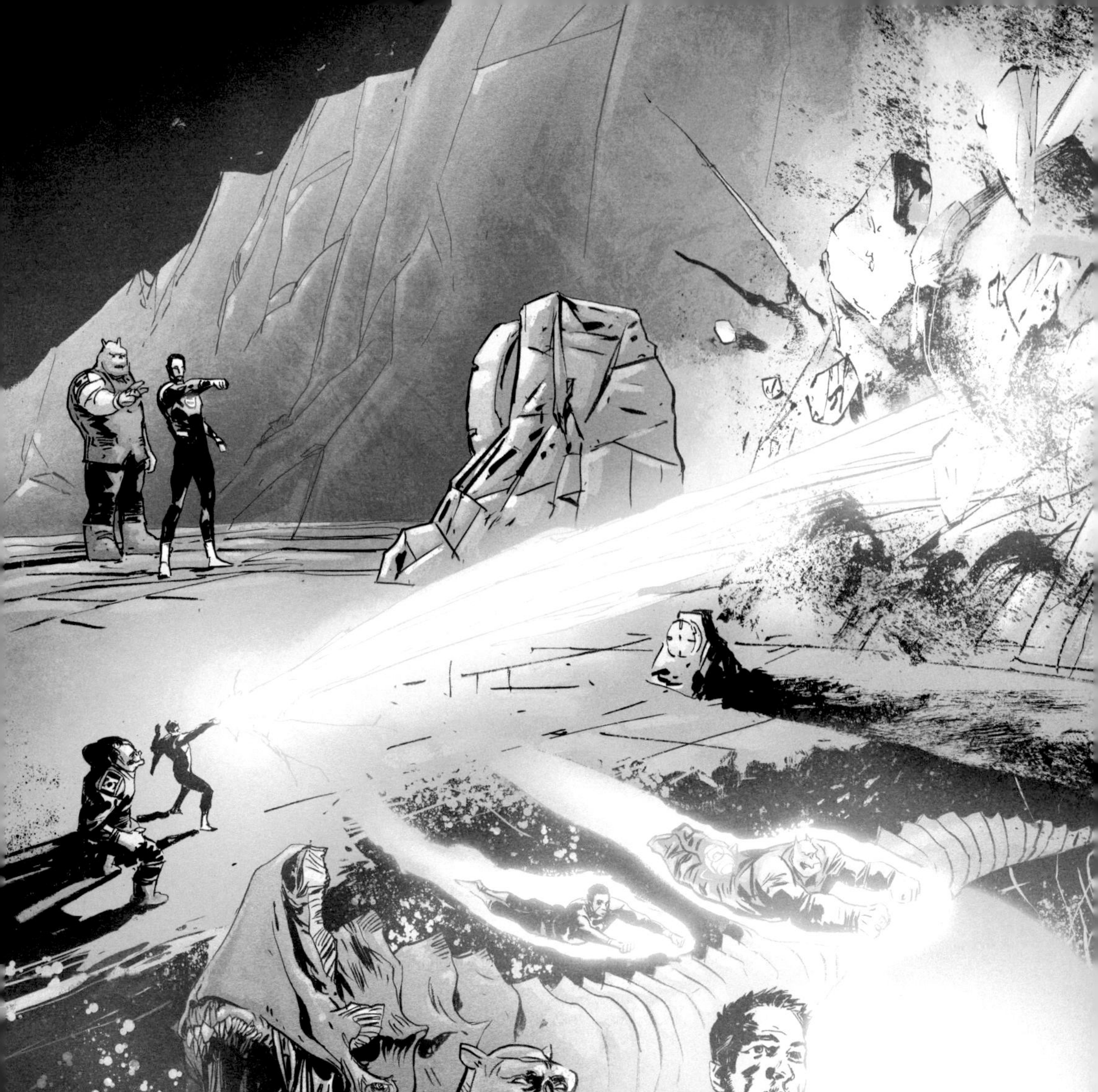

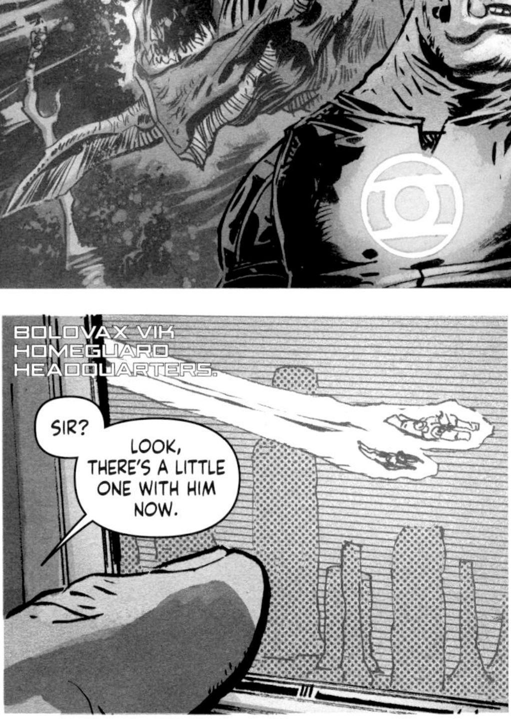
BOLOVAX VIK
HOMEGUARD
HEADQUARTERS.
SIR?
LOOK, THERE'S A LITTLE ONE WITH HIM NOW.

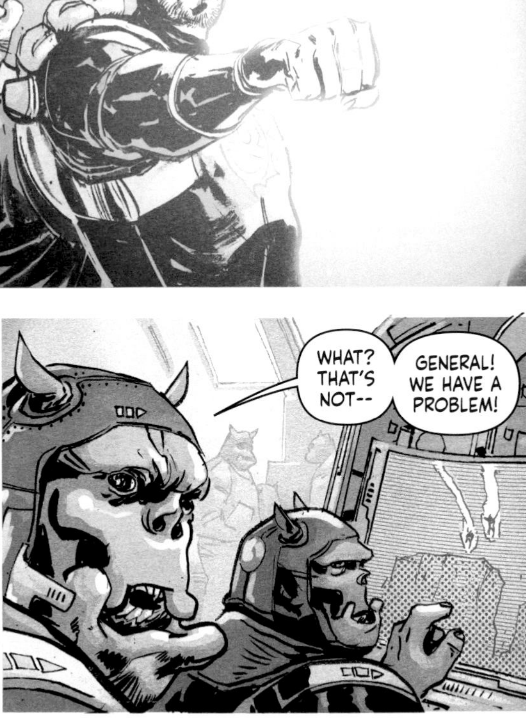
GENERAL! WE HAVE A PROBLEM!
WHAT? THAT'S NOT--

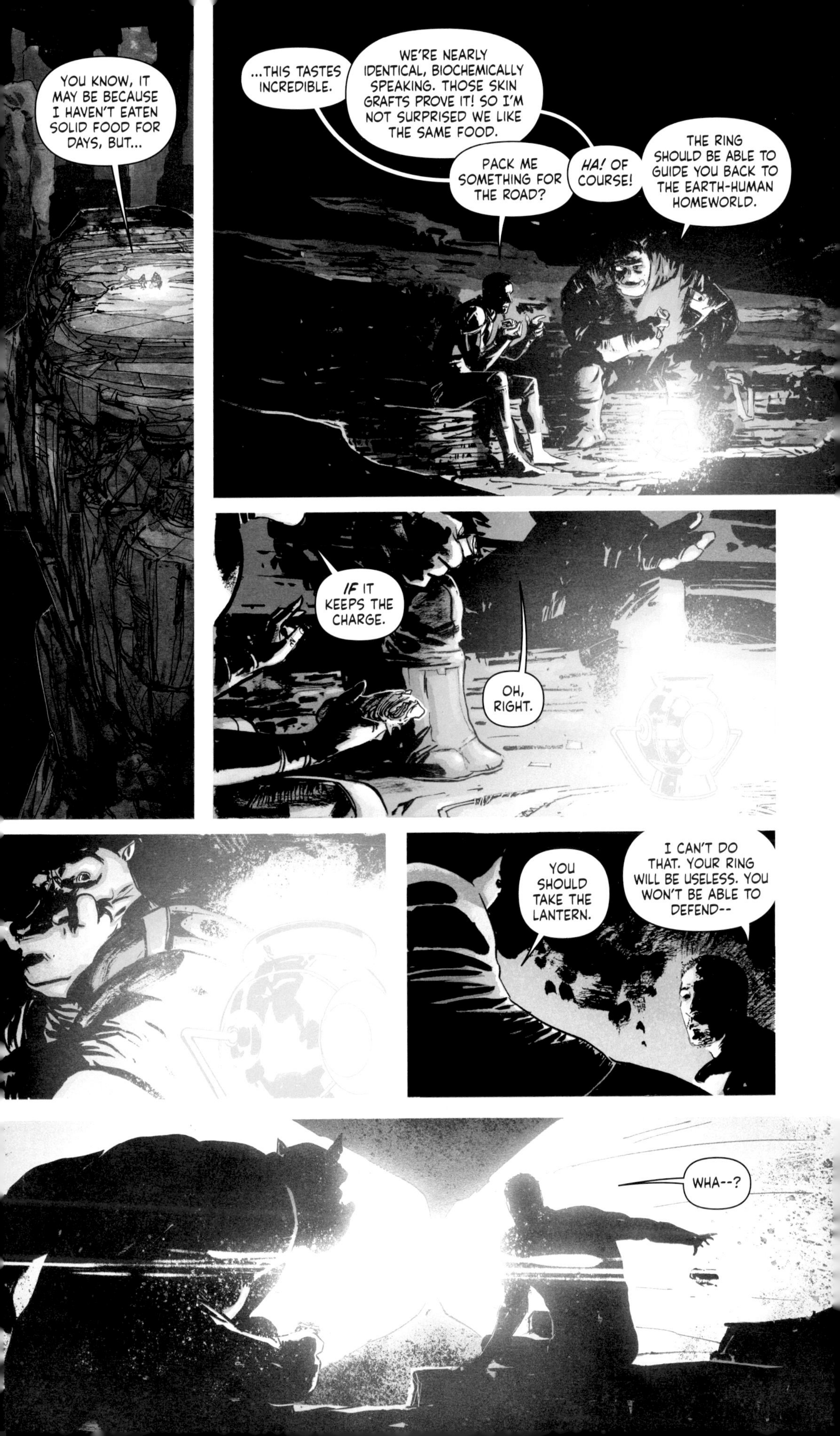
YOU KNOW, IT MAY BE BECAUSE I HAVEN'T EATEN SOLID FOOD FOR DAYS, BUT...
...THIS TASTES INCREDIBLE.
WE'RE NEARLY IDENTICAL, BIOCHEMICALLY SPEAKING. THOSE SKIN GRAFTS PROVE IT! SO I'M NOT SURPRISED WE LIKE THE SAME FOOD.
PACK ME SOMETHING FOR THE ROAD?
HA! OF COURSE!
THE RING SHOULD BE ABLE TO GUIDE YOU BACK TO THE EARTH-HUMAN HOMEWORLD.
IF IT KEEPS THE CHARGE.
OH, RIGHT.
YOU SHOULD TAKE THE LANTERN.
I CAN'T DO THAT. YOUR RING WILL BE USELESS. YOU WON'T BE ABLE TO DEFEND--
WHA--?

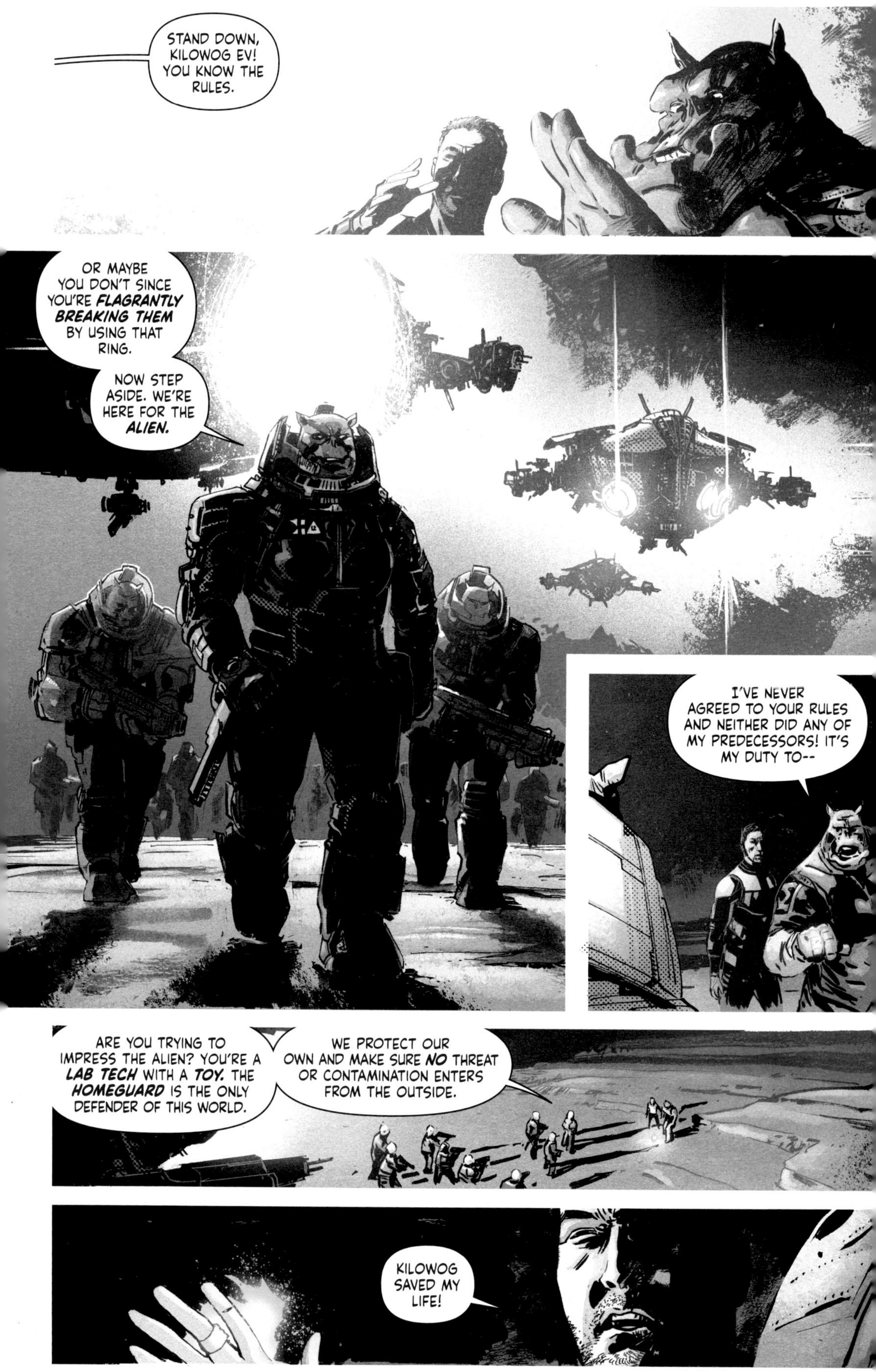
STAND DOWN, KILOWOG EV! YOU KNOW THE RULES.
OR MAYBE YOU DON'T SINCE YOU'RE **FLAGRANTLY BREAKING THEM** BY USING THAT RING.
NOW STEP ASIDE. WE'RE HERE FOR THE ***ALIEN.***
I'VE NEVER AGREED TO YOUR RULES AND NEITHER DID ANY OF MY PREDECESSORS! IT'S MY DUTY TO--
ARE YOU TRYING TO IMPRESS THE ALIEN? YOU'RE A ***LAB TECH*** WITH A ***TOY.*** THE ***HOMEGUARD*** IS THE ONLY DEFENDER OF THIS WORLD.
WE PROTECT OUR OWN AND MAKE SURE ***NO*** THREAT OR CONTAMINATION ENTERS FROM THE OUTSIDE.
KILOWOG SAVED MY LIFE!

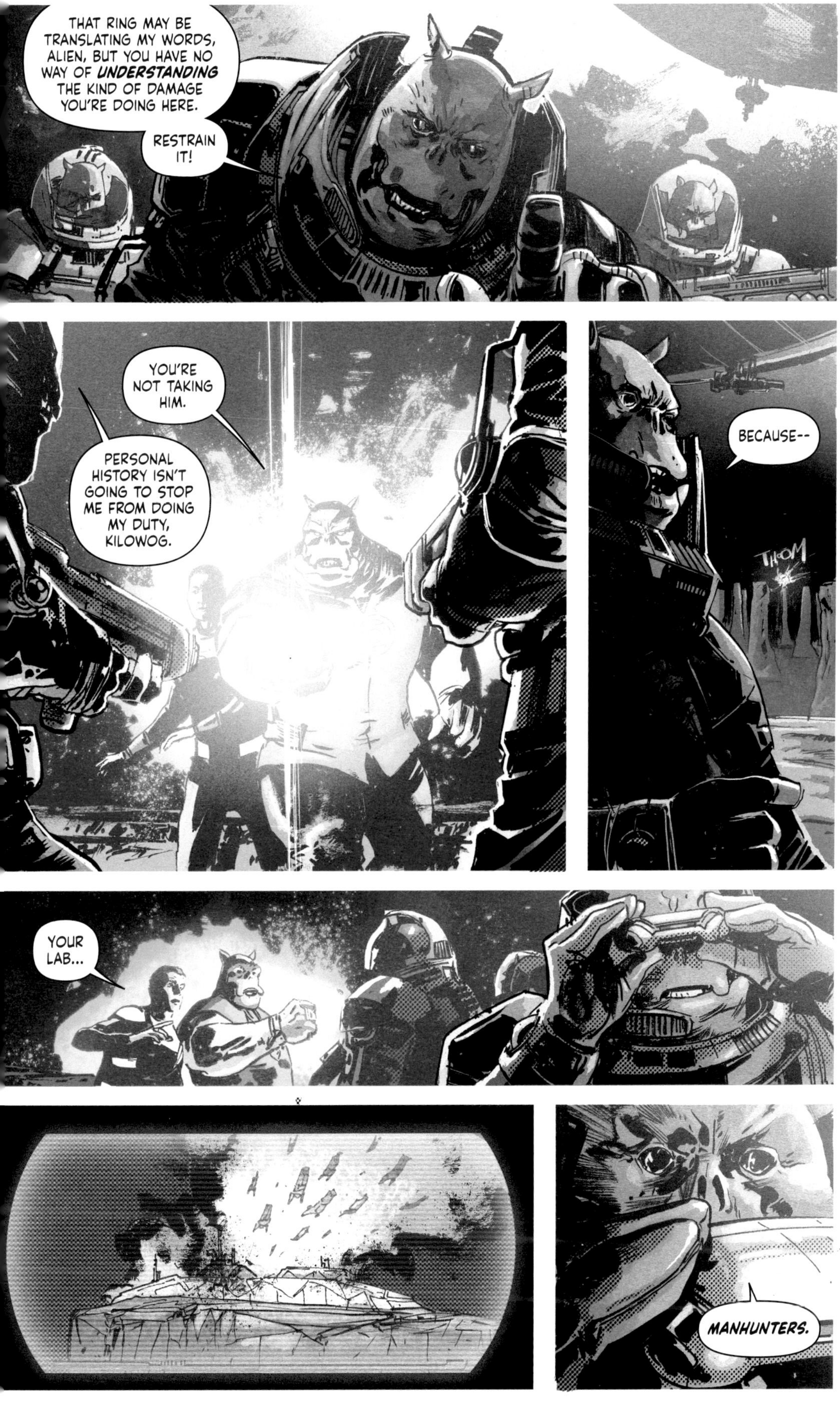
THAT RING MAY BE TRANSLATING MY WORDS, ALIEN, BUT YOU HAVE NO WAY OF **UNDERSTANDING** THE KIND OF DAMAGE YOU'RE DOING HERE.
RESTRAIN IT!
YOU'RE NOT TAKING HIM.
PERSONAL HISTORY ISN'T GOING TO STOP ME FROM DOING MY DUTY, KILOWOG.
BECAUSE--
THOOM
YOUR LAB...
MANHUNTERS.

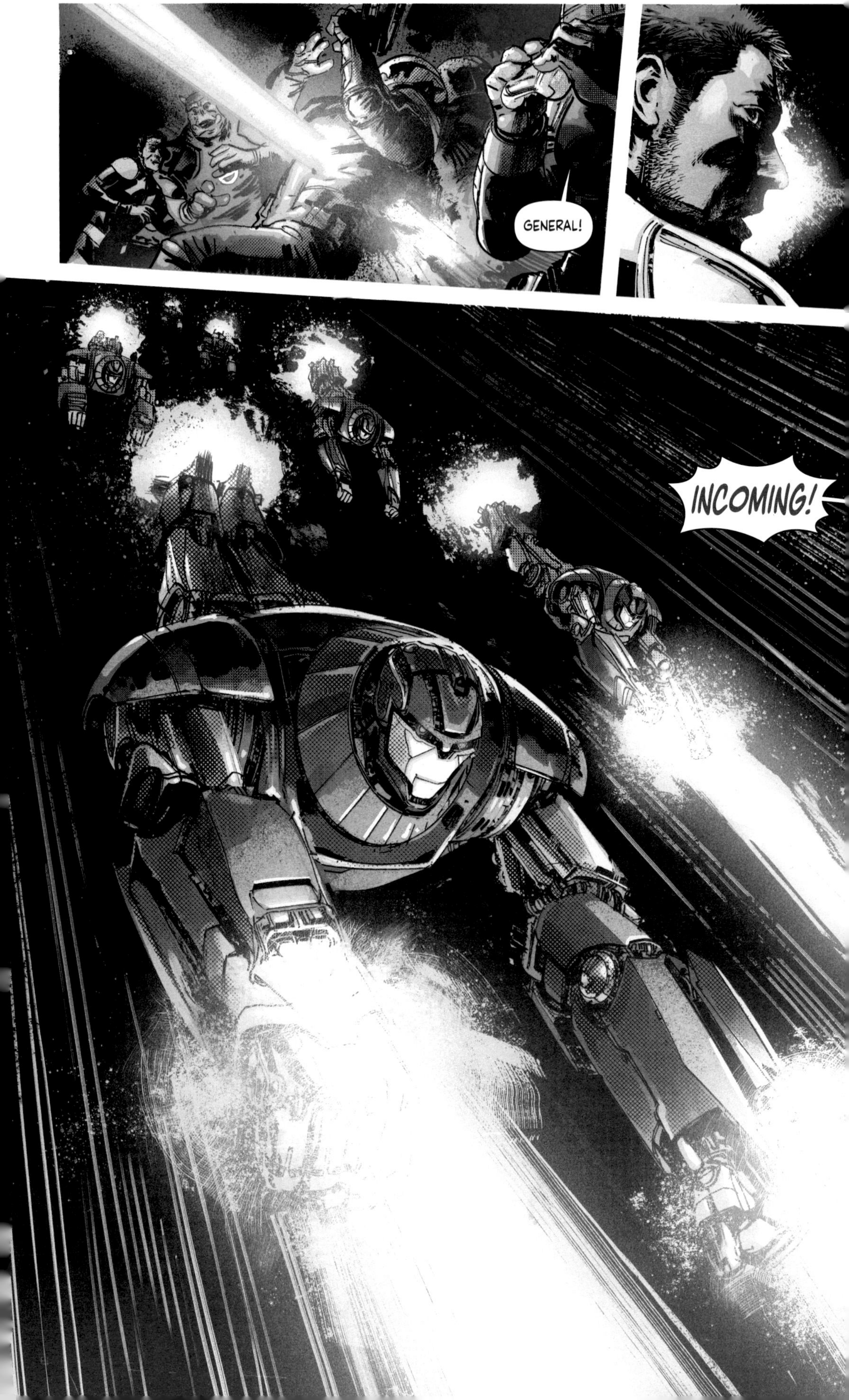
GENERAL!
INCOMING!

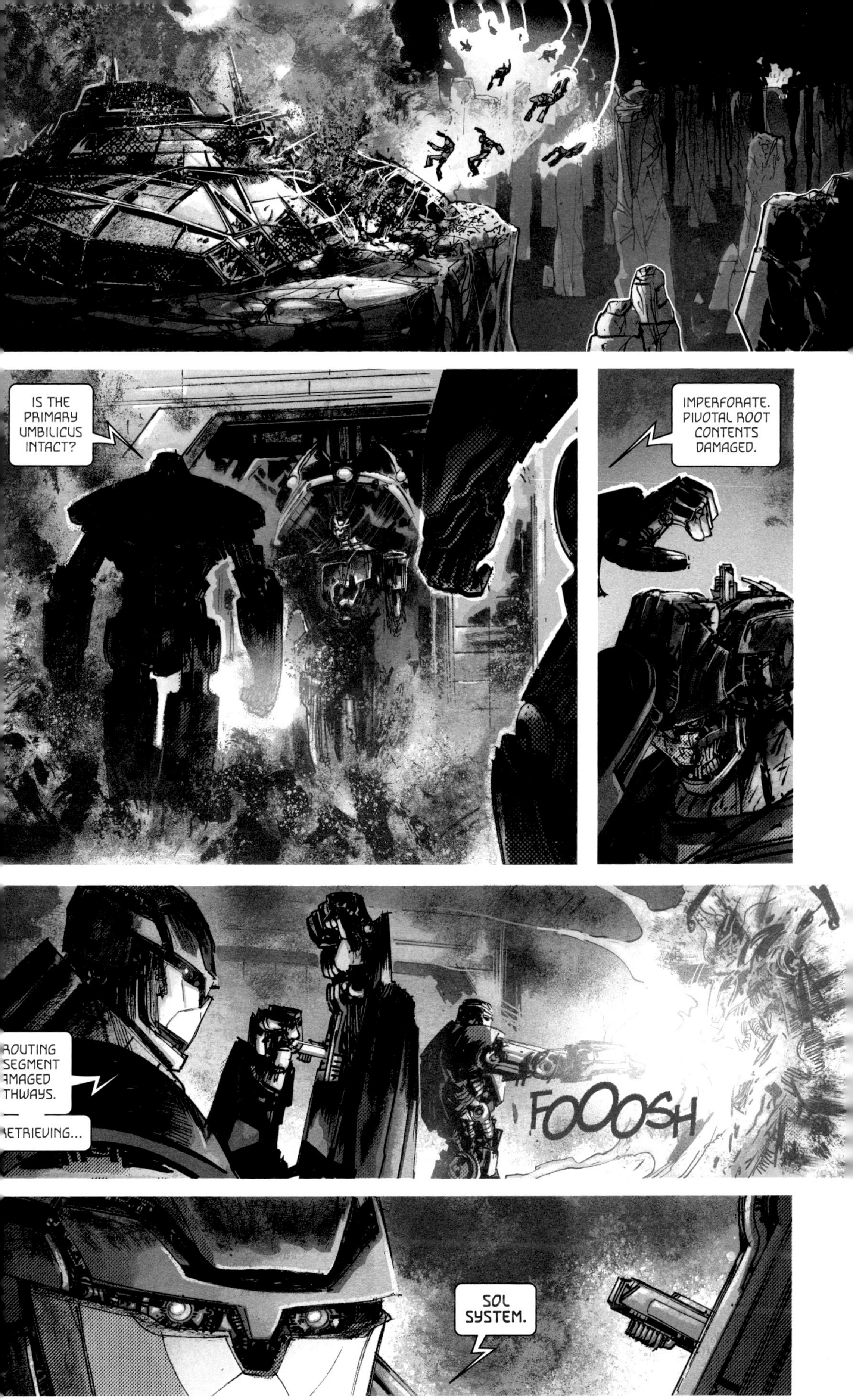
IS THE PRIMARY UMBILICUS INTACT?
IMPERFORATE. PIVOTAL ROOT CONTENTS DAMAGED.
ROUTING SEGMENT AMAGED THWAYS.
ETRIEVING...
FOOOSH
SOL SYSTEM.

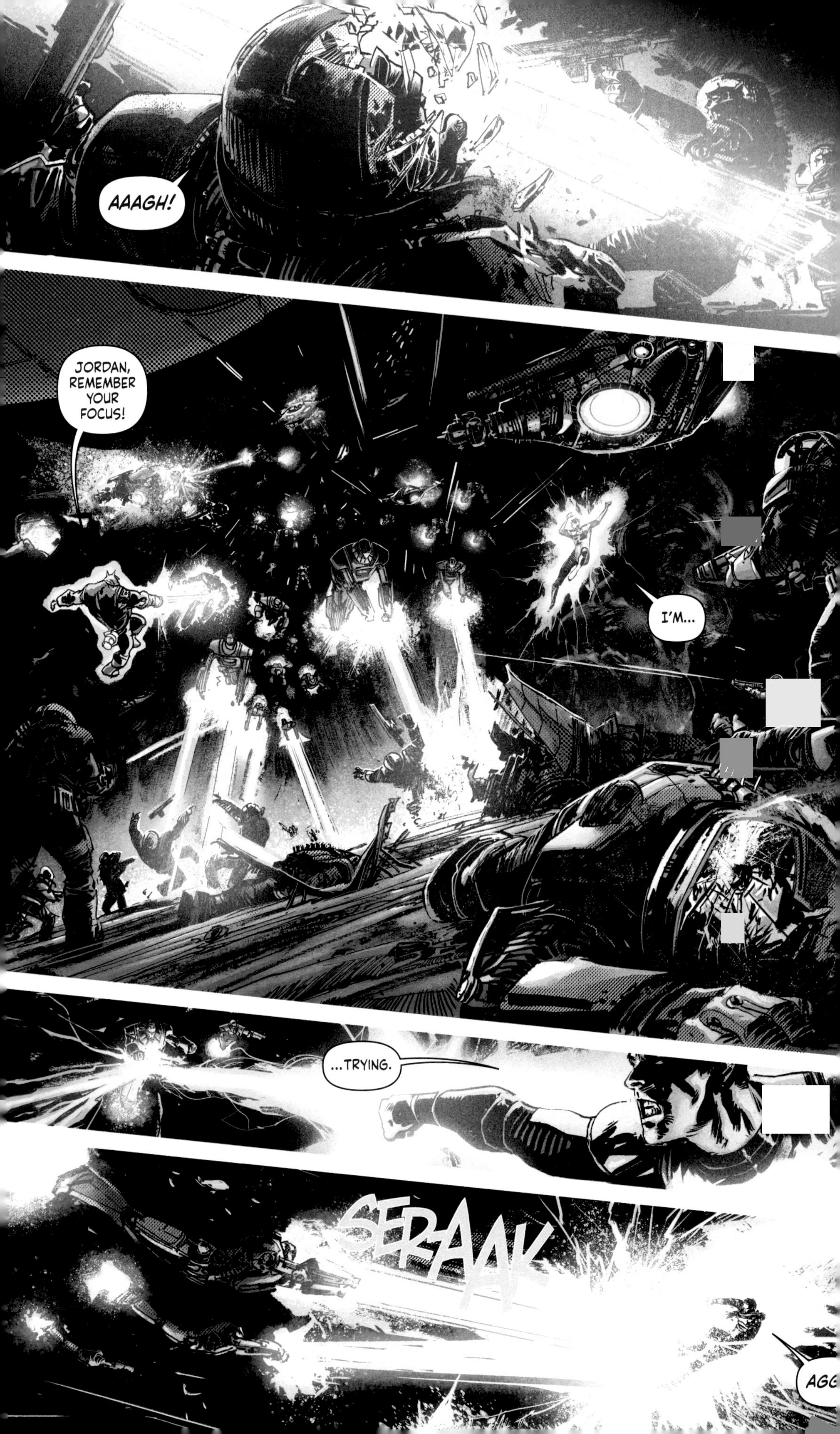
AAAGH!
JORDAN, REMEMBER YOUR FOCUS!
I'M...
...TRYING.
SCRAAK

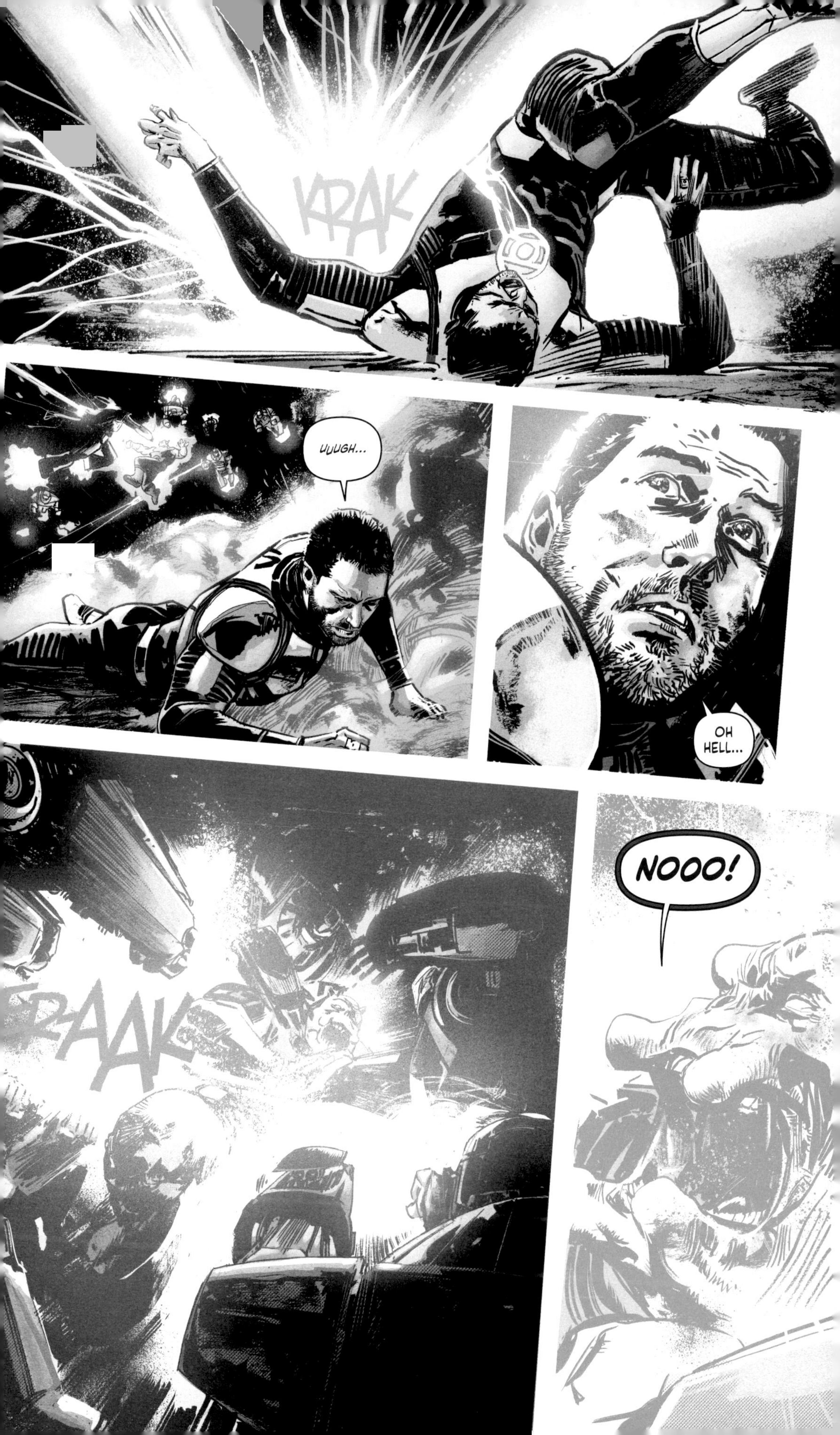
KRAK
UUUGH...
OH HELL...
KRAAK
NOOO!

WHA--?

HOLD ON!

SCRAAK

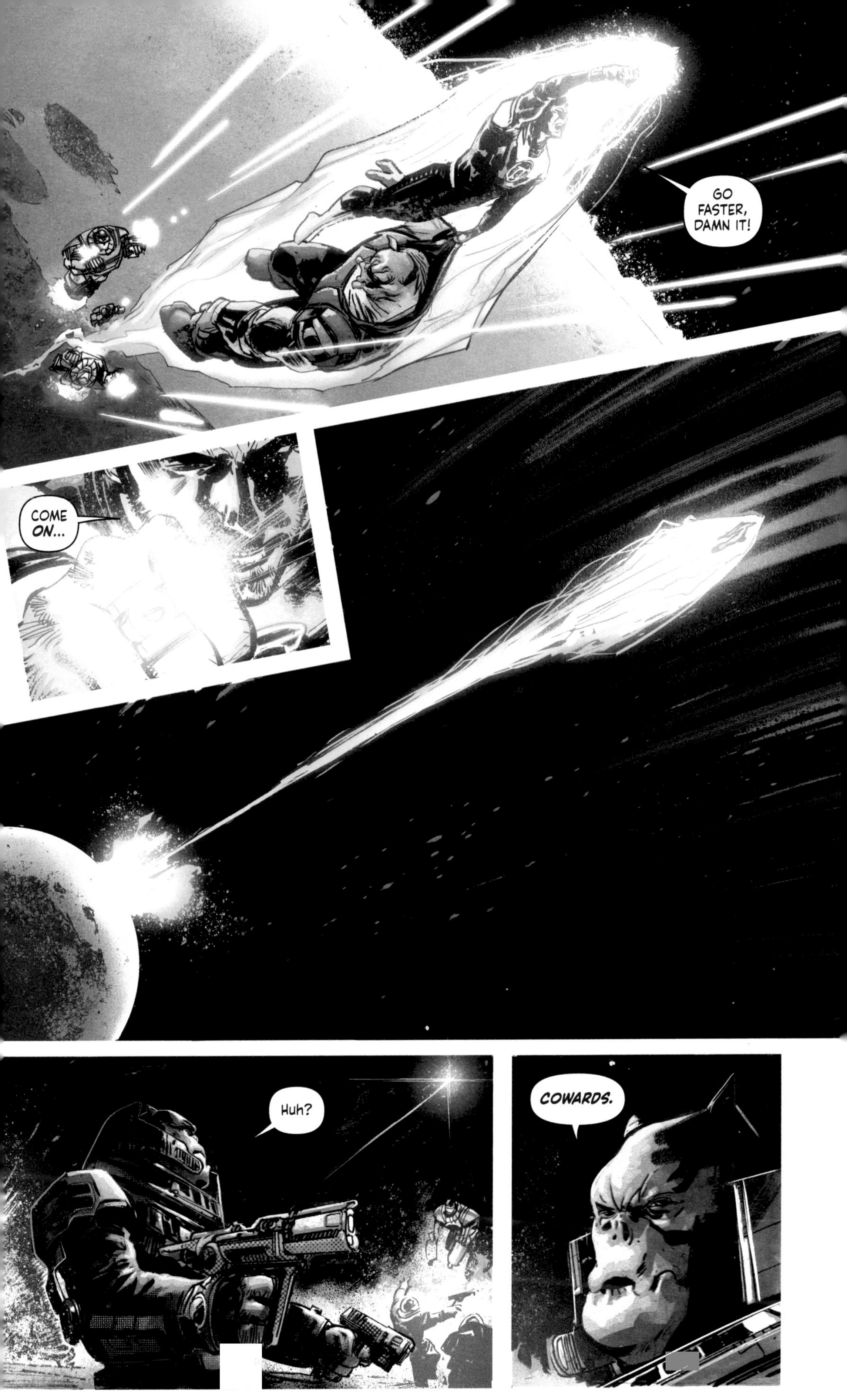
GO FASTER, DAMN IT!
COME ON...
Huh?
COWARDS.

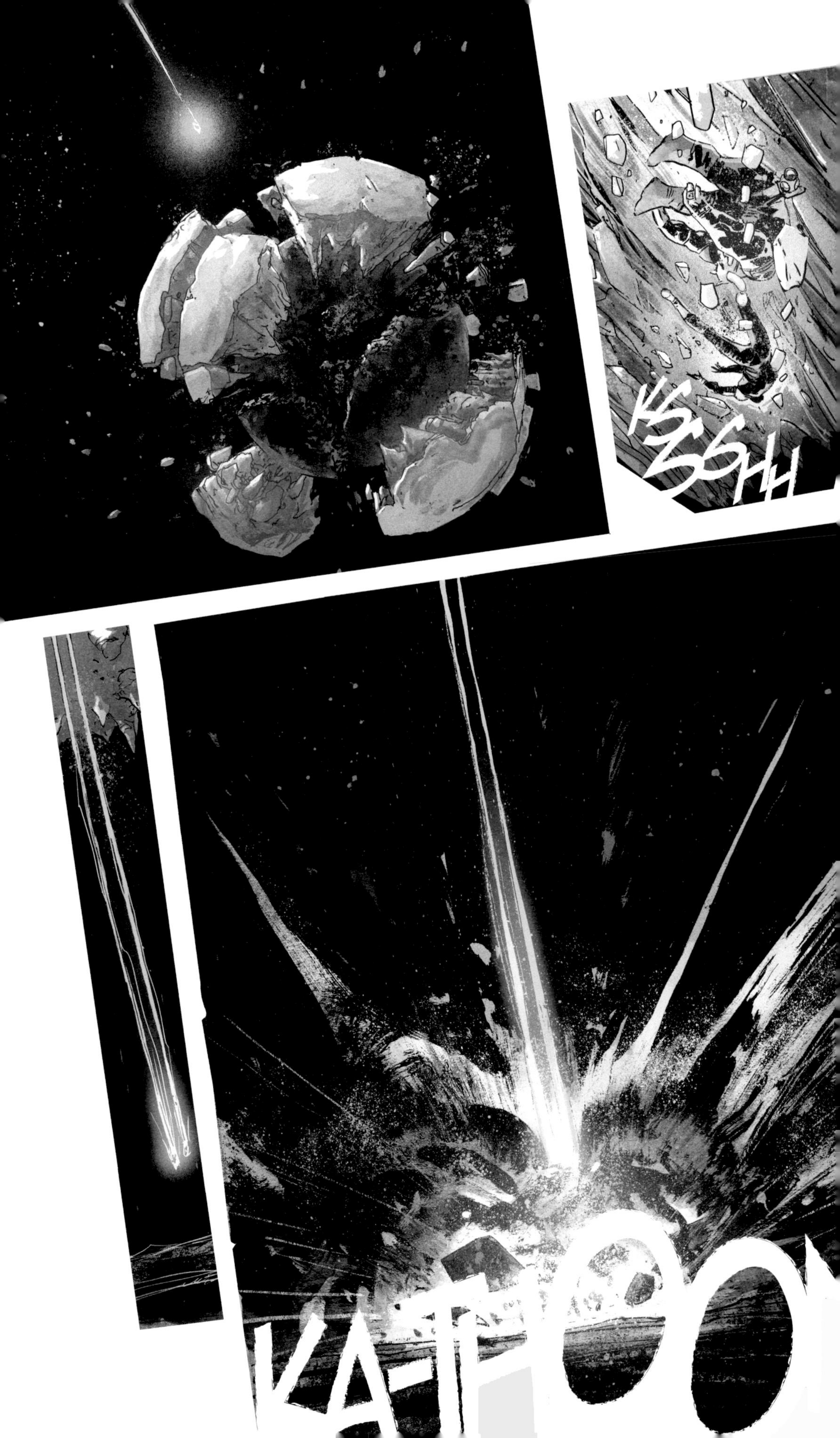
KSSSHH
KA-THOOM

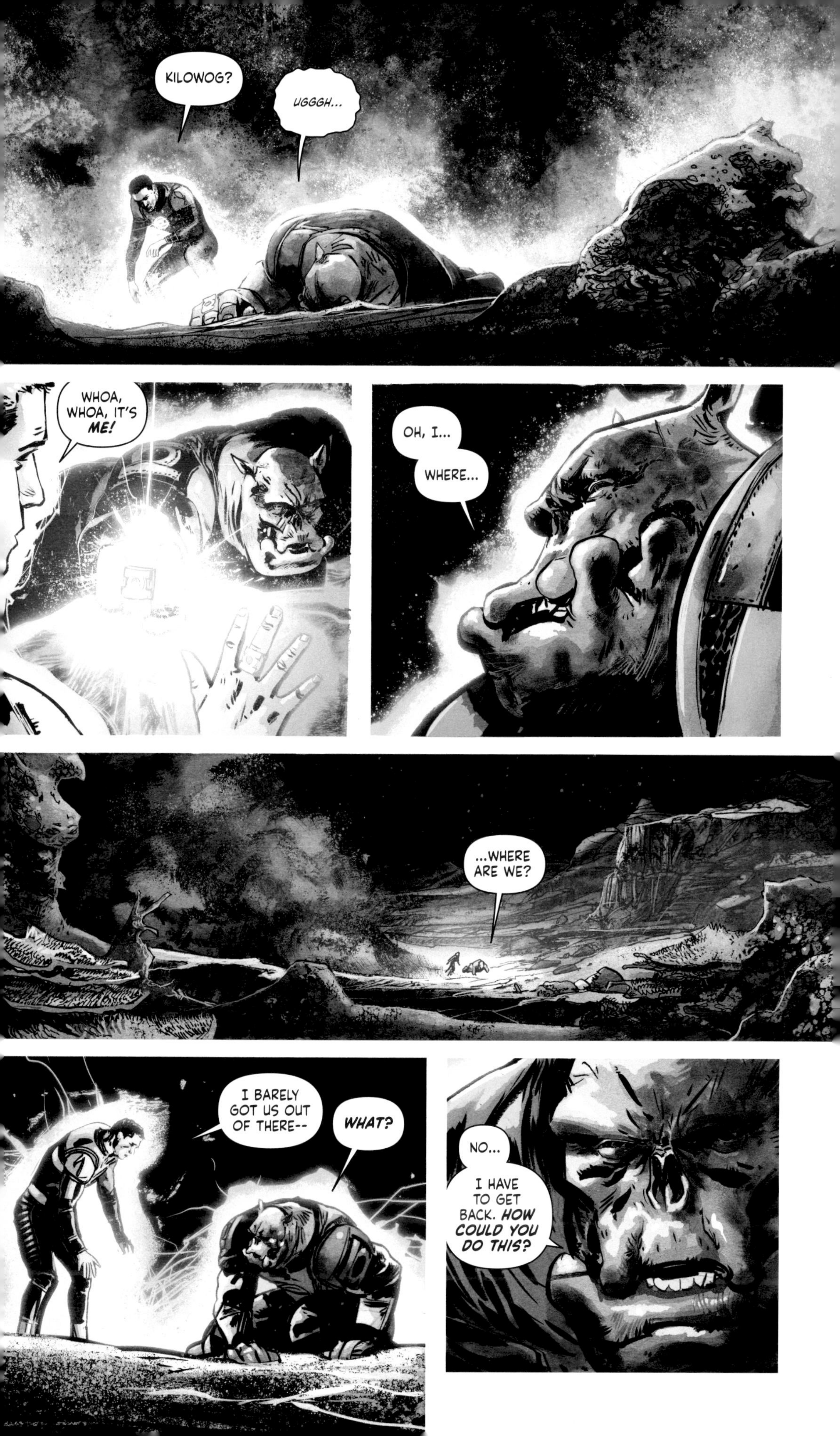
KILOWOG?
UGGGH...
WHOA, WHOA, IT'S *ME!*
OH, I...
WHERE...
...WHERE ARE WE?
I BARELY GOT US OUT OF THERE--
WHAT?
NO...
I HAVE TO GET BACK. *HOW COULD YOU DO THIS?*

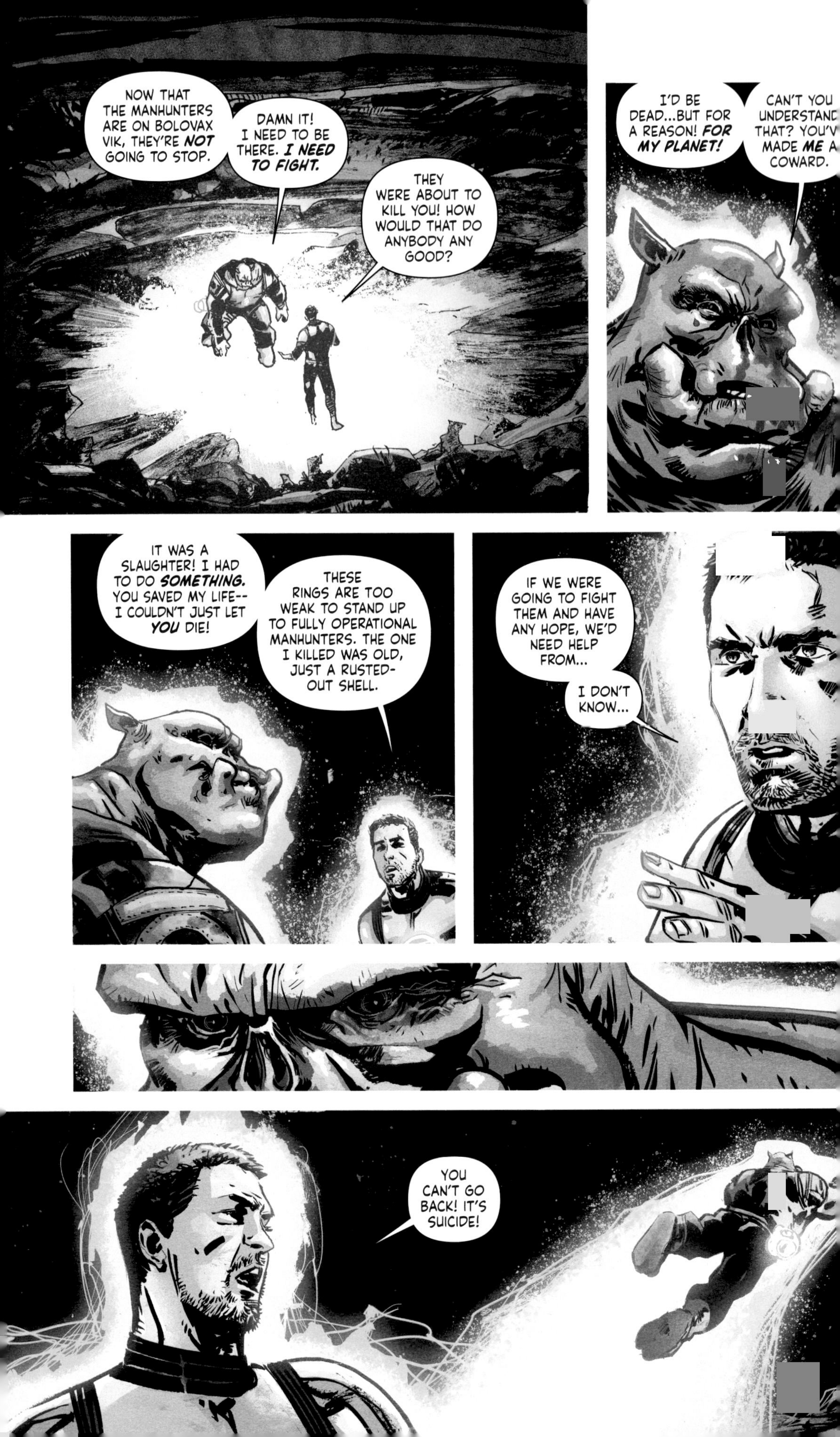
NOW THAT THE MANHUNTERS ARE ON BOLOVAX VIK, THEY'RE **NOT** GOING TO STOP.
DAMN IT! I NEED TO BE THERE. ***I NEED TO FIGHT.***
THEY WERE ABOUT TO KILL YOU! HOW WOULD THAT DO ANYBODY ANY GOOD?
I'D BE DEAD...BUT FOR A REASON! ***FOR MY PLANET!***
CAN'T YOU UNDERSTAND THAT? YOU'VE MADE **ME** A COWARD.
IT WAS A SLAUGHTER! I HAD TO DO ***SOMETHING.*** YOU SAVED MY LIFE-- I COULDN'T JUST LET ***YOU*** DIE!
THESE RINGS ARE TOO WEAK TO STAND UP TO FULLY OPERATIONAL MANHUNTERS. THE ONE I KILLED WAS OLD, JUST A RUSTED-OUT SHELL.
IF WE WERE GOING TO FIGHT THEM AND HAVE ANY HOPE, WE'D NEED HELP FROM...
I DON'T KNOW...
YOU CAN'T GO BACK! IT'S SUICIDE!

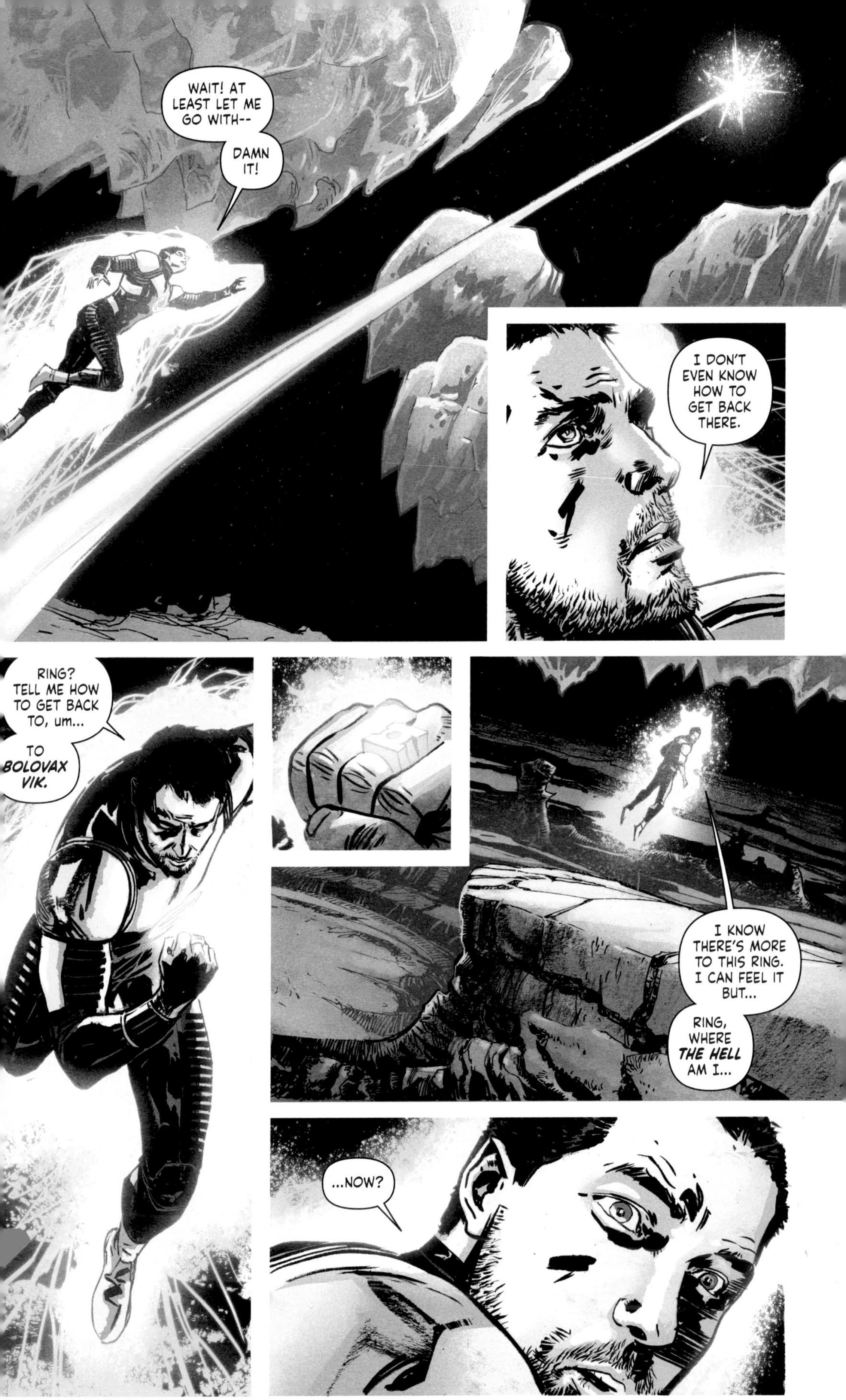
WAIT! AT LEAST LET ME GO WITH--
DAMN IT!
I DON'T EVEN KNOW HOW TO GET BACK THERE.
RING? TELL ME HOW TO GET BACK TO, um...
TO *BOLOVAX VIK.*
I KNOW THERE'S MORE TO THIS RING. I CAN FEEL IT BUT...
RING, WHERE *THE HELL* AM I...
...NOW?

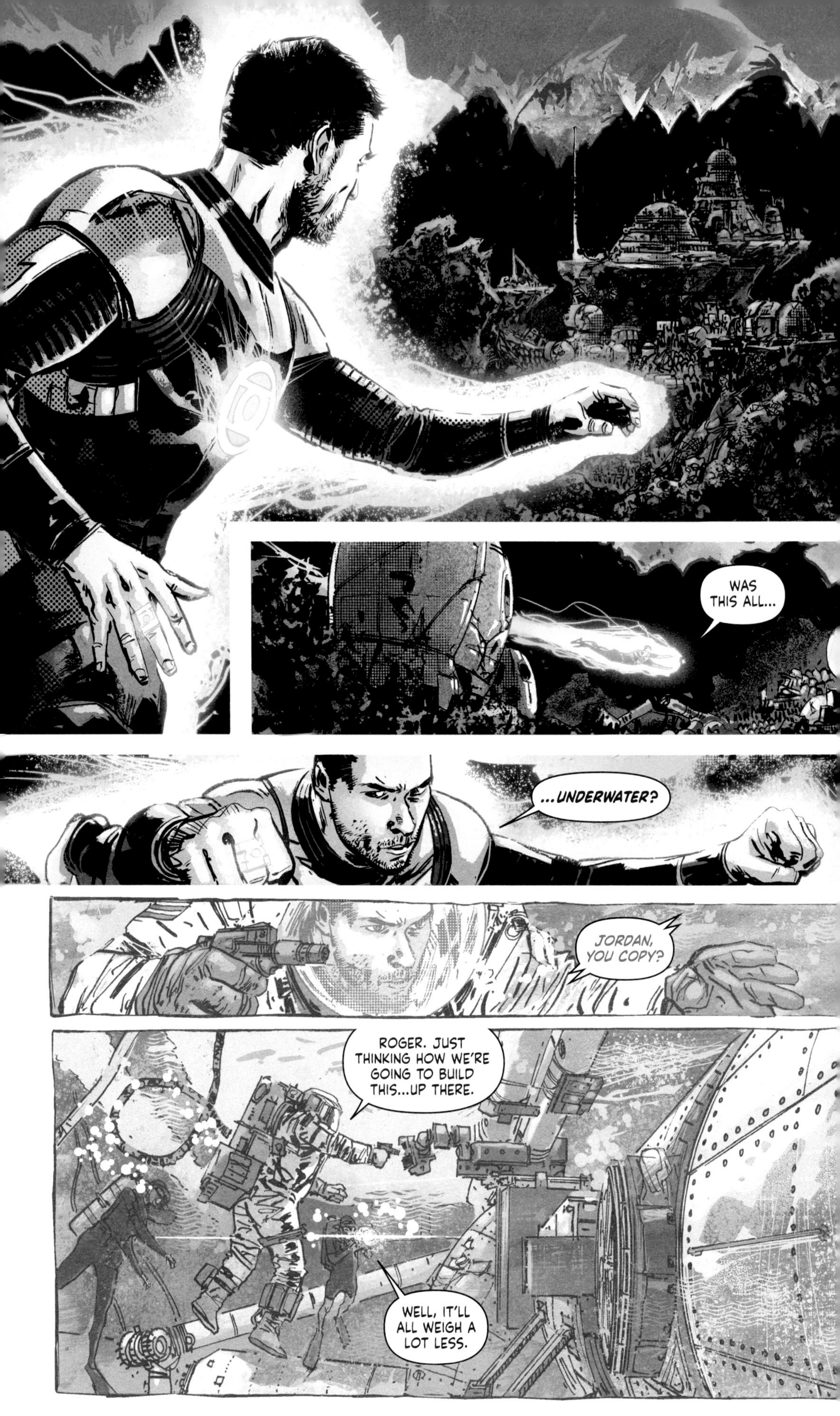
WAS THIS ALL...
...UNDERWATER?
JORDAN, YOU COPY?
ROGER. JUST THINKING HOW WE'RE GOING TO BUILD THIS...UP THERE.
WELL, IT'LL ALL WEIGH A LOT LESS.

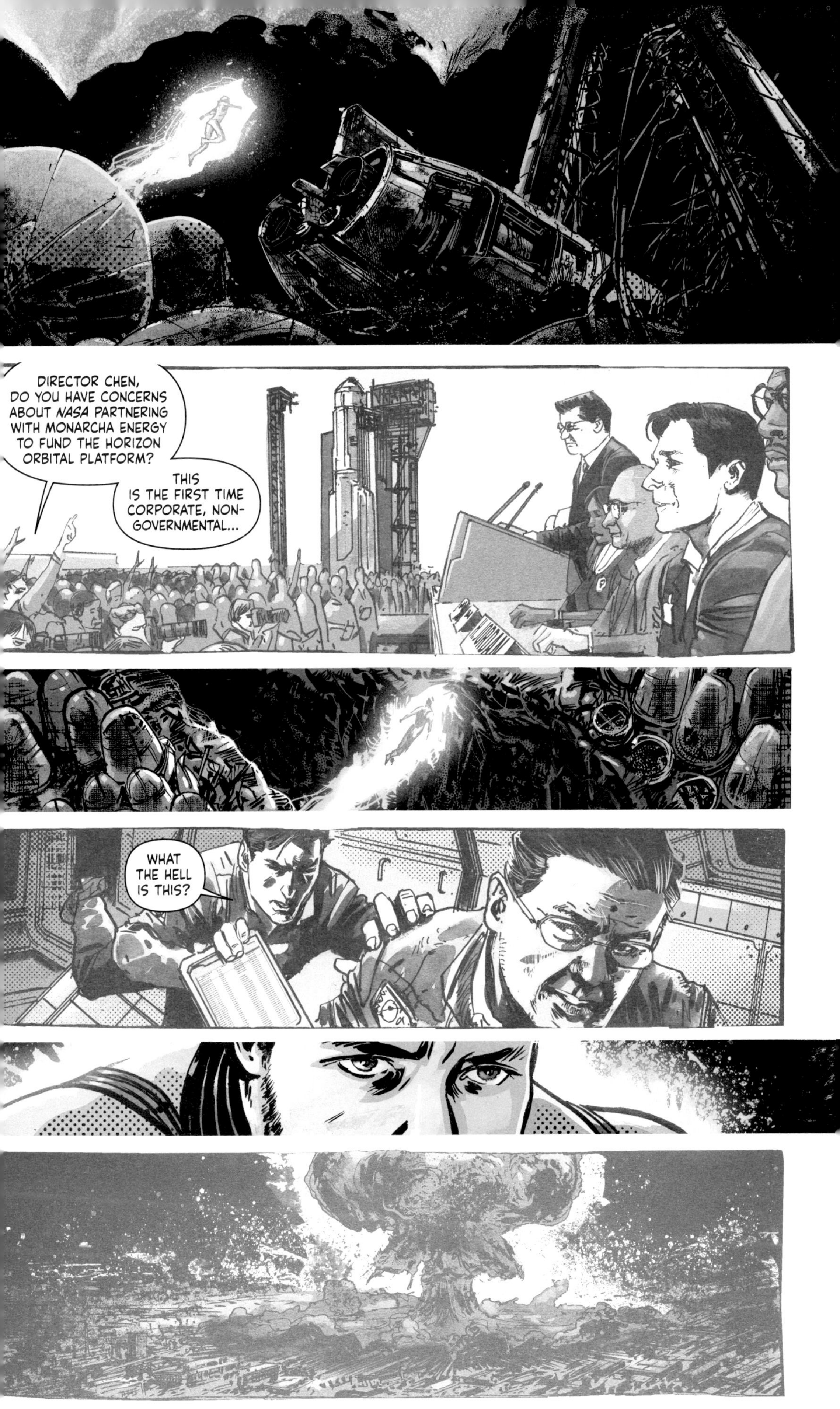
DIRECTOR CHEN, DO YOU HAVE CONCERNS ABOUT NASA PARTNERING WITH MONARCHA ENERGY TO FUND THE HORIZON ORBITAL PLATFORM?
THIS IS THE FIRST TIME CORPORATE, NON-GOVERNMENTAL...
WHAT THE HELL IS THIS?

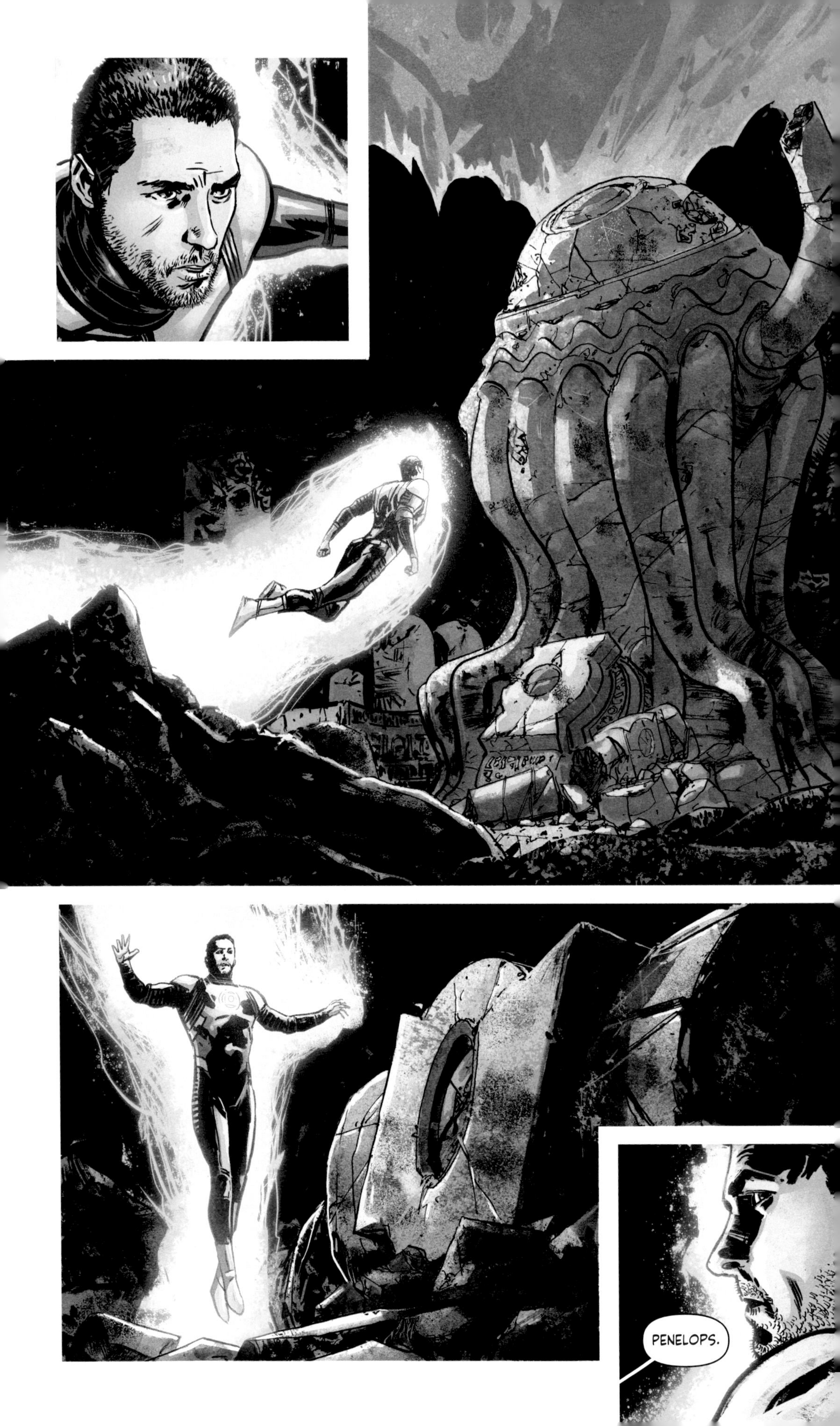
PENELOPS.

WHA--?

PENELOPS WAS THE GREEN LANTERN OF THIS SECTOR. THIS WAS HIS WORLD--PENELO. THEY SOUND ALMOST THE SAME. I THINK THE RING HAS A HARD TIME TRANSLATING THEIR LANGUAGE.

YOU WERE RIGHT. I CAN'T DO THIS ALONE.

DO YOU THINK THERE ARE MORE RINGS OUT THERE? MORE LANTERNS?

THE RINGS AND BATTERIES SEEM NEARLY INDESTRUCTIBLE.

THOUGH THEY SAY THE MANHUNTERS DESTROYED THE CENTRAL BATTERY ON OA. THAT'S WHY NONE OF THE RINGS HAVE THE POWER THEY ONCE DID.

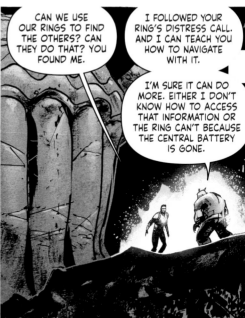

CAN WE USE OUR RINGS TO FIND THE OTHERS? CAN THEY DO THAT? YOU FOUND ME.

I FOLLOWED YOUR RING'S DISTRESS CALL. AND I CAN TEACH YOU HOW TO NAVIGATE WITH IT.

I'M SURE IT CAN DO MORE. EITHER I DON'T KNOW HOW TO ACCESS THAT INFORMATION OR THE RING CAN'T BECAUSE THE CENTRAL BATTERY IS GONE.

SO THIS ISN'T GOING TO BE EASY.

WHAT EVER IS?

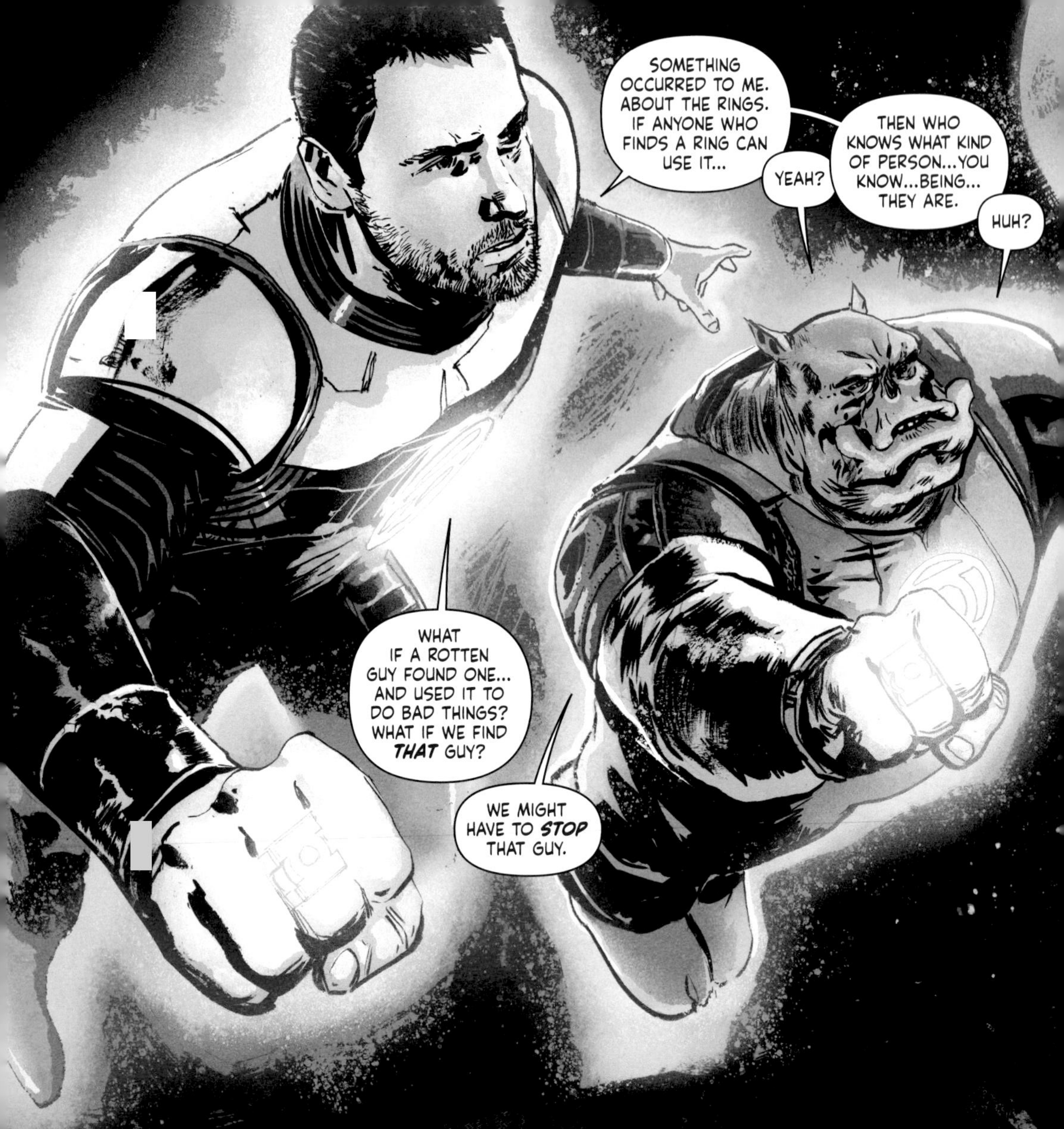
SOMETHING OCCURRED TO ME. ABOUT THE RINGS. IF ANYONE WHO FINDS A RING CAN USE IT...
YEAH?
THEN WHO KNOWS WHAT KIND OF PERSON...YOU KNOW...BEING... THEY ARE.
HUH?
WHAT IF A ROTTEN GUY FOUND ONE... AND USED IT TO DO BAD THINGS? WHAT IF WE FIND *THAT* GUY?
WE MIGHT HAVE TO *STOP* THAT GUY.

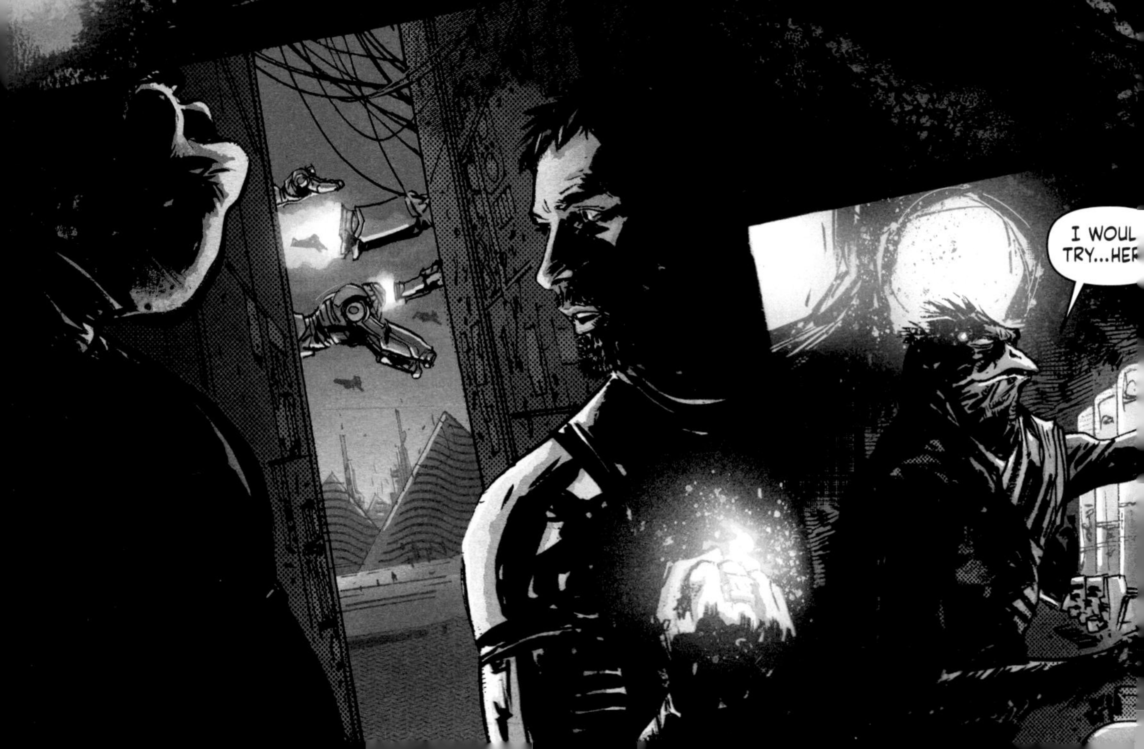

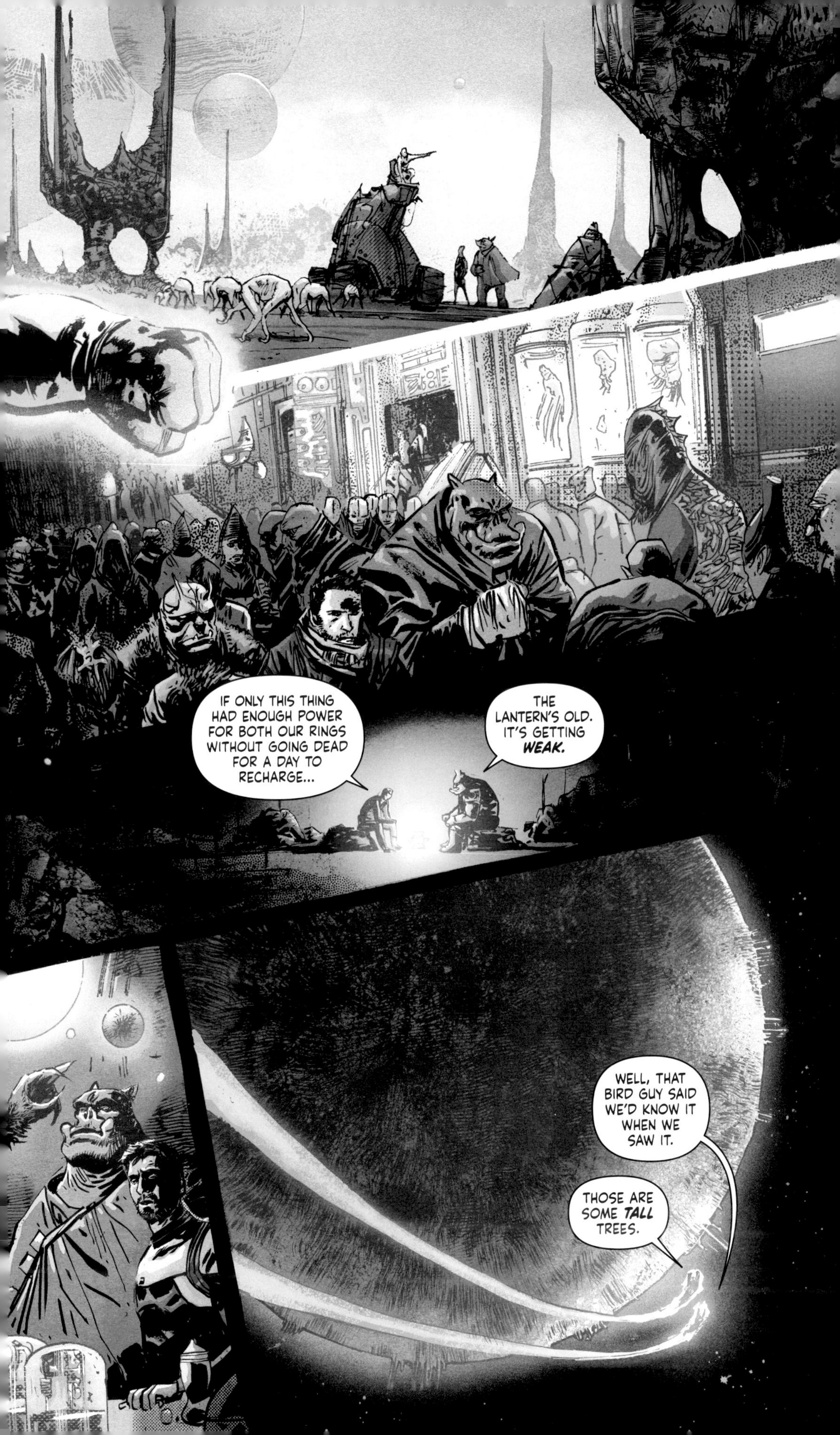
IF ONLY THIS THING HAD ENOUGH POWER FOR BOTH OUR RINGS WITHOUT GOING DEAD FOR A DAY TO RECHARGE...
THE LANTERN'S OLD. IT'S GETTING **WEAK.**
WELL, THAT BIRD GUY SAID WE'D KNOW IT WHEN WE SAW IT.
THOSE ARE SOME ***TALL*** TREES.

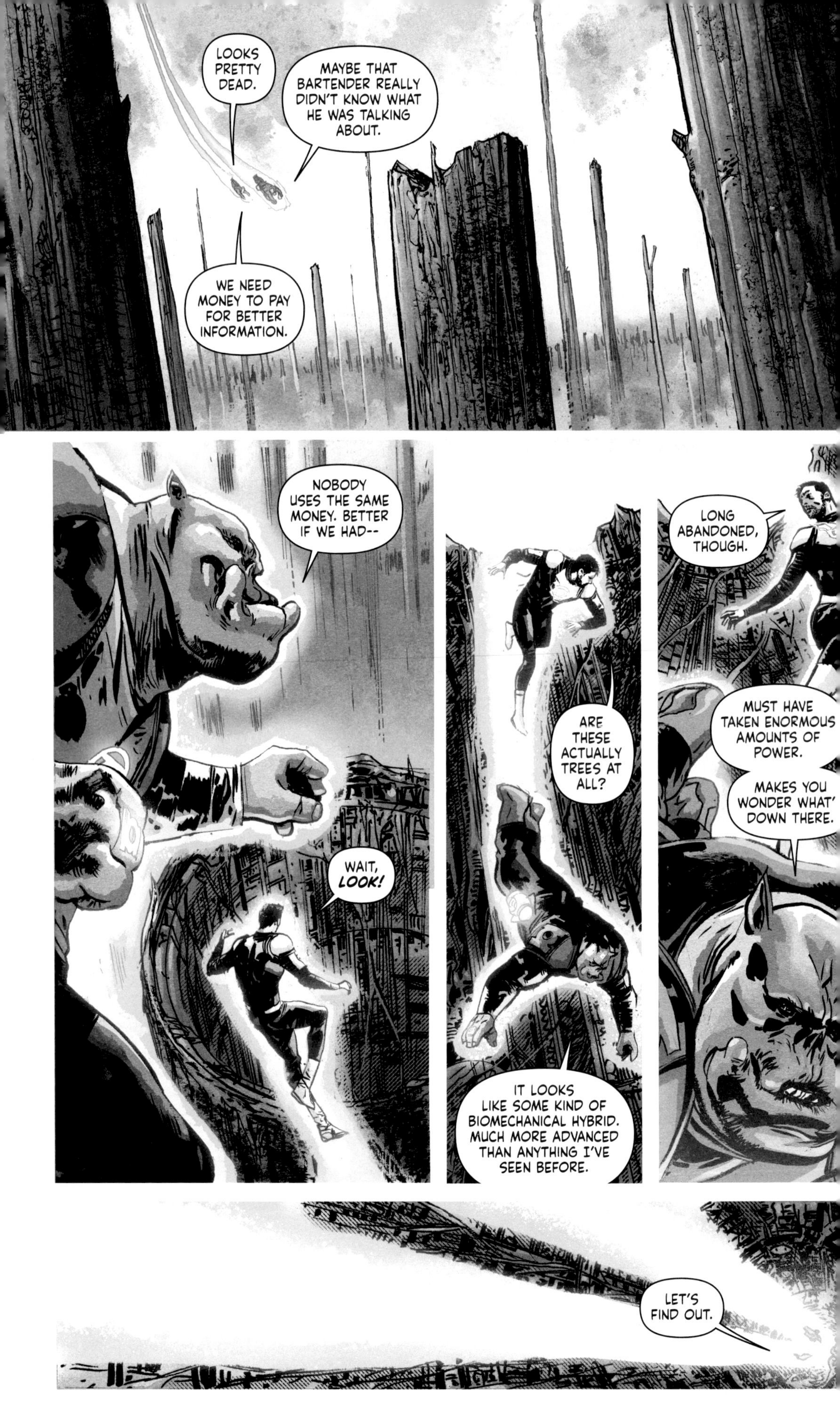
LOOKS PRETTY DEAD.
MAYBE THAT BARTENDER REALLY DIDN'T KNOW WHAT HE WAS TALKING ABOUT.
WE NEED MONEY TO PAY FOR BETTER INFORMATION.
NOBODY USES THE SAME MONEY. BETTER IF WE HAD--
WAIT, **LOOK!**
ARE THESE ACTUALLY TREES AT ALL?
IT LOOKS LIKE SOME KIND OF BIOMECHANICAL HYBRID. MUCH MORE ADVANCED THAN ANYTHING I'VE SEEN BEFORE.
LONG ABANDONED, THOUGH.
MUST HAVE TAKEN ENORMOUS AMOUNTS OF POWER.
MAKES YOU WONDER WHAT' DOWN THERE.
LET'S FIND OUT.

WOW.

IS IT SOME KIND OF BUDDING FRUIT? MAYBE IT'S EDIBLE?

ONLY IF YOU EAT GLASS.

IT'S SILICA. MAYBE *EVERYTHING* HERE WAS BIO-MECHANICALLY GROWN.

OR MAYBE THEY JUST ATE GLASS.

YOU KNOW, THAT'S NOT ENTIRELY--

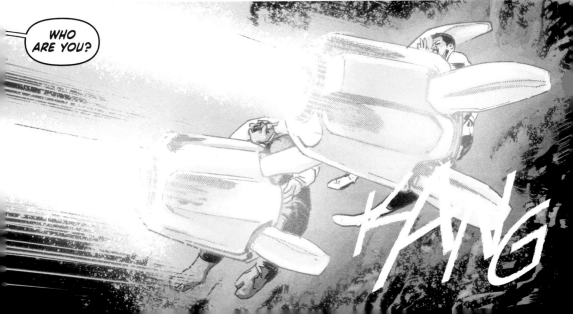

WHO ARE YOU?

KANG

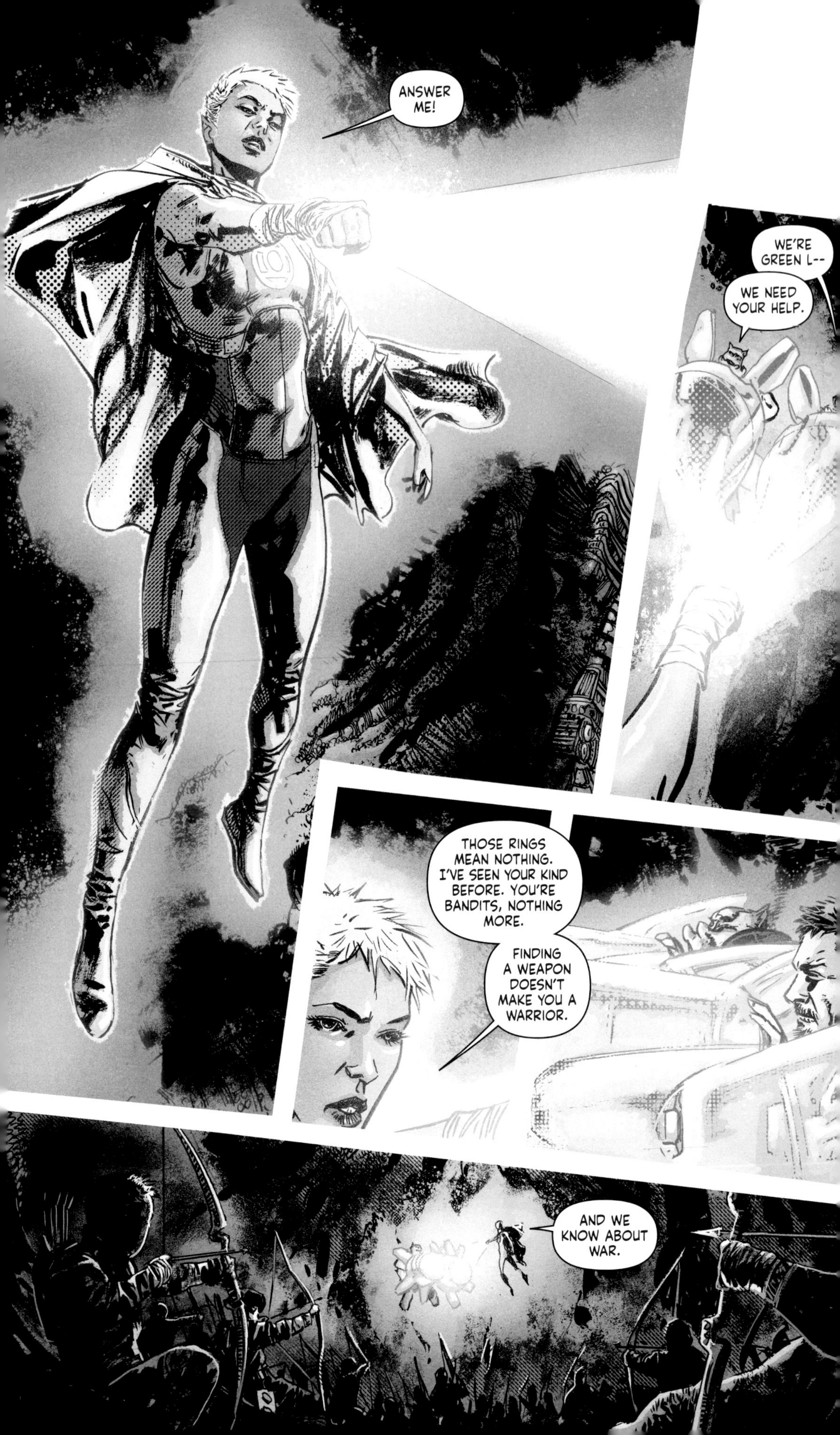
ANSWER ME!
WE'RE GREEN L--
WE NEED YOUR HELP.
THOSE RINGS MEAN NOTHING. I'VE SEEN YOUR KIND BEFORE. YOU'RE BANDITS, NOTHING MORE.
FINDING A WEAPON DOESN'T MAKE YOU A WARRIOR.
AND WE KNOW ABOUT WAR.

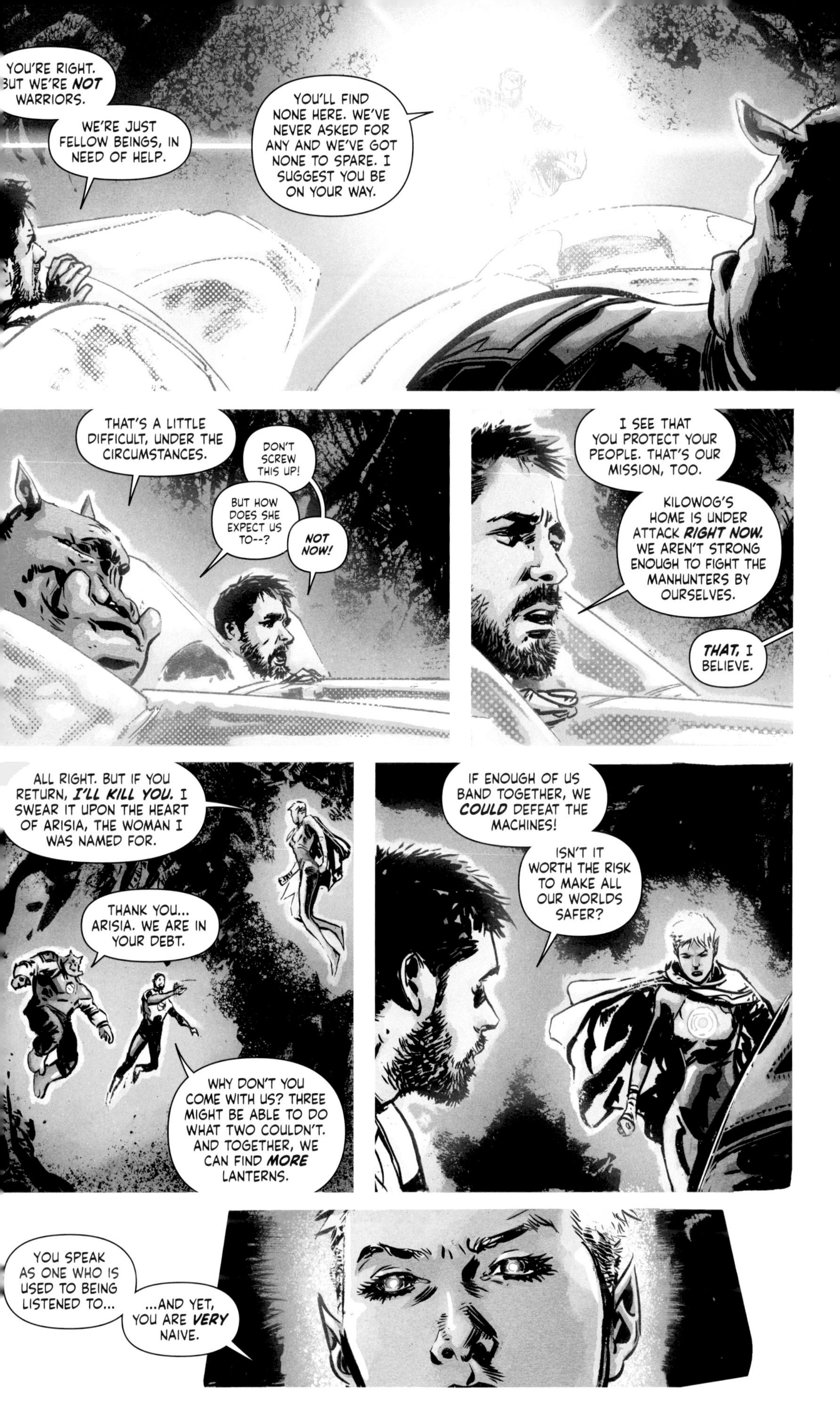

YOU'RE RIGHT. BUT WE'RE NOT WARRIORS.
WE'RE JUST FELLOW BEINGS, IN NEED OF HELP.
YOU'LL FIND NONE HERE. WE'VE NEVER ASKED FOR ANY AND WE'VE GOT NONE TO SPARE. I SUGGEST YOU BE ON YOUR WAY.
THAT'S A LITTLE DIFFICULT, UNDER THE CIRCUMSTANCES.
DON'T SCREW THIS UP!
BUT HOW DOES SHE EXPECT US TO--?
NOT NOW!
I SEE THAT YOU PROTECT YOUR PEOPLE. THAT'S OUR MISSION, TOO.
KILOWOG'S HOME IS UNDER ATTACK RIGHT NOW. WE AREN'T STRONG ENOUGH TO FIGHT THE MANHUNTERS BY OURSELVES.
THAT, I BELIEVE.
ALL RIGHT. BUT IF YOU RETURN, I'LL KILL YOU. I SWEAR IT UPON THE HEART OF ARISIA, THE WOMAN I WAS NAMED FOR.
THANK YOU... ARISIA. WE ARE IN YOUR DEBT.
WHY DON'T YOU COME WITH US? THREE MIGHT BE ABLE TO DO WHAT TWO COULDN'T. AND TOGETHER, WE CAN FIND MORE LANTERNS.
IF ENOUGH OF US BAND TOGETHER, WE COULD DEFEAT THE MACHINES!
ISN'T IT WORTH THE RISK TO MAKE ALL OUR WORLDS SAFER?
YOU SPEAK AS ONE WHO IS USED TO BEING LISTENED TO...
...AND YET, YOU ARE VERY NAIVE.

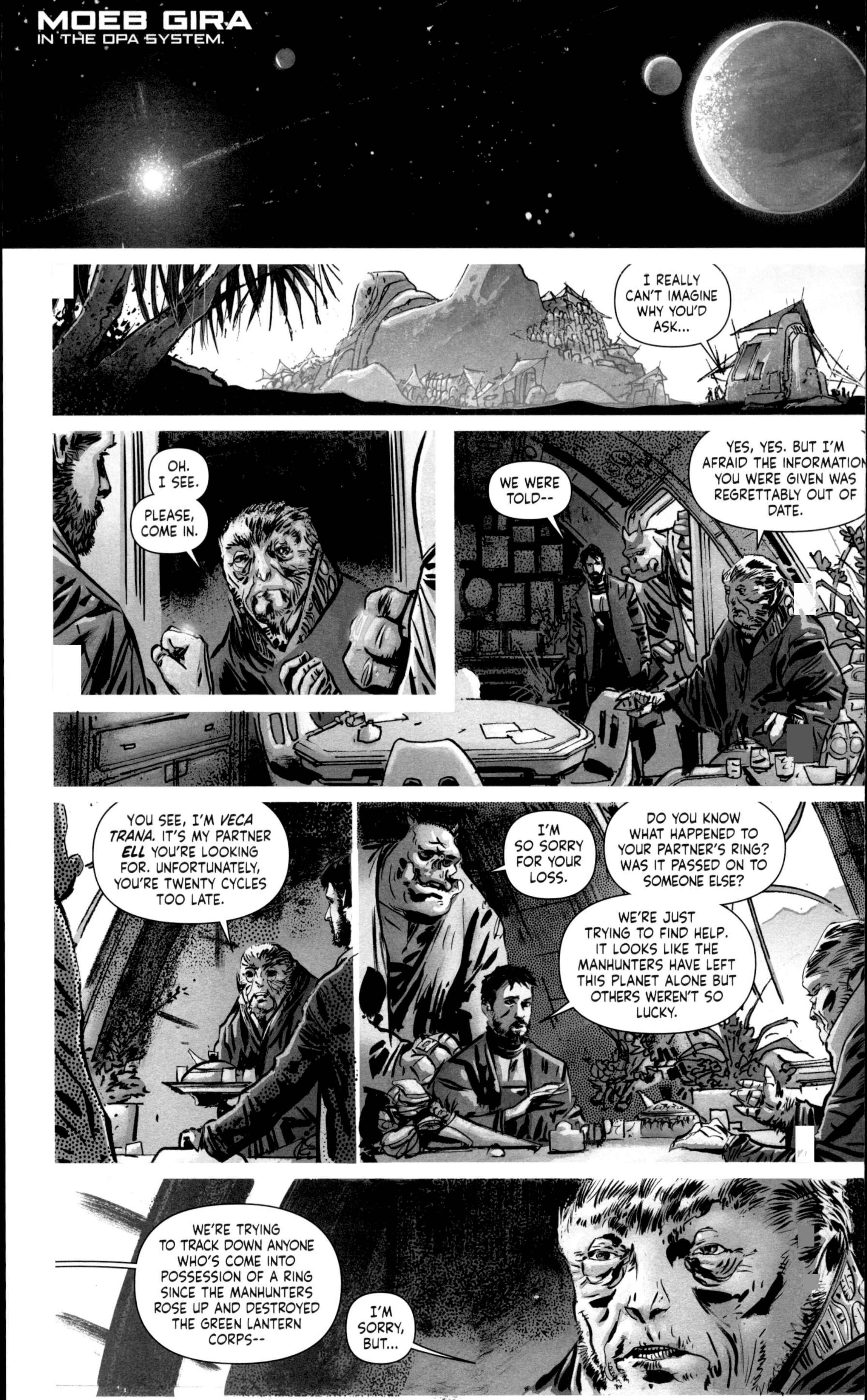
MOEB GIRA
IN THE OPA SYSTEM.
I REALLY CAN'T IMAGINE WHY YOU'D ASK...
OH. I SEE.
PLEASE, COME IN.
WE WERE TOLD--
YES, YES. BUT I'M AFRAID THE INFORMATION YOU WERE GIVEN WAS REGRETTABLY OUT OF DATE.
YOU SEE, I'M VECA TRANA. IT'S MY PARTNER ELL YOU'RE LOOKING FOR. UNFORTUNATELY, YOU'RE TWENTY CYCLES TOO LATE.
I'M SO SORRY FOR YOUR LOSS.
DO YOU KNOW WHAT HAPPENED TO YOUR PARTNER'S RING? WAS IT PASSED ON TO SOMEONE ELSE?
WE'RE JUST TRYING TO FIND HELP. IT LOOKS LIKE THE MANHUNTERS HAVE LEFT THIS PLANET ALONE BUT OTHERS WEREN'T SO LUCKY.
WE'RE TRYING TO TRACK DOWN ANYONE WHO'S COME INTO POSSESSION OF A RING SINCE THE MANHUNTERS ROSE UP AND DESTROYED THE GREEN LANTERN CORPS--
I'M SORRY, BUT...

WHAT EXACTLY DO YOU THINK HAPPENED TO THE LANTERN CORPS?

WELL, I...I DON'T KNOW FOR SURE. I WAS TOLD--

PERHAPS I SHOULD CLEAR THIS UP FOR YOU. BECAUSE I WASN'T *TOLD* THESE THINGS, I *EXPERIENCED* THEM.

WHAT DO YOU KNOW OF THE OANS?

VERY LITTLE. THEY CREATED THE LANTERNS TO BRING ORDER TO THE GALAXY?

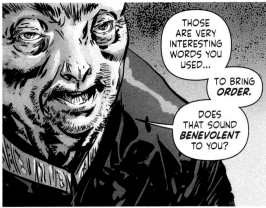

THOSE ARE VERY INTERESTING WORDS YOU USED...

TO BRING *ORDER.*

DOES THAT SOUND *BENEVOLENT* TO YOU?

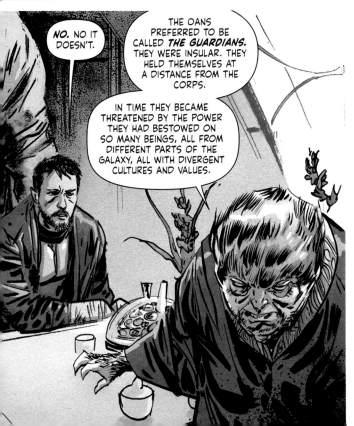

NO. NO IT DOESN'T.

THE OANS PREFERRED TO BE CALLED *THE GUARDIANS.* THEY WERE INSULAR. THEY HELD THEMSELVES AT A DISTANCE FROM THE CORPS.

IN TIME THEY BECAME THREATENED BY THE POWER THEY HAD BESTOWED ON SO MANY BEINGS, ALL FROM DIFFERENT PARTS OF THE GALAXY, ALL WITH DIVERGENT CULTURES AND VALUES.

THE MANHUNTERS DIDN'T RISE UP. THEY WERE CREATED BY THE OANS--THE GUARDIANS--TO DESTROY THIS *THING* THAT HAD GOTTEN TOO DIVERSE AND UNWIELDY FOR THEM TO CONTROL.

THE MANHUNTERS WERE CREATED TO *DESTROY* THE GREEN LANTERN CORPS AND THAT'S EXACTLY WHAT THEY DID.

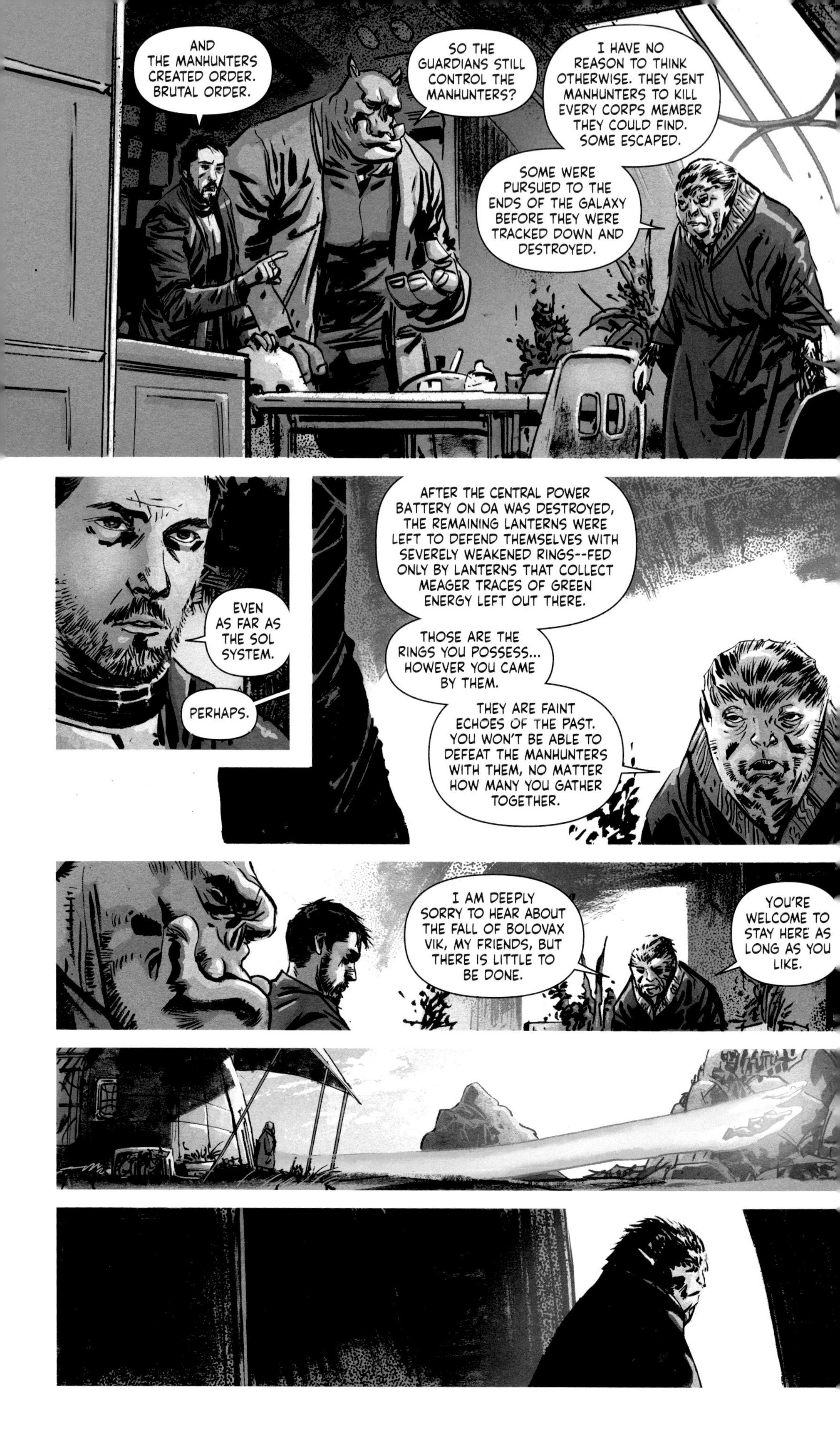
AND THE MANHUNTERS CREATED ORDER. BRUTAL ORDER.
SO THE GUARDIANS STILL CONTROL THE MANHUNTERS?
I HAVE NO REASON TO THINK OTHERWISE. THEY SENT MANHUNTERS TO KILL EVERY CORPS MEMBER THEY COULD FIND. SOME ESCAPED.
SOME WERE PURSUED TO THE ENDS OF THE GALAXY BEFORE THEY WERE TRACKED DOWN AND DESTROYED.
EVEN AS FAR AS THE SOL SYSTEM.
PERHAPS.
AFTER THE CENTRAL POWER BATTERY ON OA WAS DESTROYED, THE REMAINING LANTERNS WERE LEFT TO DEFEND THEMSELVES WITH SEVERELY WEAKENED RINGS--FED ONLY BY LANTERNS THAT COLLECT MEAGER TRACES OF GREEN ENERGY LEFT OUT THERE.
THOSE ARE THE RINGS YOU POSSESS... HOWEVER YOU CAME BY THEM.
THEY ARE FAINT ECHOES OF THE PAST. YOU WON'T BE ABLE TO DEFEAT THE MANHUNTERS WITH THEM, NO MATTER HOW MANY YOU GATHER TOGETHER.
I AM DEEPLY SORRY TO HEAR ABOUT THE FALL OF BOLOVAX VIK, MY FRIENDS, BUT THERE IS LITTLE TO BE DONE.
YOU'RE WELCOME TO STAY HERE AS LONG AS YOU LIKE.

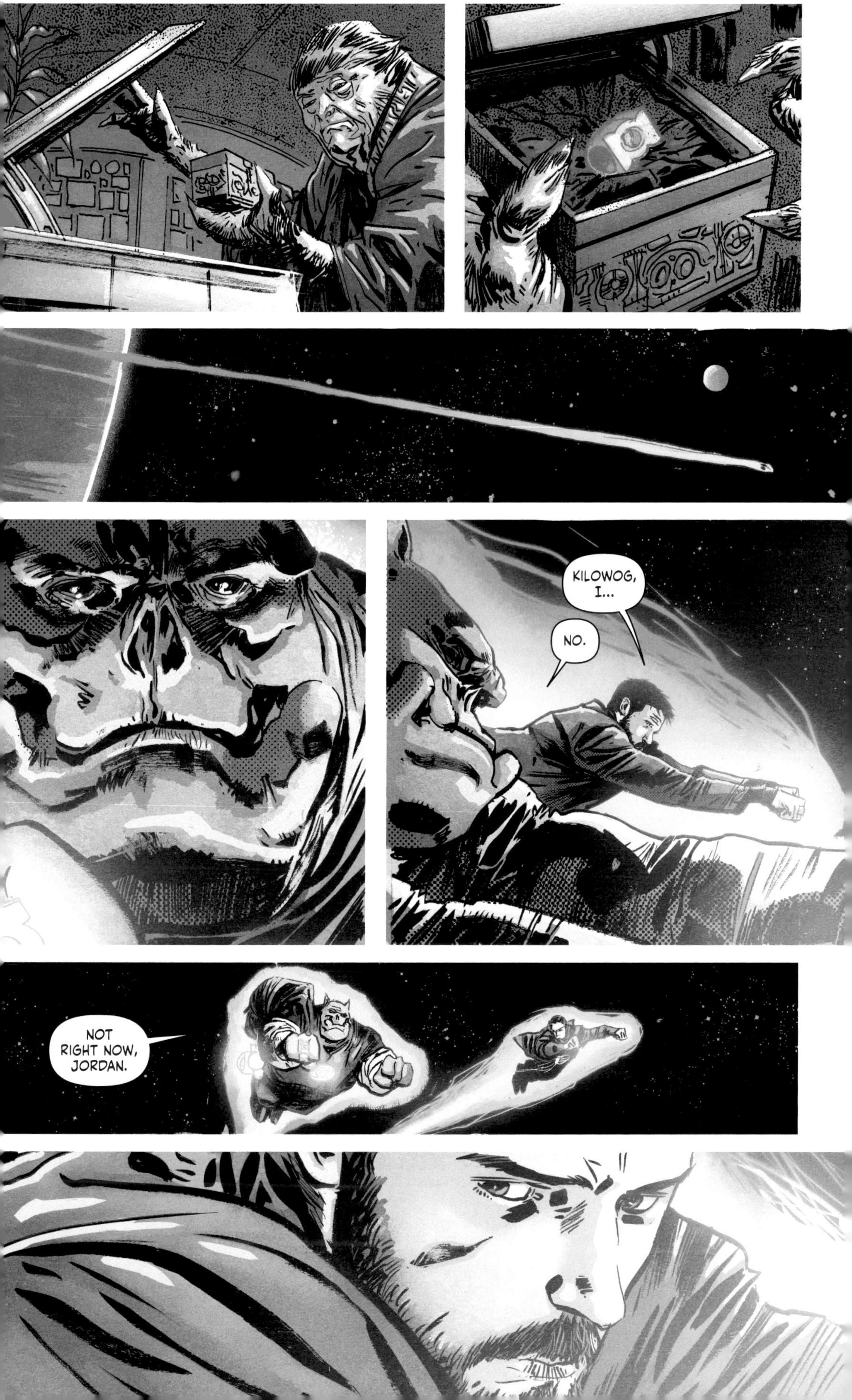
KILOWOG, I...
NO.
NOT RIGHT NOW, JORDAN.

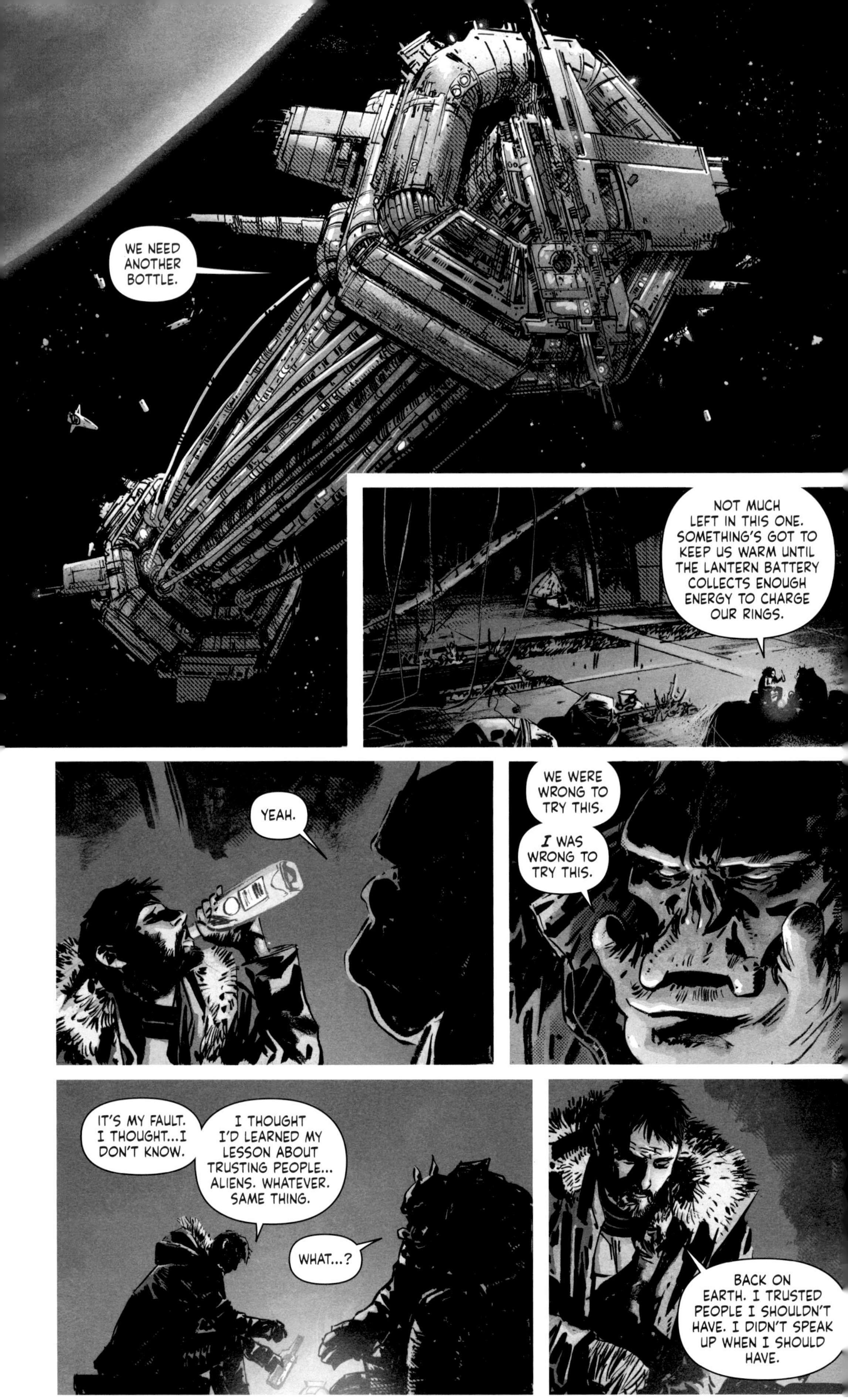
WE NEED ANOTHER BOTTLE.
NOT MUCH LEFT IN THIS ONE. SOMETHING'S GOT TO KEEP US WARM UNTIL THE LANTERN BATTERY COLLECTS ENOUGH ENERGY TO CHARGE OUR RINGS.
YEAH.
WE WERE WRONG TO TRY THIS.
I WAS WRONG TO TRY THIS.
IT'S MY FAULT. I THOUGHT...I DON'T KNOW.
I THOUGHT I'D LEARNED MY LESSON ABOUT TRUSTING PEOPLE... ALIENS. WHATEVER. SAME THING.
WHAT...?
BACK ON EARTH. I TRUSTED PEOPLE I SHOULDN'T HAVE. I DIDN'T SPEAK UP WHEN I SHOULD HAVE.

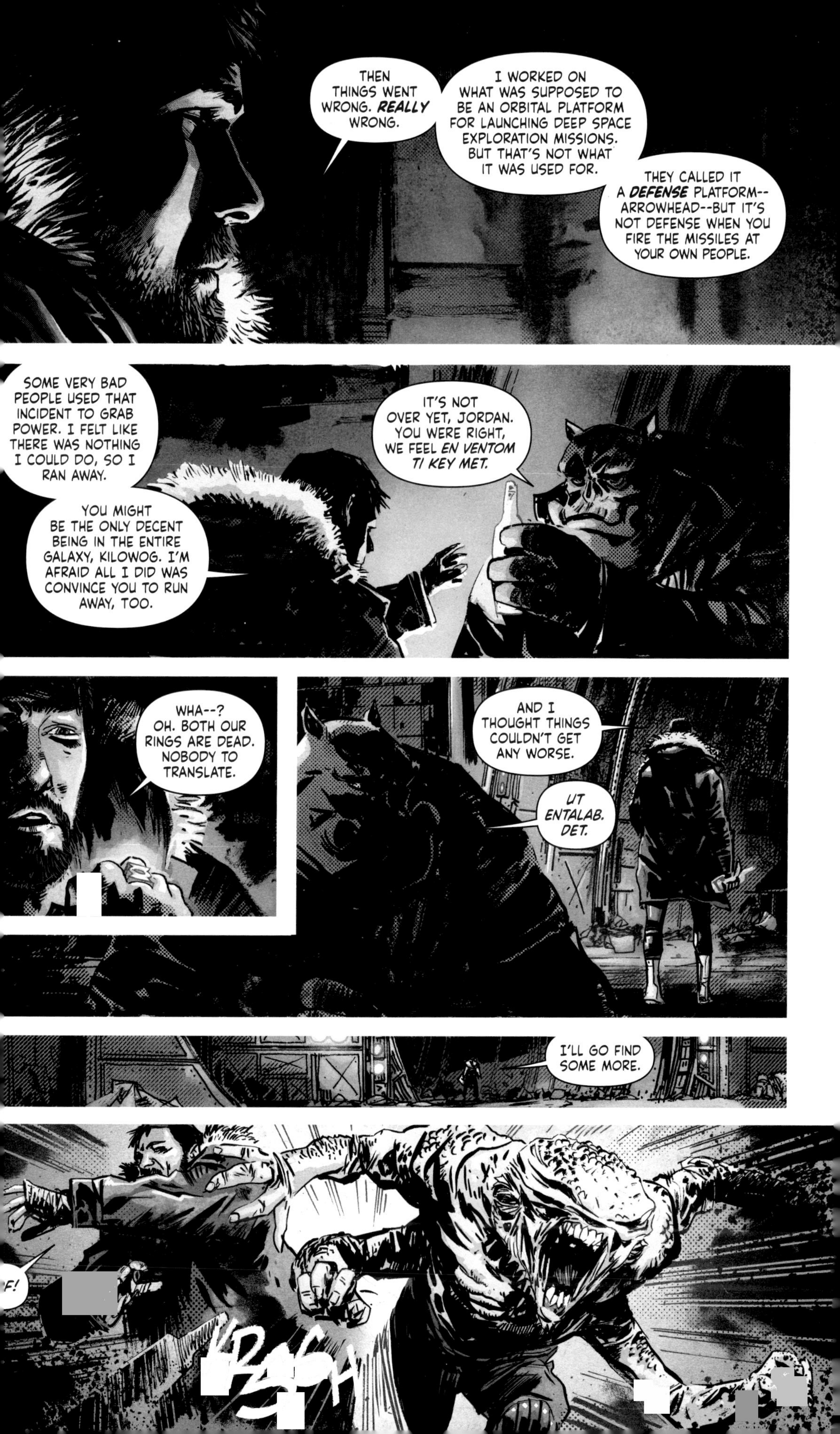
THEN THINGS WENT WRONG. *REALLY* WRONG.
I WORKED ON WHAT WAS SUPPOSED TO BE AN ORBITAL PLATFORM FOR LAUNCHING DEEP SPACE EXPLORATION MISSIONS. BUT THAT'S NOT WHAT IT WAS USED FOR.
THEY CALLED IT A *DEFENSE* PLATFORM--ARROWHEAD--BUT IT'S NOT DEFENSE WHEN YOU FIRE THE MISSILES AT YOUR OWN PEOPLE.
SOME VERY BAD PEOPLE USED THAT INCIDENT TO GRAB POWER. I FELT LIKE THERE WAS NOTHING I COULD DO, SO I RAN AWAY.
YOU MIGHT BE THE ONLY DECENT BEING IN THE ENTIRE GALAXY, KILOWOG. I'M AFRAID ALL I DID WAS CONVINCE YOU TO RUN AWAY, TOO.
IT'S NOT OVER YET, JORDAN. YOU WERE RIGHT, WE FEEL *EN VENTOM TI KEY MET.*
WHA--? OH. BOTH OUR RINGS ARE DEAD. NOBODY TO TRANSLATE.
AND I THOUGHT THINGS COULDN'T GET ANY WORSE.
UT ENTALAB. DET.
I'LL GO FIND SOME MORE.
KRASH

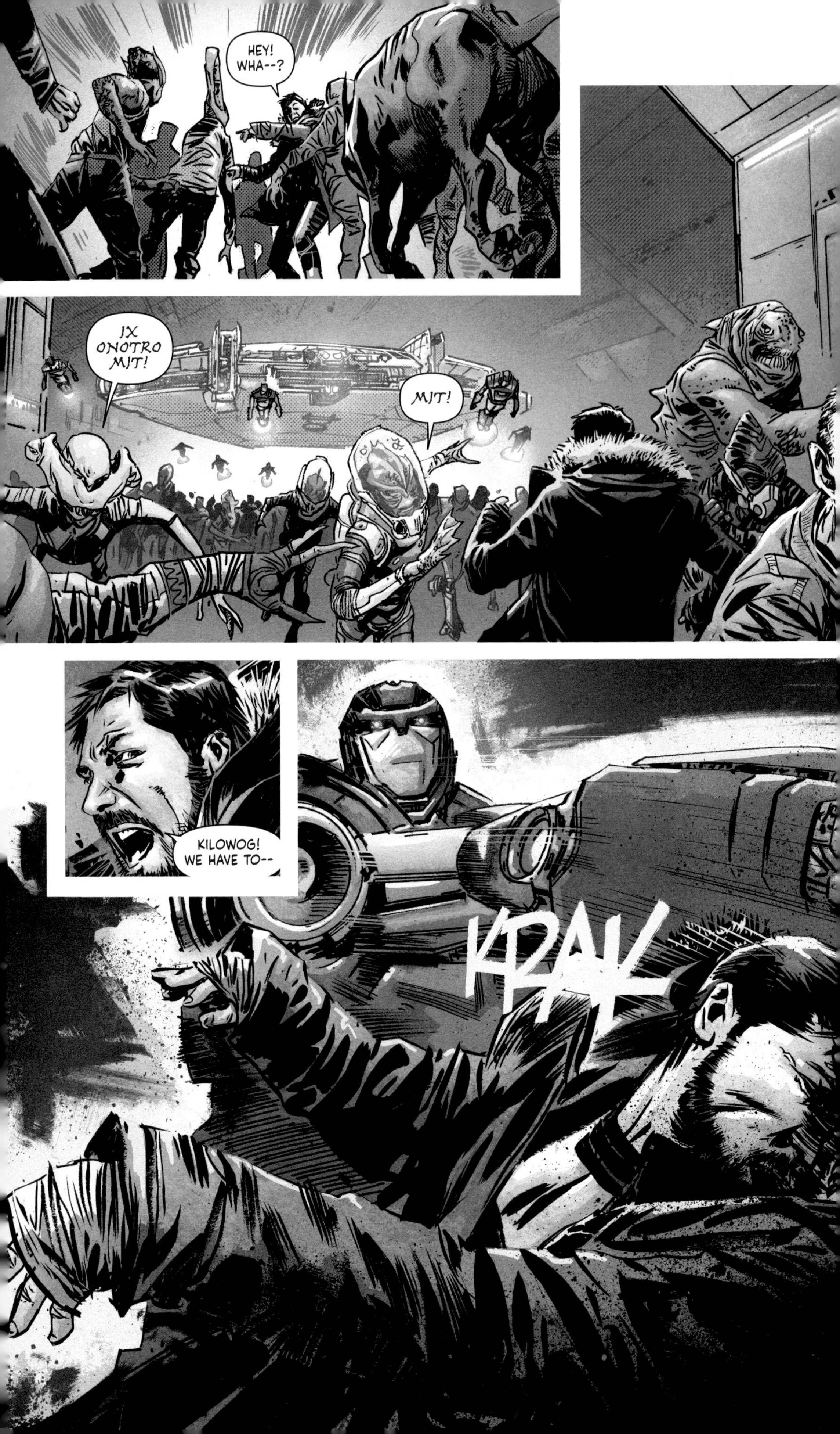
HEY! WHA--?
IX ONOTRO MIT!
MIT!
KILOWOG! WE HAVE TO--
KRAK

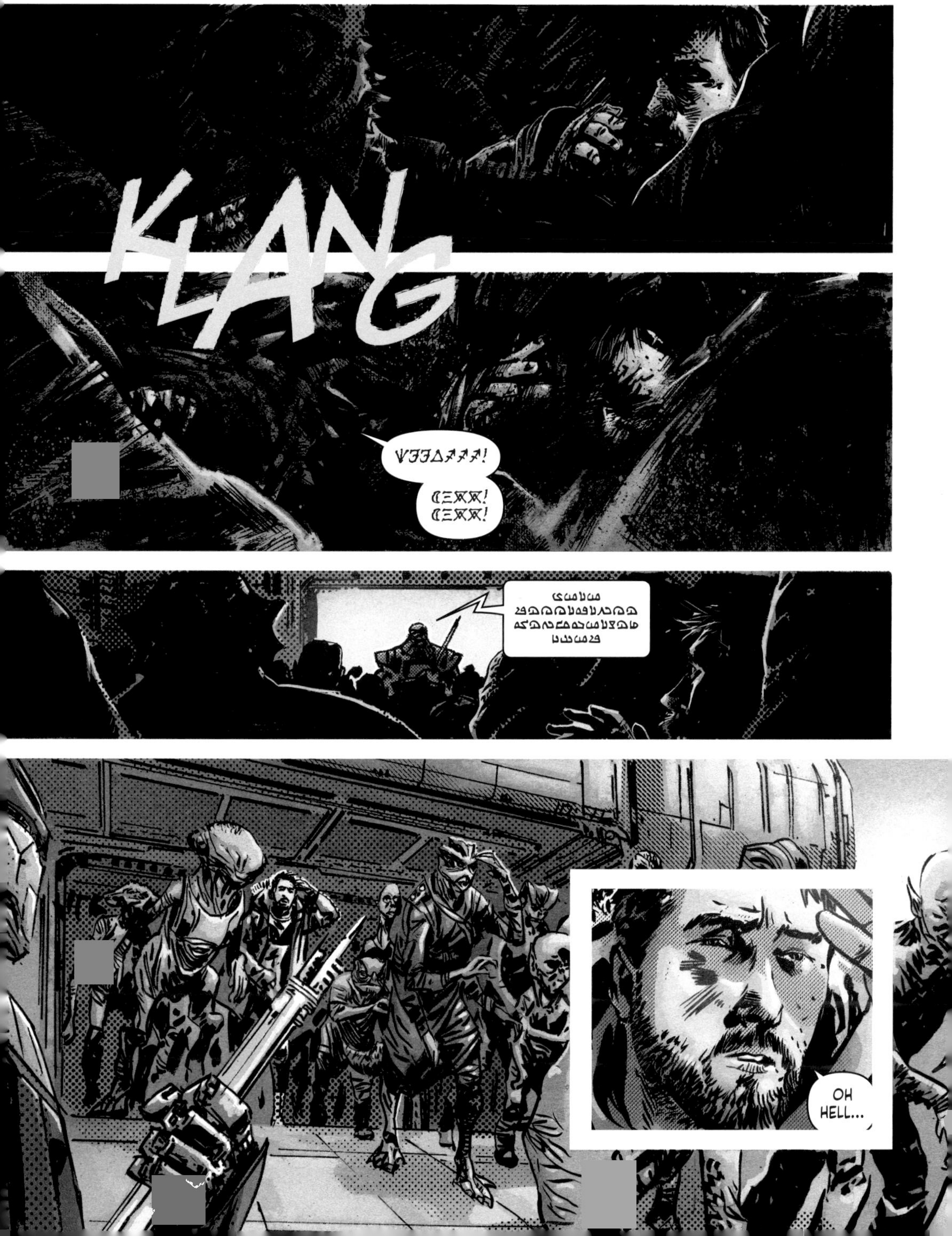
KLANG
OH HELL...

WHERE... WHAT IS THIS PLACE?

THIS PLANET?

ᑌᔕᐃ ᒪᔭᒪᐃᔕᔕ ᖴᔕᔕᔕᐳᐸᑎᖴ.

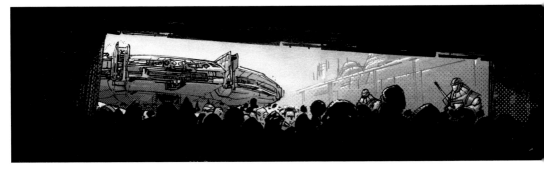

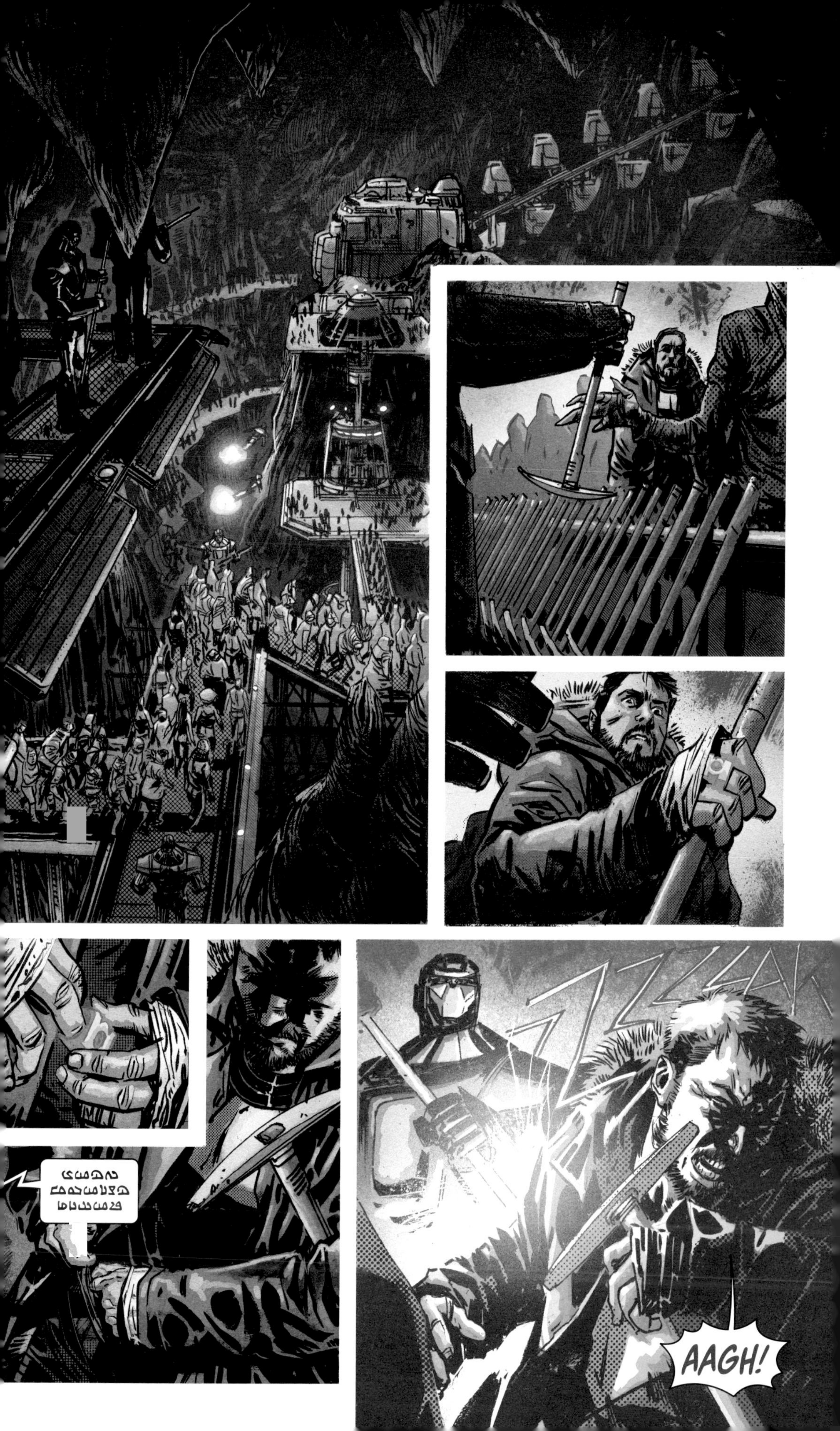
ZZZZAK
AAGH!

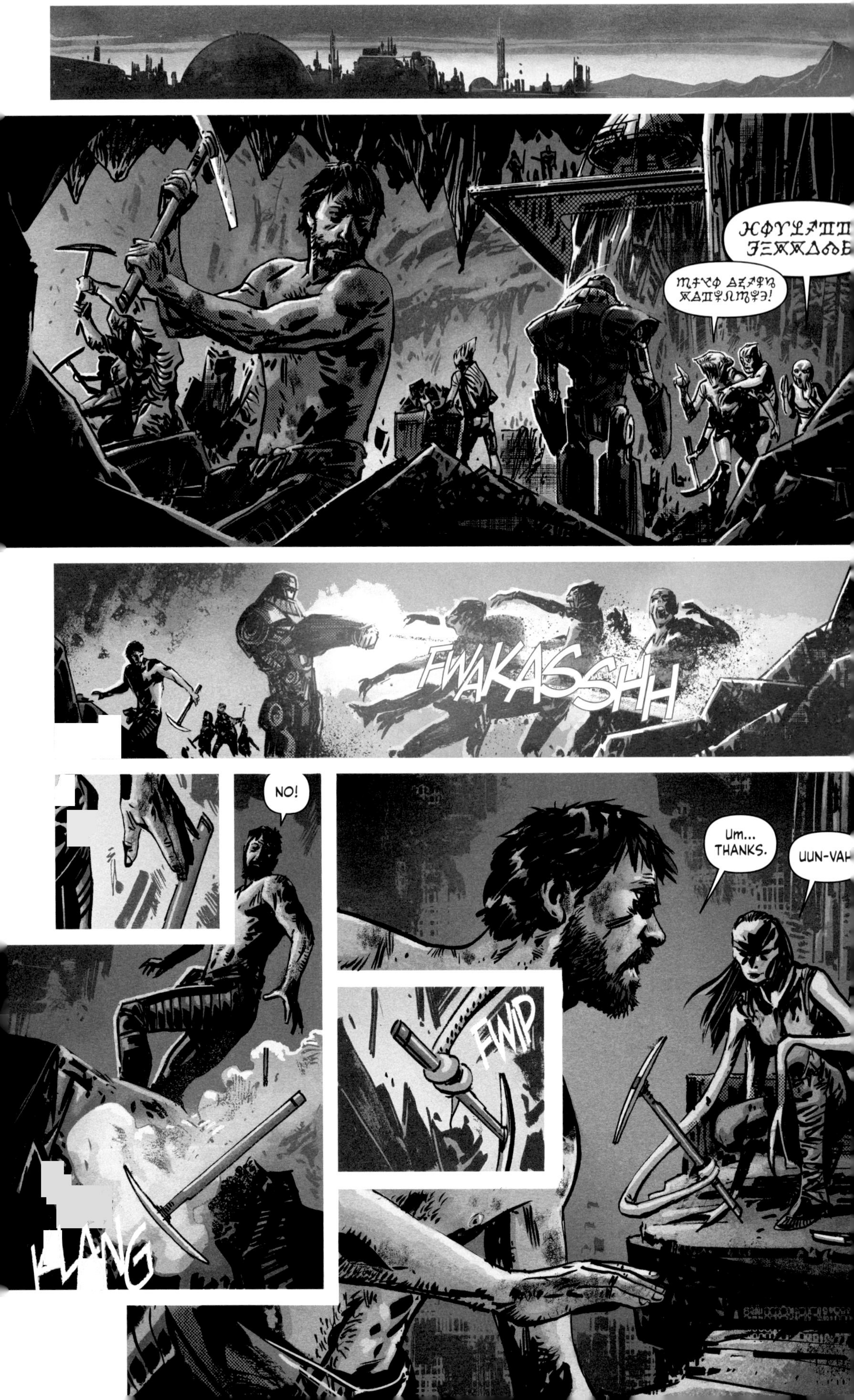
FWAKASSHH
NO!
KLANG
FWIP
Um... THANKS.
UUN-VAH

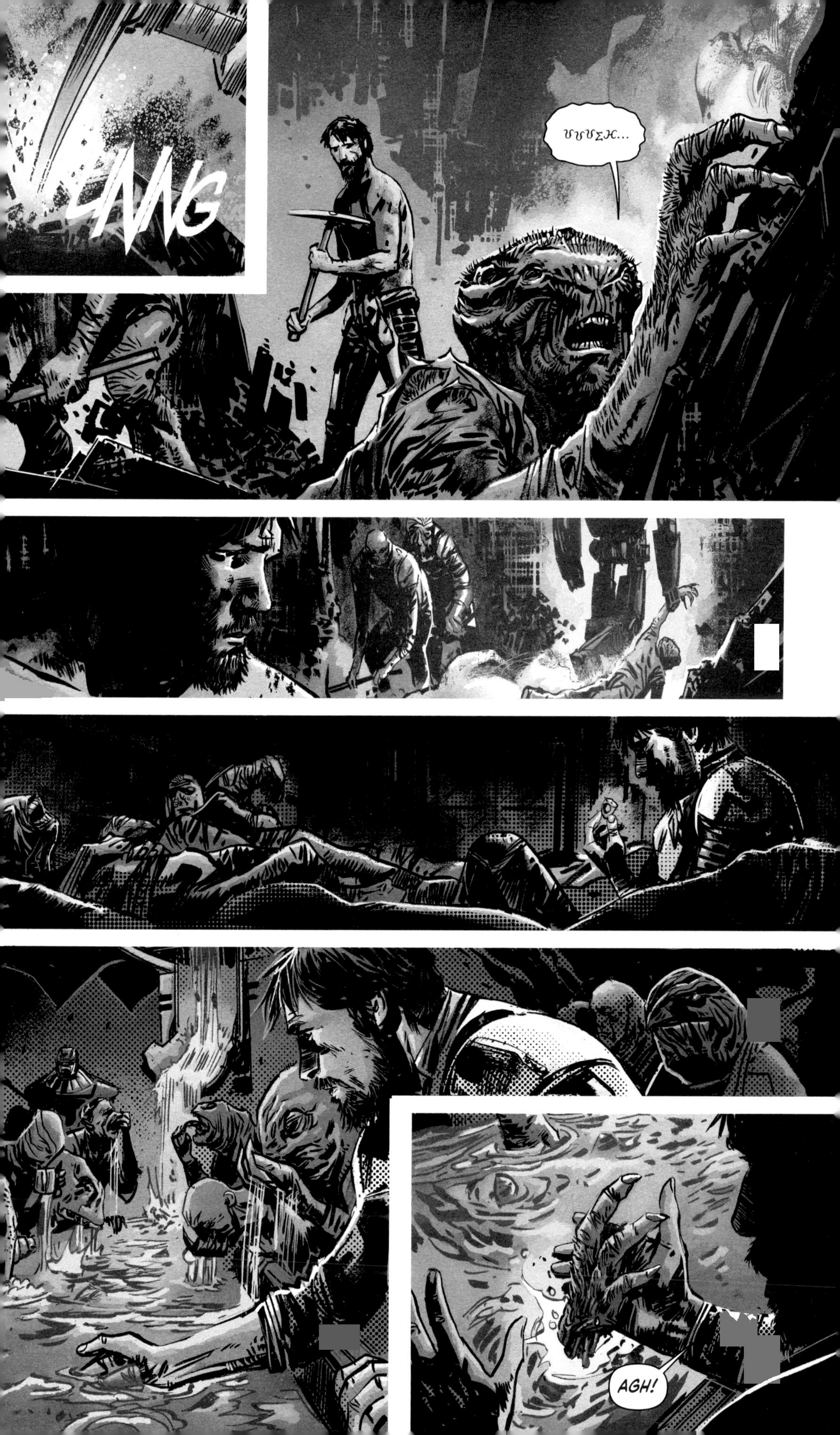
AGH!

VET IN THE MINES.

WHAT IF I GIVE YOU HALF MY MEAL FOR *THREE* CYCLES?

IS THAT ENOUGH TO MAKE IT WORTH YOU WHILE?

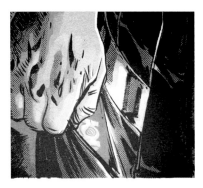

WHAT THE HELL?

WHAT COULD BE CHARGING...?

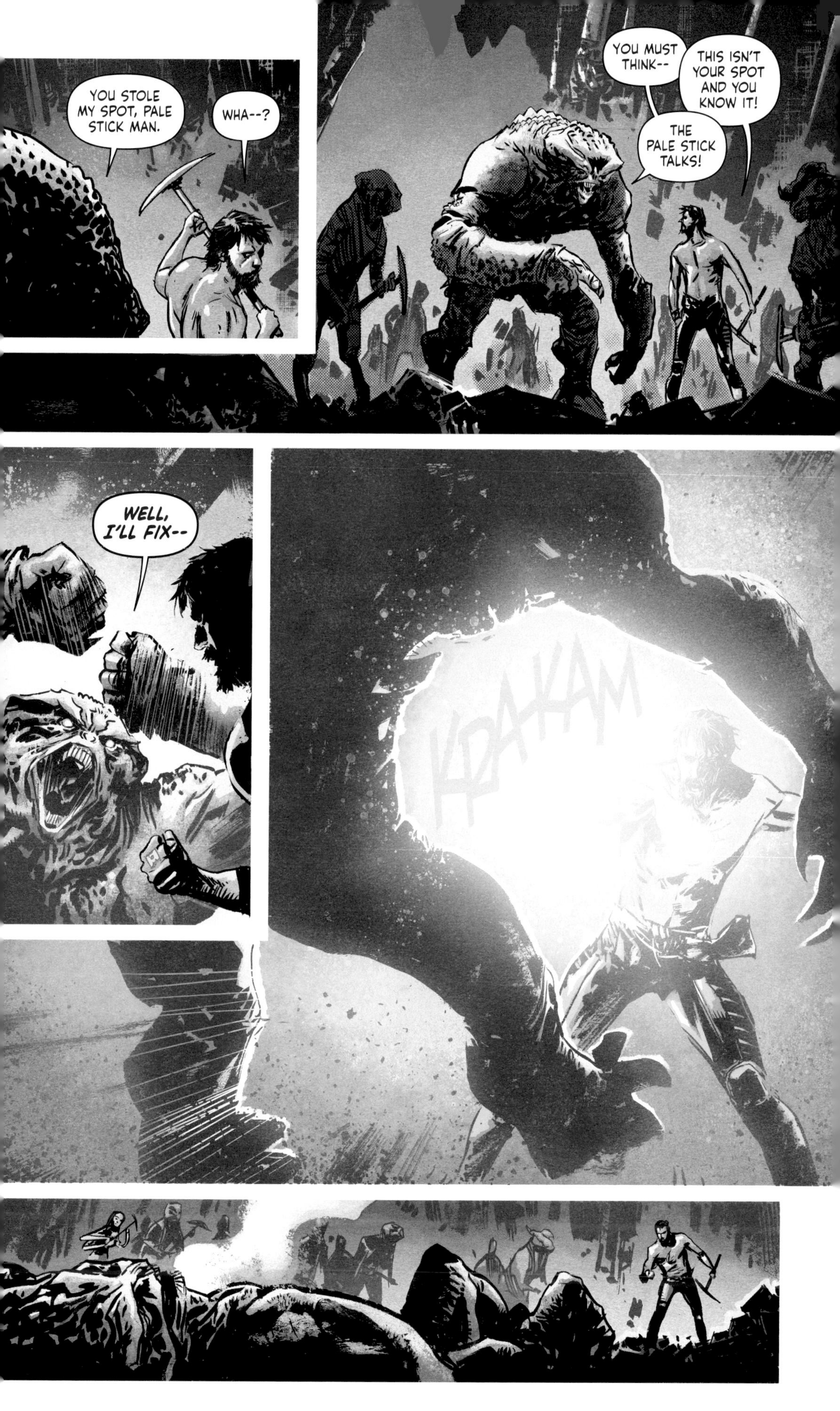
YOU STOLE MY SPOT, PALE STICK MAN.
WHA--?
YOU MUST THINK--
THE PALE STICK TALKS!
THIS ISN'T YOUR SPOT AND YOU KNOW IT!
WELL, I'LL FIX--
KRAKAM

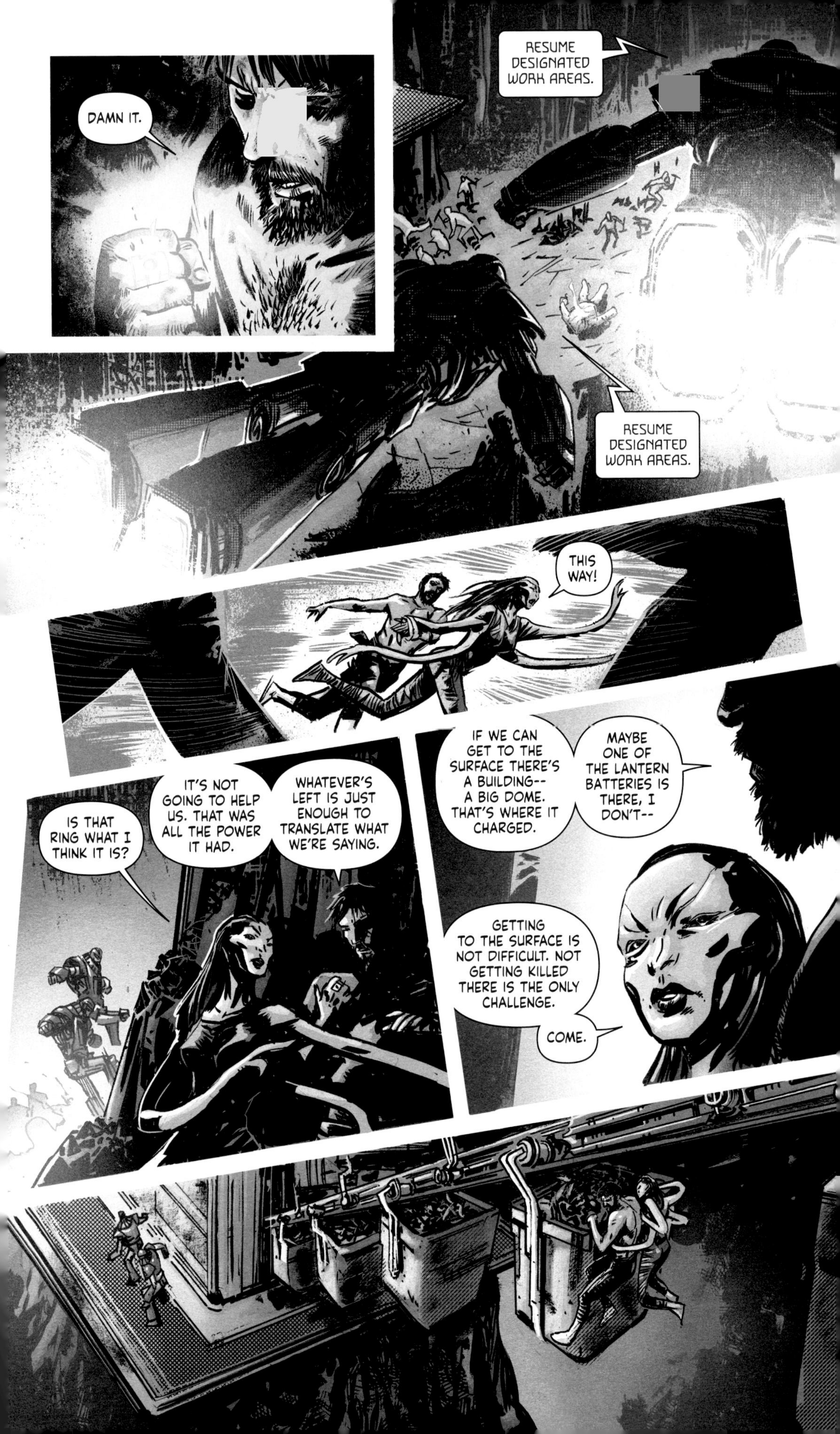

DAMN IT.
RESUME DESIGNATED WORK AREAS.
RESUME DESIGNATED WORK AREAS.
THIS WAY!
IS THAT RING WHAT I THINK IT IS?
IT'S NOT GOING TO HELP US. THAT WAS ALL THE POWER IT HAD.
WHATEVER'S LEFT IS JUST ENOUGH TO TRANSLATE WHAT WE'RE SAYING.
IF WE CAN GET TO THE SURFACE THERE'S A BUILDING-- A BIG DOME. THAT'S WHERE IT CHARGED.
MAYBE ONE OF THE LANTERN BATTERIES IS THERE, I DON'T--
GETTING TO THE SURFACE IS NOT DIFFICULT. NOT GETTING KILLED THERE IS THE ONLY CHALLENGE.
COME.

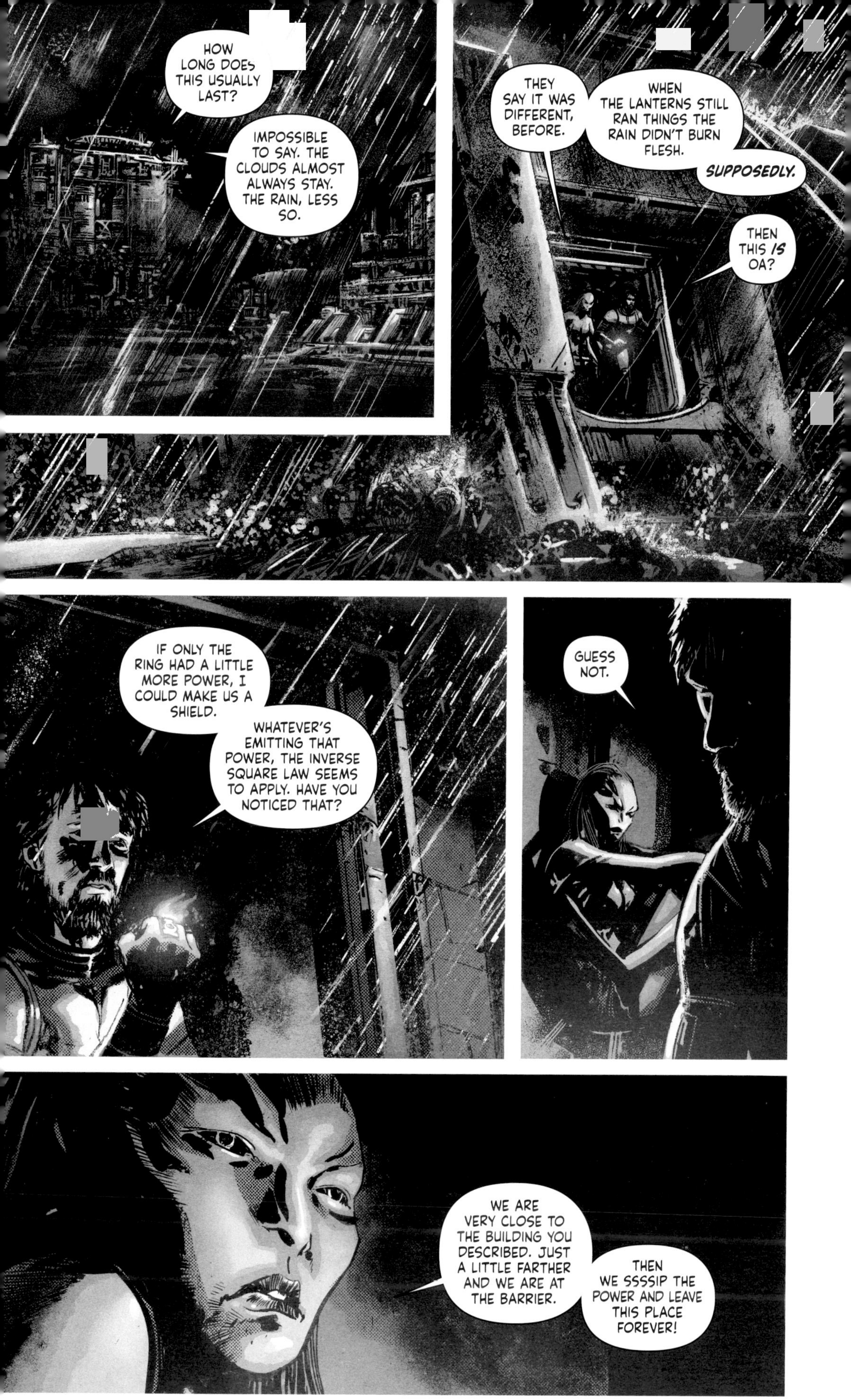
HOW LONG DOES THIS USUALLY LAST?
IMPOSSIBLE TO SAY. THE CLOUDS ALMOST ALWAYS STAY. THE RAIN, LESS SO.
THEY SAY IT WAS DIFFERENT, BEFORE.
WHEN THE LANTERNS STILL RAN THINGS THE RAIN DIDN'T BURN FLESH.
SUPPOSEDLY.
THEN THIS IS OA?
IF ONLY THE RING HAD A LITTLE MORE POWER, I COULD MAKE US A SHIELD.
WHATEVER'S EMITTING THAT POWER, THE INVERSE SQUARE LAW SEEMS TO APPLY. HAVE YOU NOTICED THAT?
GUESS NOT.
WE ARE VERY CLOSE TO THE BUILDING YOU DESCRIBED. JUST A LITTLE FARTHER AND WE ARE AT THE BARRIER.
THEN WE SSSSIP THE POWER AND LEAVE THIS PLACE FOREVER!

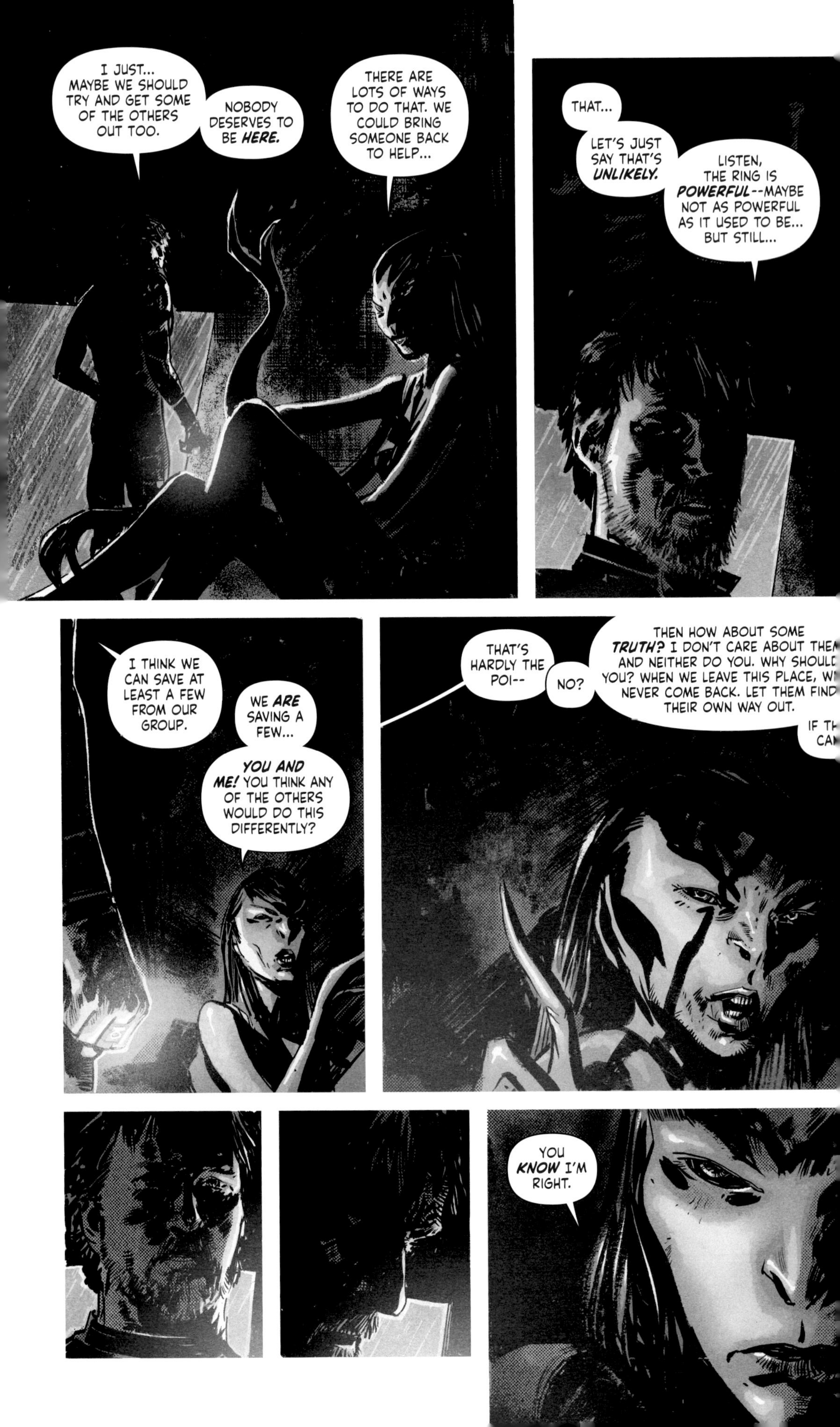
I JUST... MAYBE WE SHOULD TRY AND GET SOME OF THE OTHERS OUT TOO.
NOBODY DESERVES TO BE *HERE.*
THERE ARE LOTS OF WAYS TO DO THAT. WE COULD BRING SOMEONE BACK TO HELP...
THAT...
LET'S JUST SAY THAT'S *UNLIKELY.*
LISTEN, THE RING IS *POWERFUL*--MAYBE NOT AS POWERFUL AS IT USED TO BE... BUT STILL...
I THINK WE CAN SAVE AT LEAST A FEW FROM OUR GROUP.
WE *ARE* SAVING A FEW...
YOU AND ME! YOU THINK ANY OF THE OTHERS WOULD DO THIS DIFFERENTLY?
THAT'S HARDLY THE POI--
NO?
THEN HOW ABOUT SOME *TRUTH?* I DON'T CARE ABOUT THE AND NEITHER DO YOU. WHY SHOUL YOU? WHEN WE LEAVE THIS PLACE, W NEVER COME BACK. LET THEM FIND THEIR OWN WAY OUT.
YOU *KNOW* I'M RIGHT.

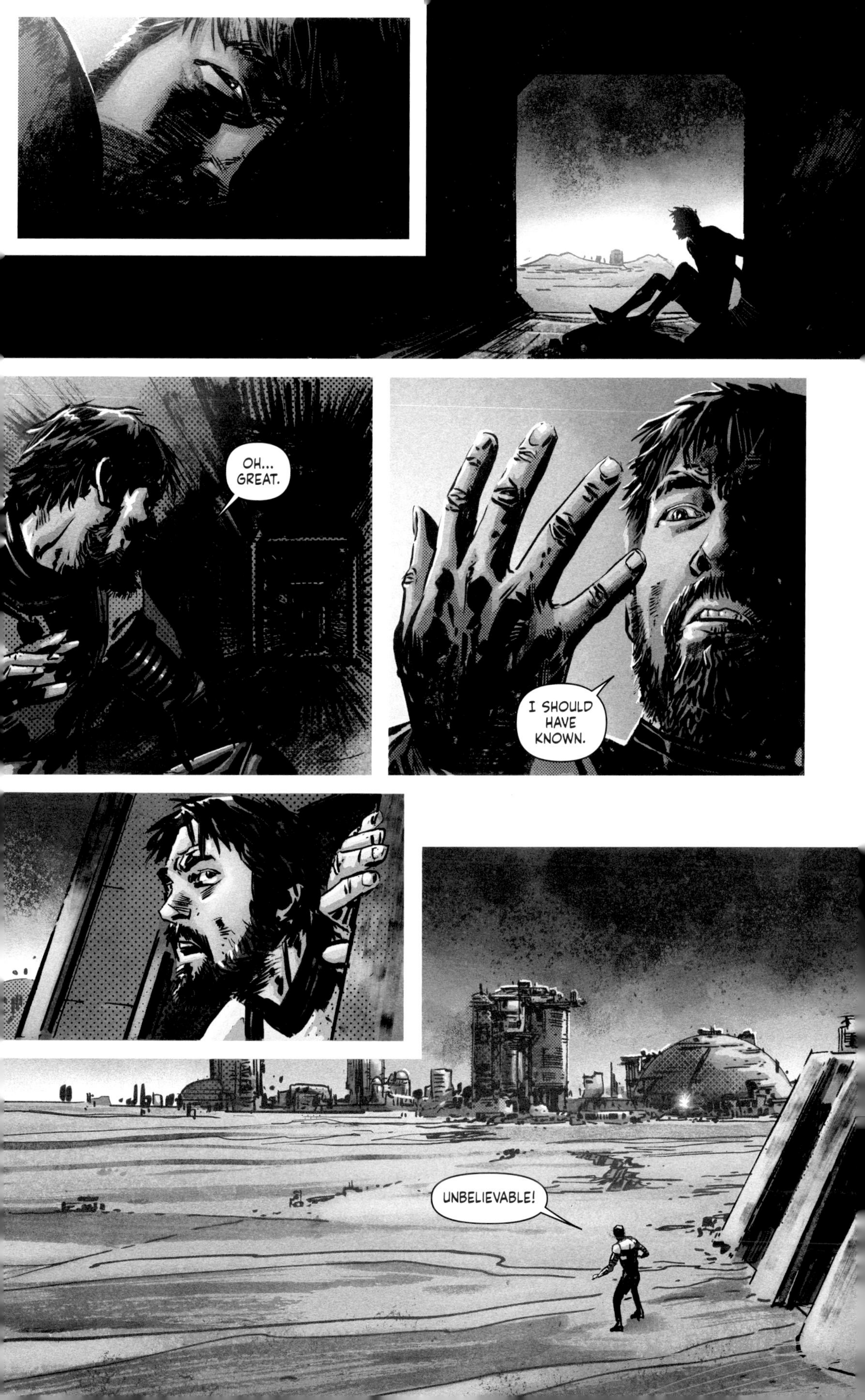
OH... GREAT.
I SHOULD HAVE KNOWN.
UNBELIEVABLE!

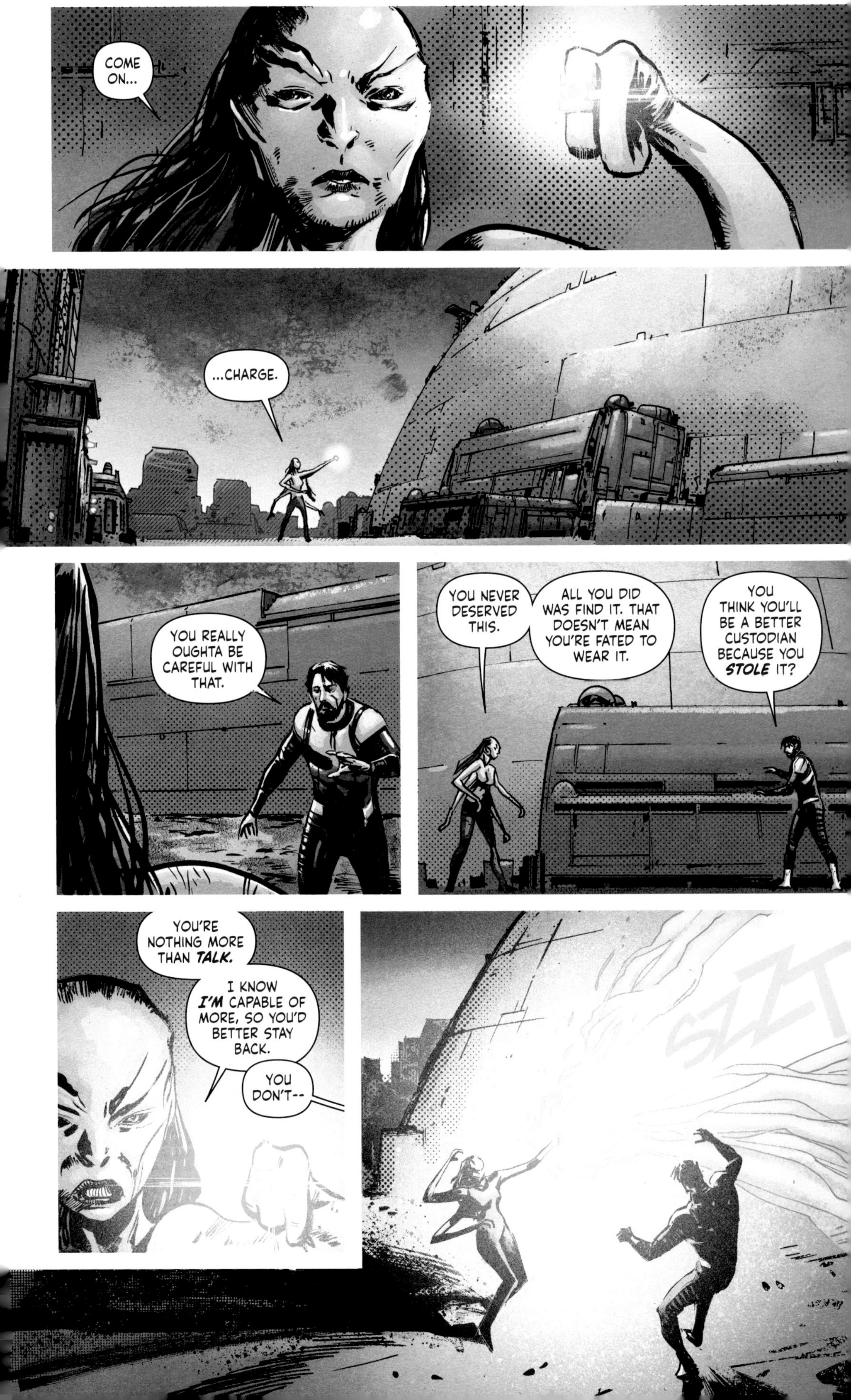
COME ON...
...CHARGE.
YOU REALLY OUGHTA BE CAREFUL WITH THAT.
YOU NEVER DESERVED THIS.
ALL YOU DID WAS FIND IT. THAT DOESN'T MEAN YOU'RE FATED TO WEAR IT.
YOU THINK YOU'LL BE A BETTER CUSTODIAN BECAUSE YOU STOLE IT?
YOU'RE NOTHING MORE THAN TALK.
I KNOW I'M CAPABLE OF MORE, SO YOU'D BETTER STAY BACK.
YOU DON'T--
SZZT

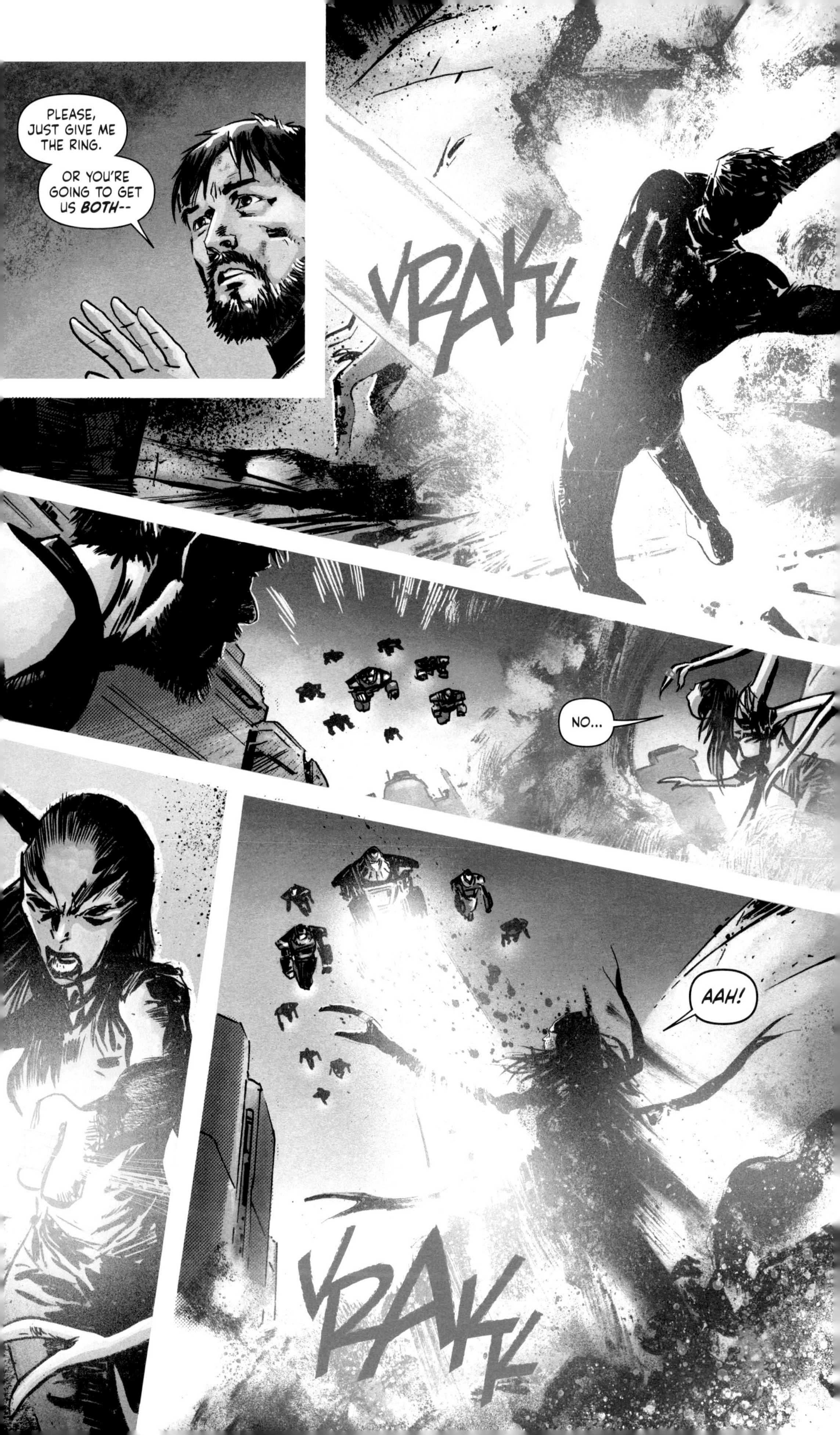
PLEASE, JUST GIVE ME THE RING.
OR YOU'RE GOING TO GET US *BOTH*--
VRAKK
NO...
AAH!
VRAKK

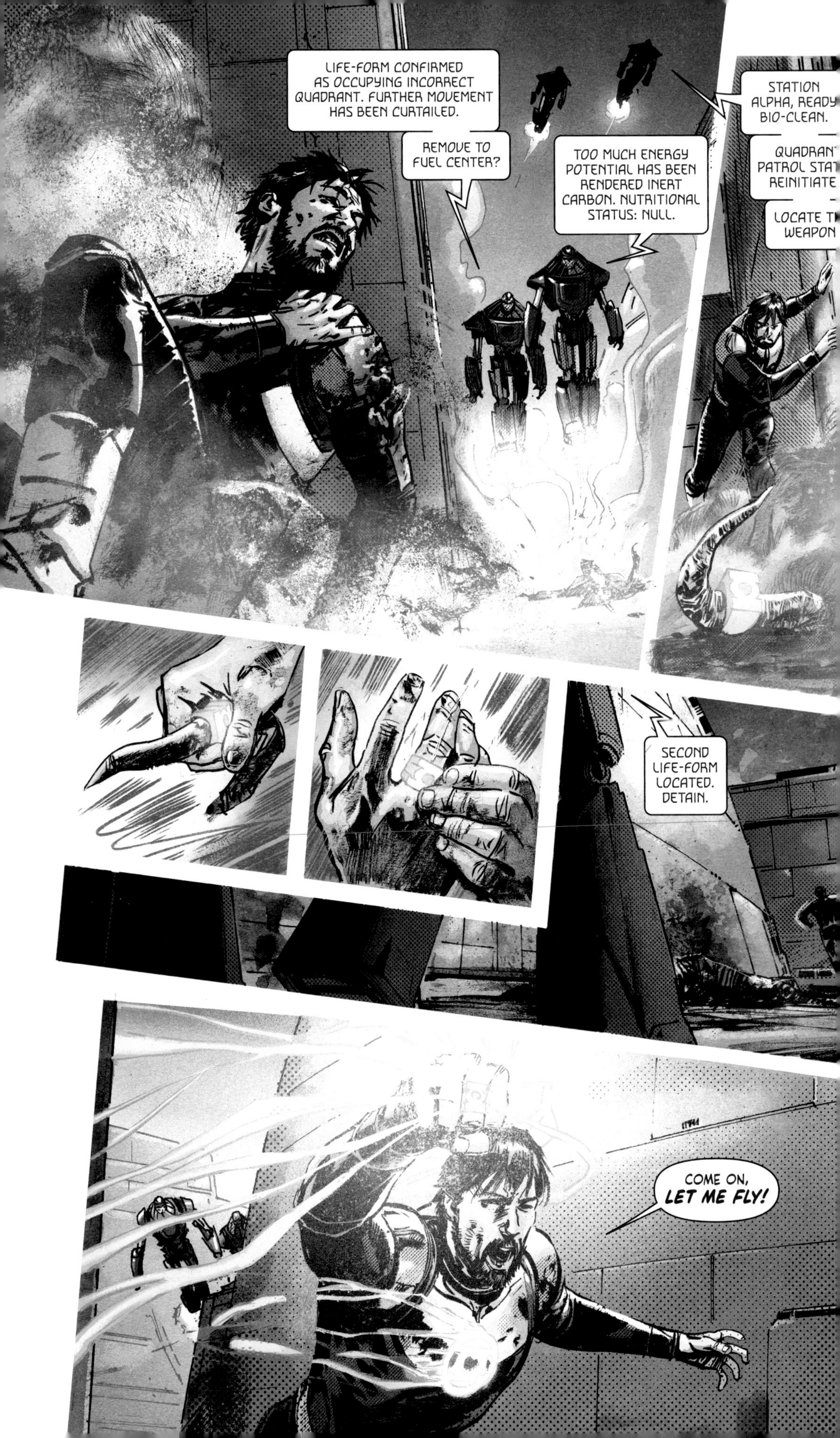
LIFE-FORM CONFIRMED AS OCCUPYING INCORRECT QUADRANT. FURTHER MOVEMENT HAS BEEN CURTAILED.
REMOVE TO FUEL CENTER?
TOO MUCH ENERGY POTENTIAL HAS BEEN RENDERED INERT CARBON. NUTRITIONAL STATUS: NULL.
STATION ALPHA, READY BIO-CLEAN.
SECOND LIFE-FORM LOCATED. DETAIN.
COME ON, LET ME FLY!

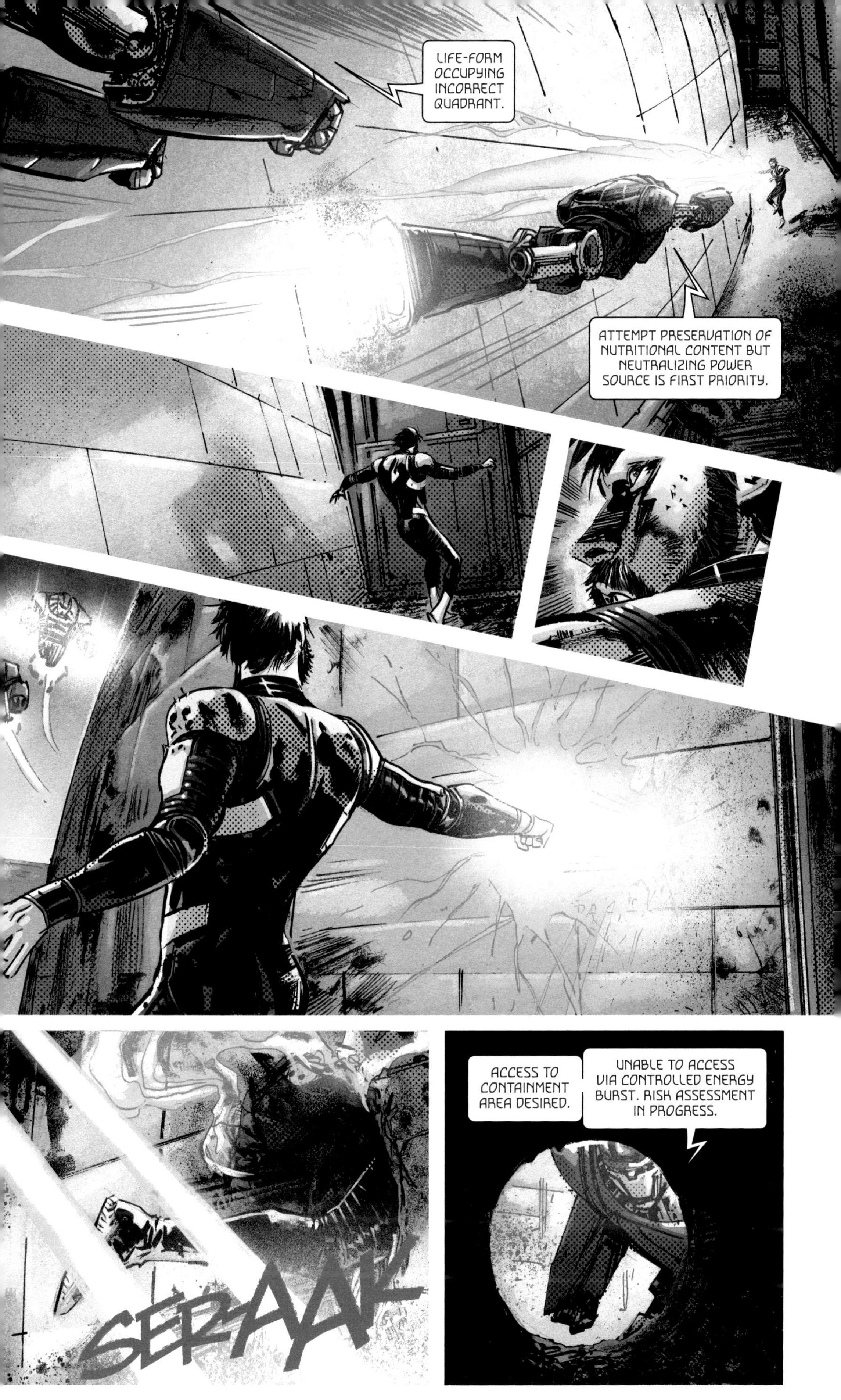
LIFE-FORM OCCUPYING INCORRECT QUADRANT.
ATTEMPT PRESERVATION OF NUTRITIONAL CONTENT BUT NEUTRALIZING POWER SOURCE IS FIRST PRIORITY.
SKRAAK
ACCESS TO CONTAINMENT AREA DESIRED.
UNABLE TO ACCESS VIA CONTROLLED ENERGY BURST. RISK ASSESSMENT IN PROGRESS.

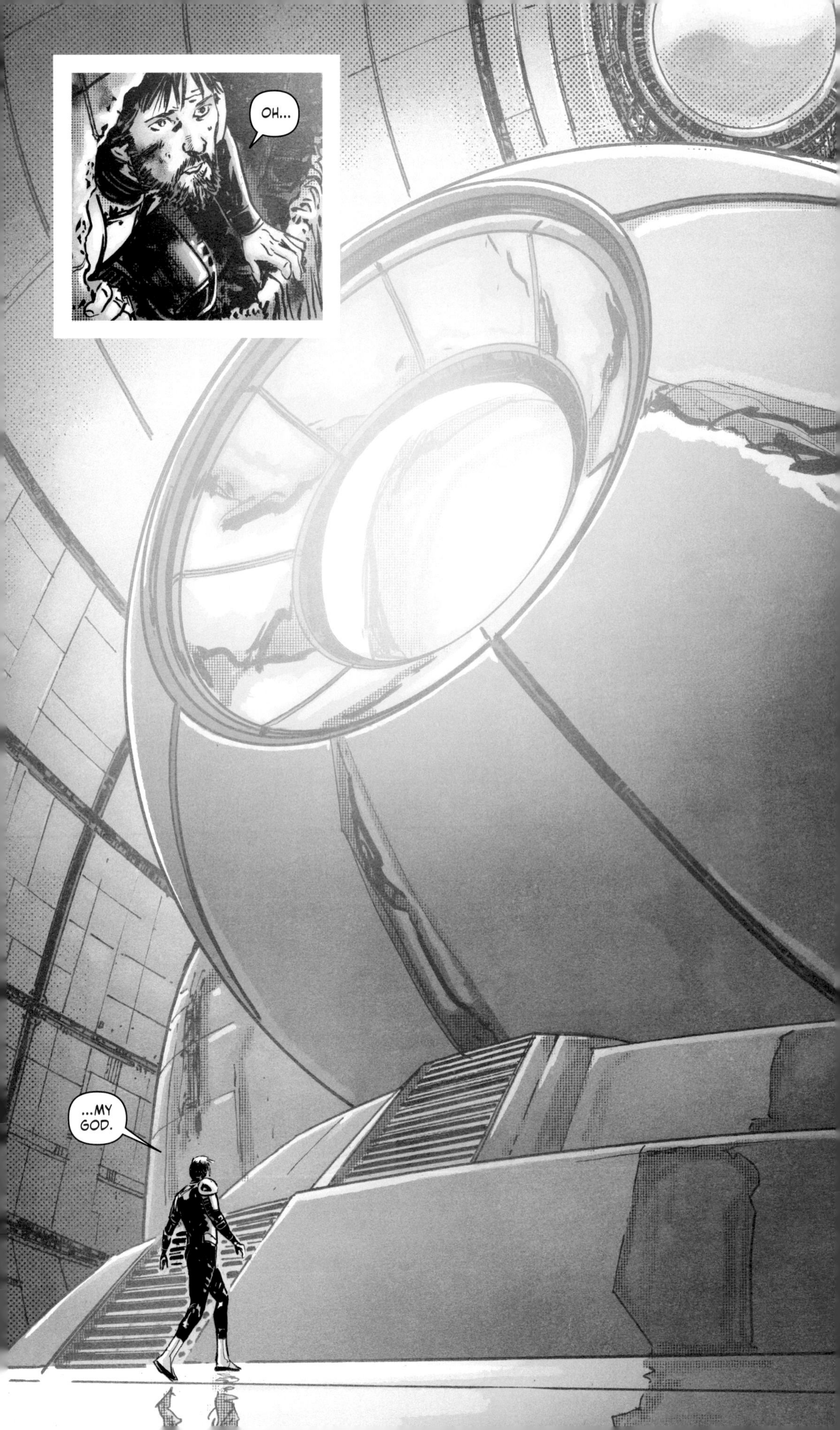
OH...
...MY GOD.

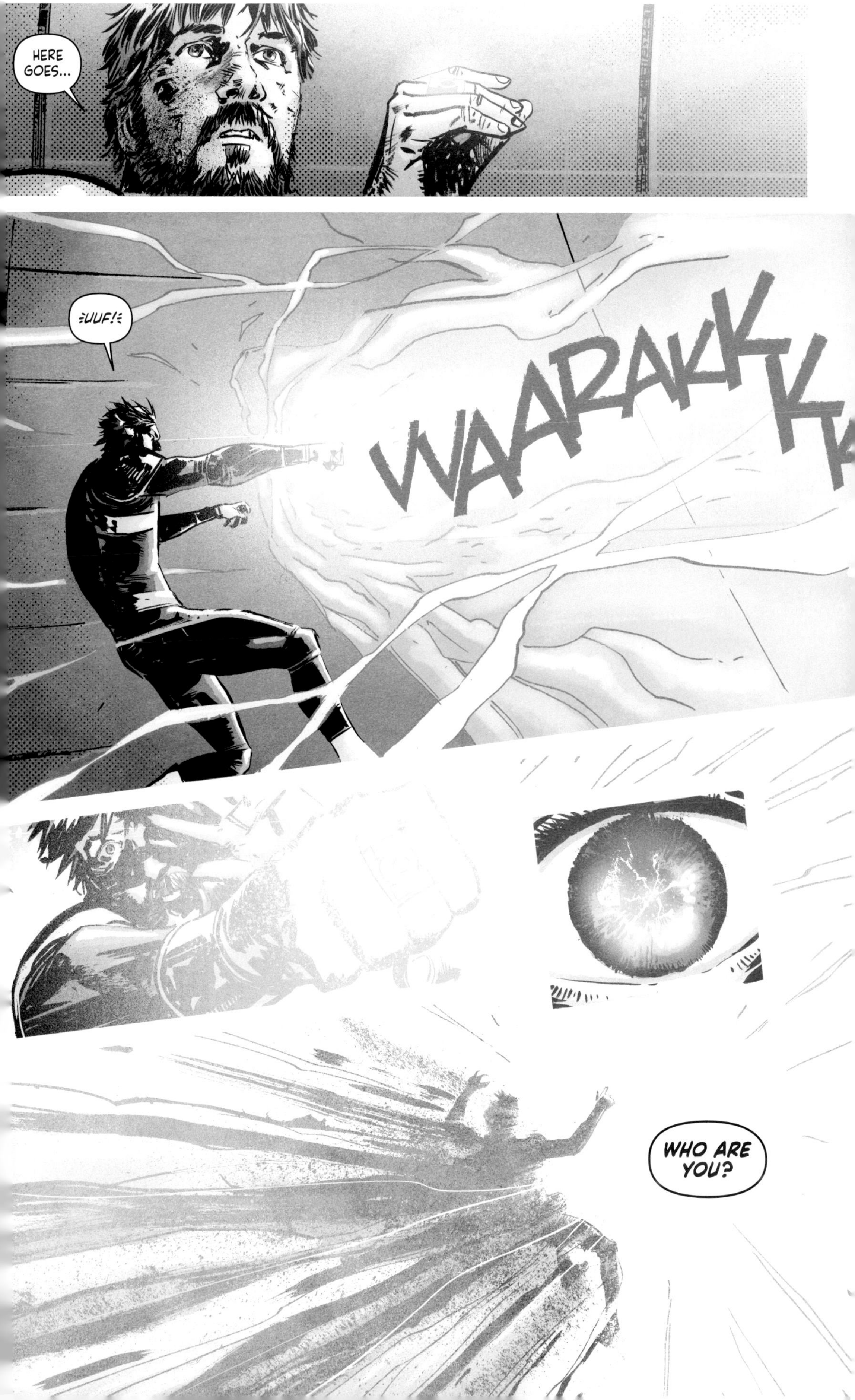
HERE GOES...
UUF!
WAARAKKK
WHO ARE YOU?

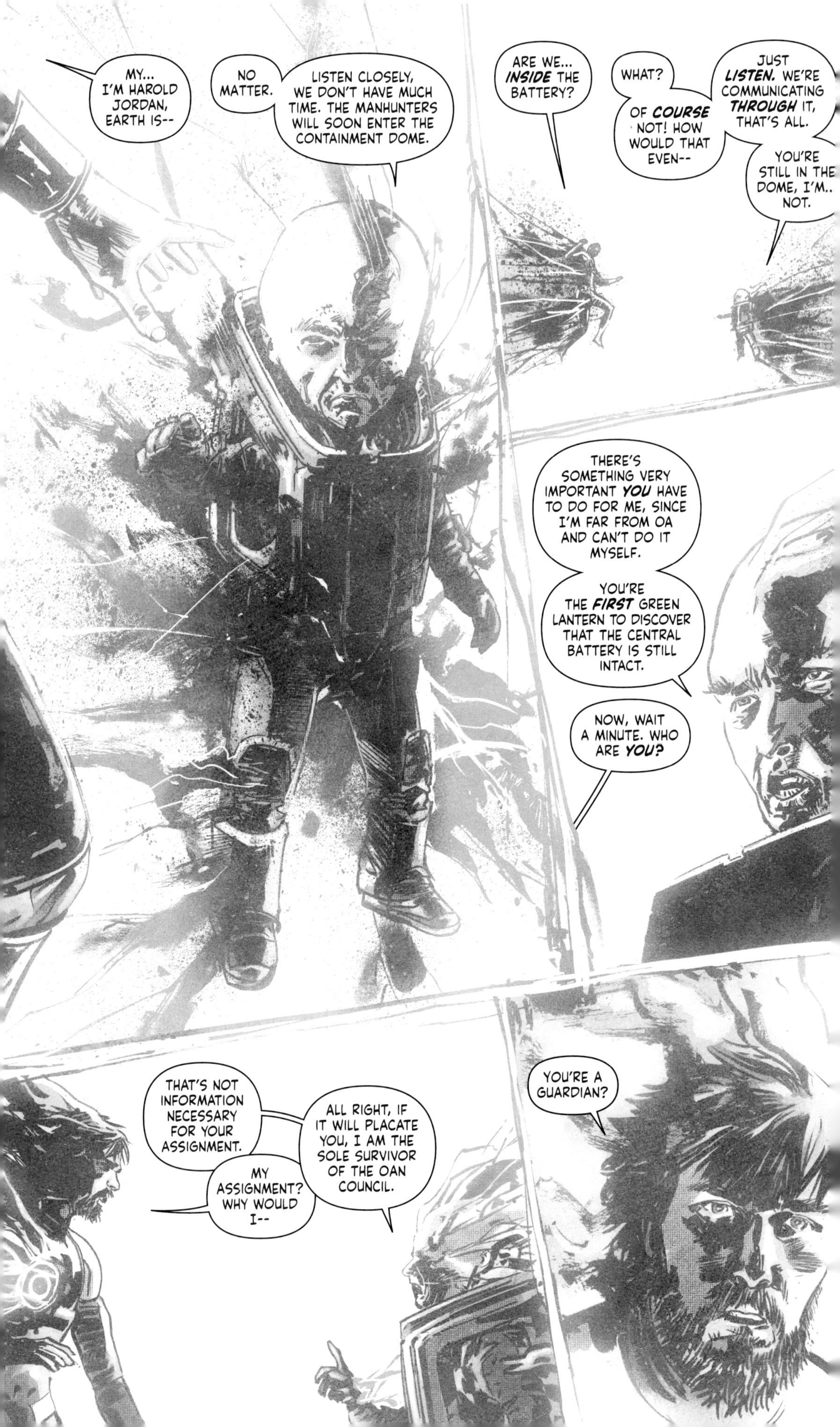
MY... I'M HAROLD JORDAN, EARTH IS--
NO MATTER.
LISTEN CLOSELY, WE DON'T HAVE MUCH TIME. THE MANHUNTERS WILL SOON ENTER THE CONTAINMENT DOME.
ARE WE... INSIDE THE BATTERY?
WHAT?
OF COURSE NOT! HOW WOULD THAT EVEN--
JUST LISTEN. WE'RE COMMUNICATING THROUGH IT, THAT'S ALL.
YOU'RE STILL IN THE DOME, I'M.. NOT.
THERE'S SOMETHING VERY IMPORTANT YOU HAVE TO DO FOR ME, SINCE I'M FAR FROM OA AND CAN'T DO IT MYSELF.
YOU'RE THE FIRST GREEN LANTERN TO DISCOVER THAT THE CENTRAL BATTERY IS STILL INTACT.
NOW, WAIT A MINUTE. WHO ARE YOU?
THAT'S NOT INFORMATION NECESSARY FOR YOUR ASSIGNMENT.
MY ASSIGNMENT? WHY WOULD I--
ALL RIGHT, IF IT WILL PLACATE YOU, I AM THE SOLE SURVIVOR OF THE OAN COUNCIL.
YOU'RE A GUARDIAN?

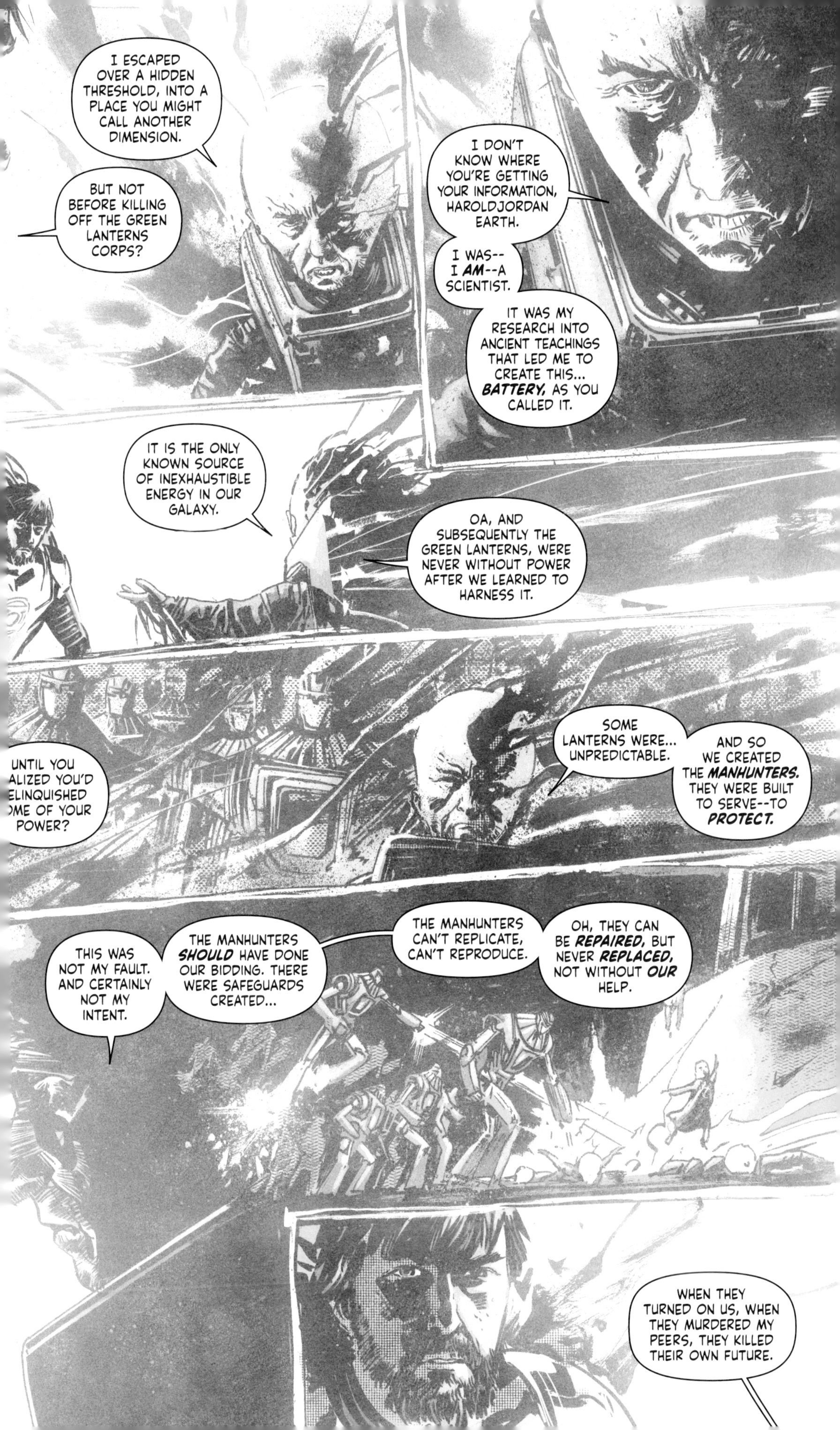
I ESCAPED OVER A HIDDEN THRESHOLD, INTO A PLACE YOU MIGHT CALL ANOTHER DIMENSION.
BUT NOT BEFORE KILLING OFF THE GREEN LANTERNS CORPS?
I DON'T KNOW WHERE YOU'RE GETTING YOUR INFORMATION, HAROLDJORDAN EARTH.
I WAS-- I AM--A SCIENTIST.
IT WAS MY RESEARCH INTO ANCIENT TEACHINGS THAT LED ME TO CREATE THIS... BATTERY, AS YOU CALLED IT.
IT IS THE ONLY KNOWN SOURCE OF INEXHAUSTIBLE ENERGY IN OUR GALAXY.
OA, AND SUBSEQUENTLY THE GREEN LANTERNS, WERE NEVER WITHOUT POWER AFTER WE LEARNED TO HARNESS IT.
UNTIL YOU ALIZED YOU'D ELINQUISHED OME OF YOUR POWER?
SOME LANTERNS WERE... UNPREDICTABLE.
AND SO WE CREATED THE MANHUNTERS. THEY WERE BUILT TO SERVE--TO PROTECT.
THIS WAS NOT MY FAULT. AND CERTAINLY NOT MY INTENT.
THE MANHUNTERS SHOULD HAVE DONE OUR BIDDING. THERE WERE SAFEGUARDS CREATED...
THE MANHUNTERS CAN'T REPLICATE, CAN'T REPRODUCE.
OH, THEY CAN BE REPAIRED, BUT NEVER REPLACED, NOT WITHOUT OUR HELP.
WHEN THEY TURNED ON US, WHEN THEY MURDERED MY PEERS, THEY KILLED THEIR OWN FUTURE.

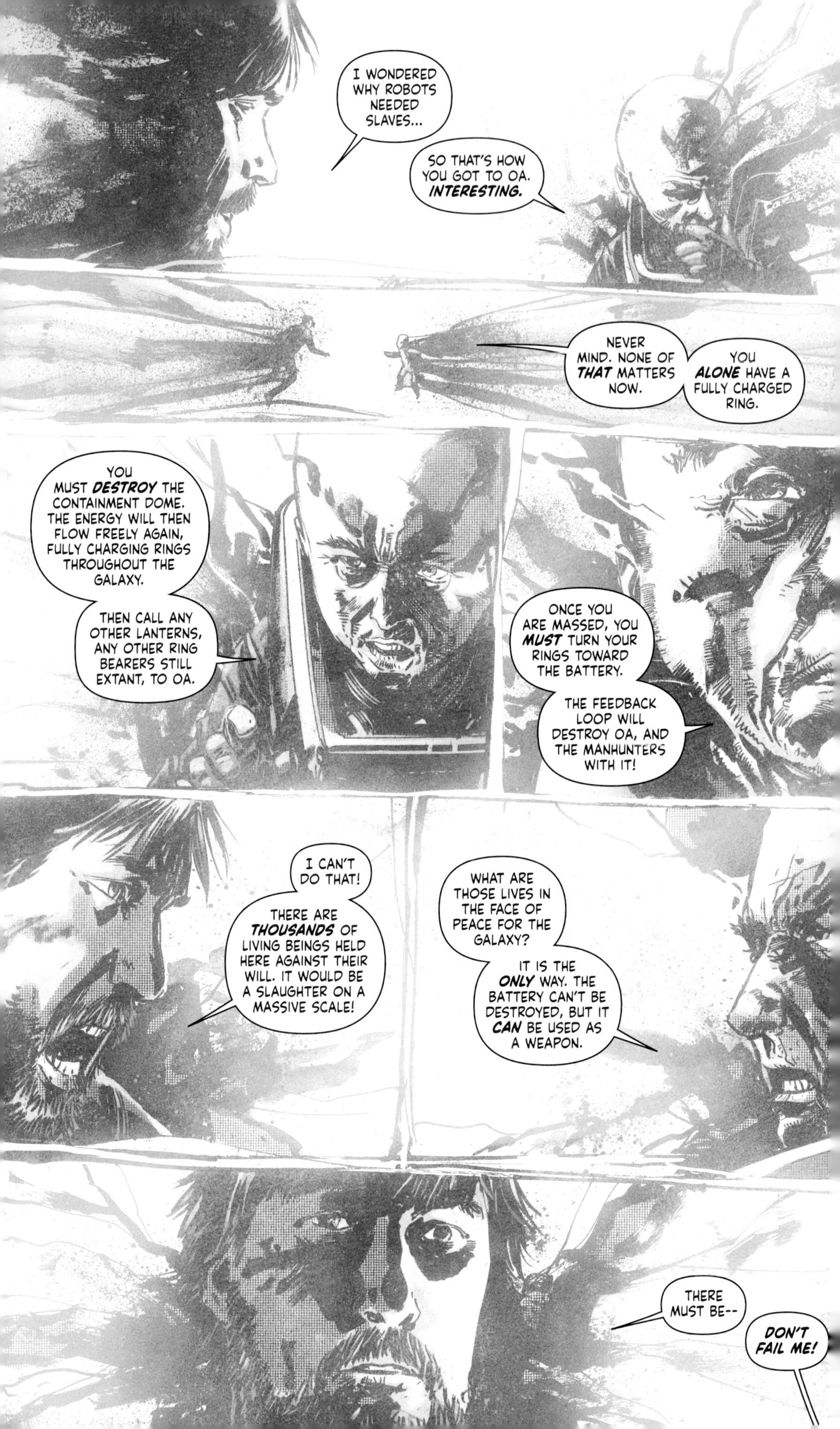
I WONDERED WHY ROBOTS NEEDED SLAVES...
SO THAT'S HOW YOU GOT TO OA. INTERESTING.
NEVER MIND. NONE OF THAT MATTERS NOW.
YOU ALONE HAVE A FULLY CHARGED RING.
YOU MUST DESTROY THE CONTAINMENT DOME. THE ENERGY WILL THEN FLOW FREELY AGAIN, FULLY CHARGING RINGS THROUGHOUT THE GALAXY.
THEN CALL ANY OTHER LANTERNS, ANY OTHER RING BEARERS STILL EXTANT, TO OA.
ONCE YOU ARE MASSED, YOU MUST TURN YOUR RINGS TOWARD THE BATTERY.
THE FEEDBACK LOOP WILL DESTROY OA, AND THE MANHUNTERS WITH IT!
I CAN'T DO THAT!
THERE ARE THOUSANDS OF LIVING BEINGS HELD HERE AGAINST THEIR WILL. IT WOULD BE A SLAUGHTER ON A MASSIVE SCALE!
WHAT ARE THOSE LIVES IN THE FACE OF PEACE FOR THE GALAXY?
IT IS THE ONLY WAY. THE BATTERY CAN'T BE DESTROYED, BUT IT CAN BE USED AS A WEAPON.
THERE MUST BE--
DON'T FAIL ME!

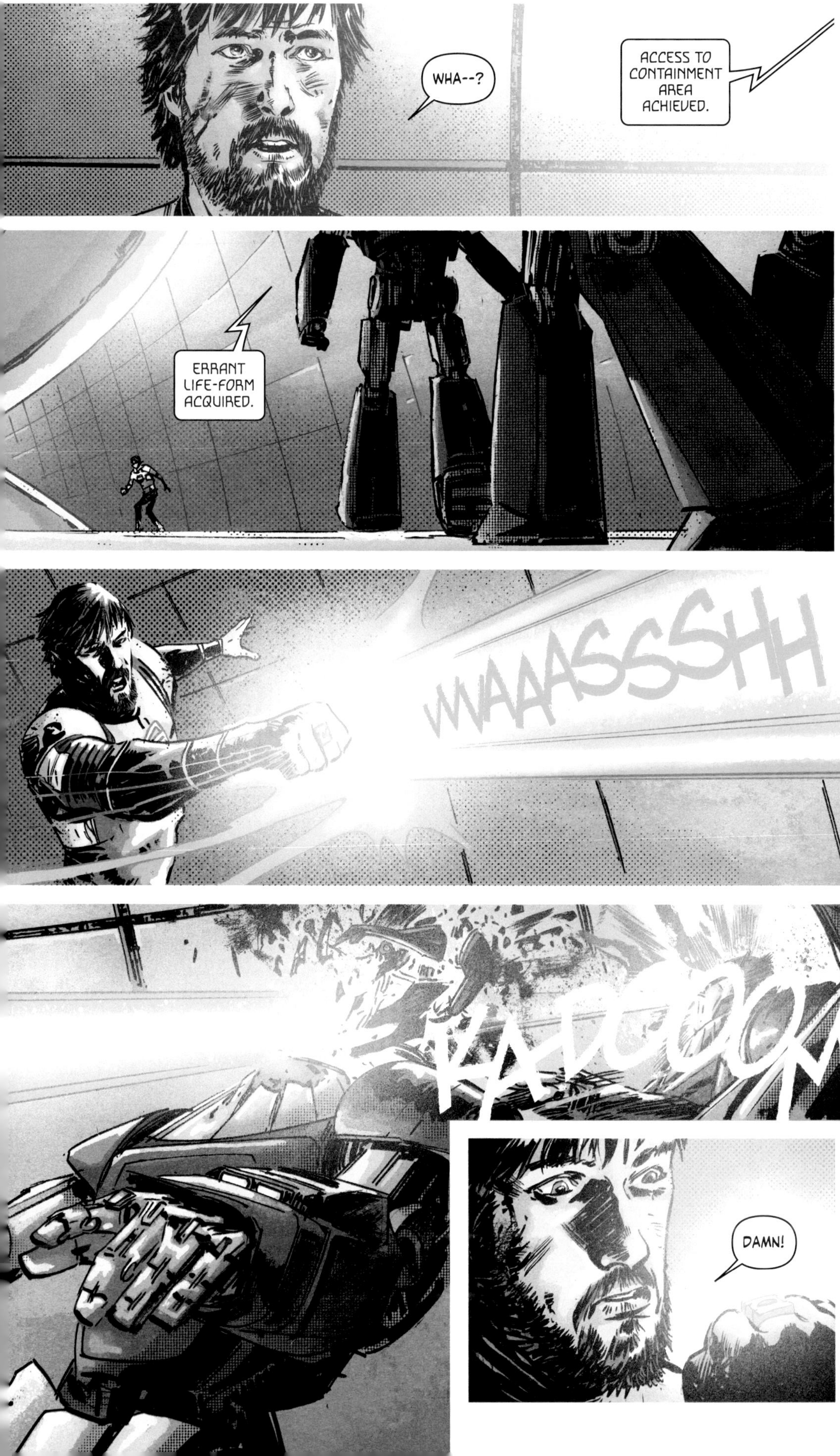
WHA--?
ACCESS TO CONTAINMENT AREA ACHIEVED.
ERRANT LIFE-FORM ACQUIRED.
WAAASSSHH
KA-DOOOM
DAMN!

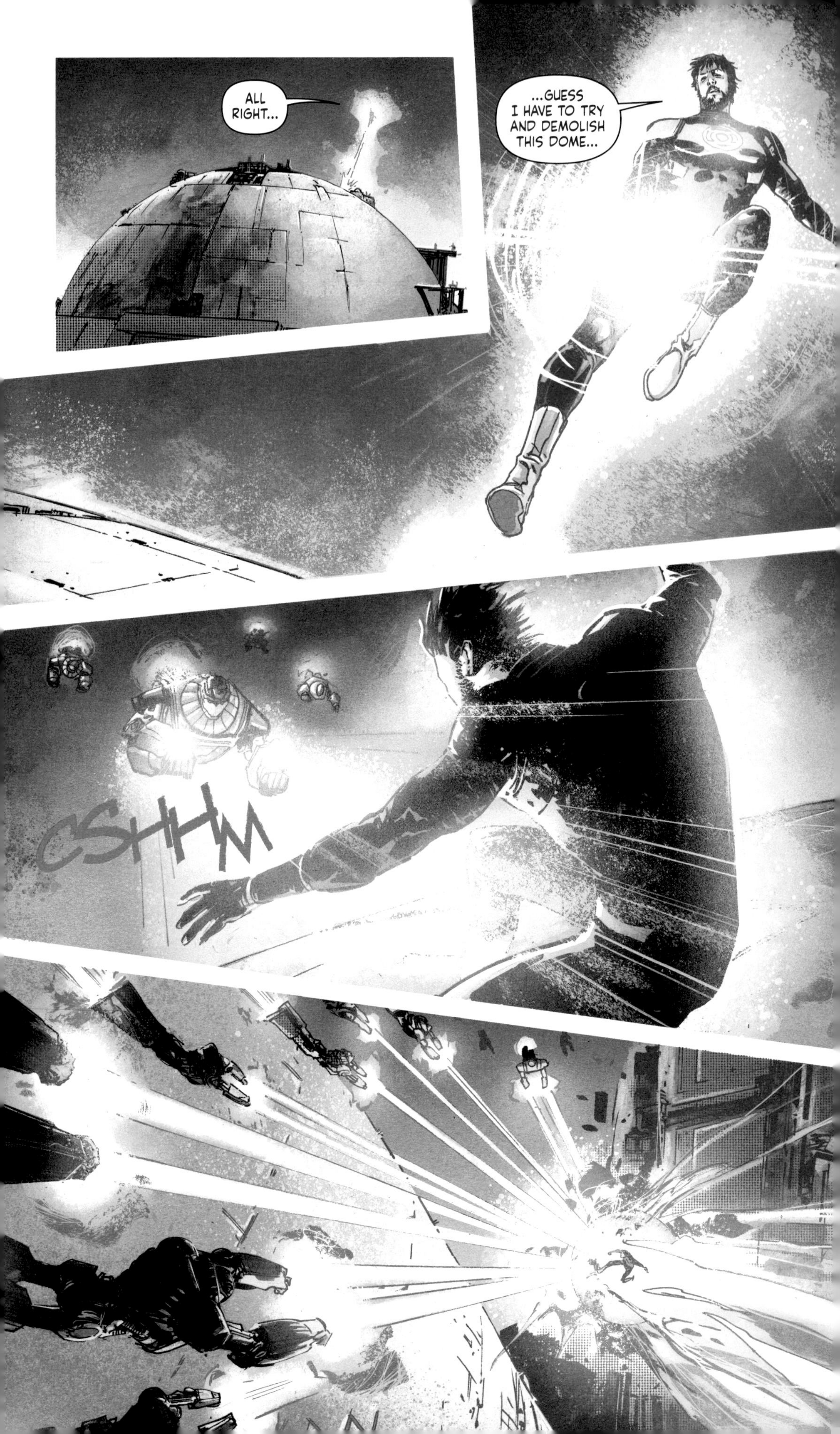
ALL RIGHT...
...GUESS I HAVE TO TRY AND DEMOLISH THIS DOME...
CSHHM

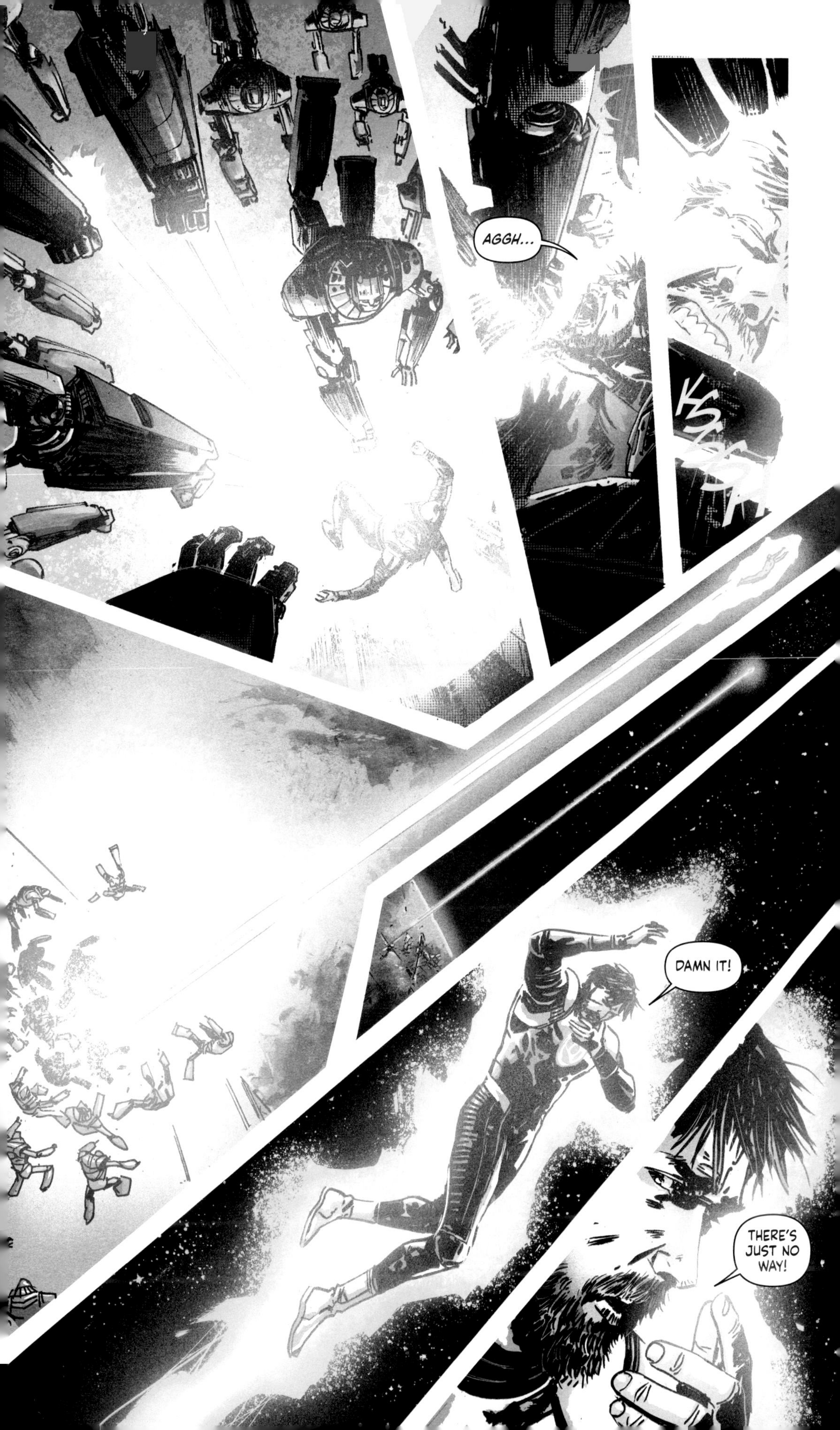
AGGH...
DAMN IT!
THERE'S JUST NO WAY!

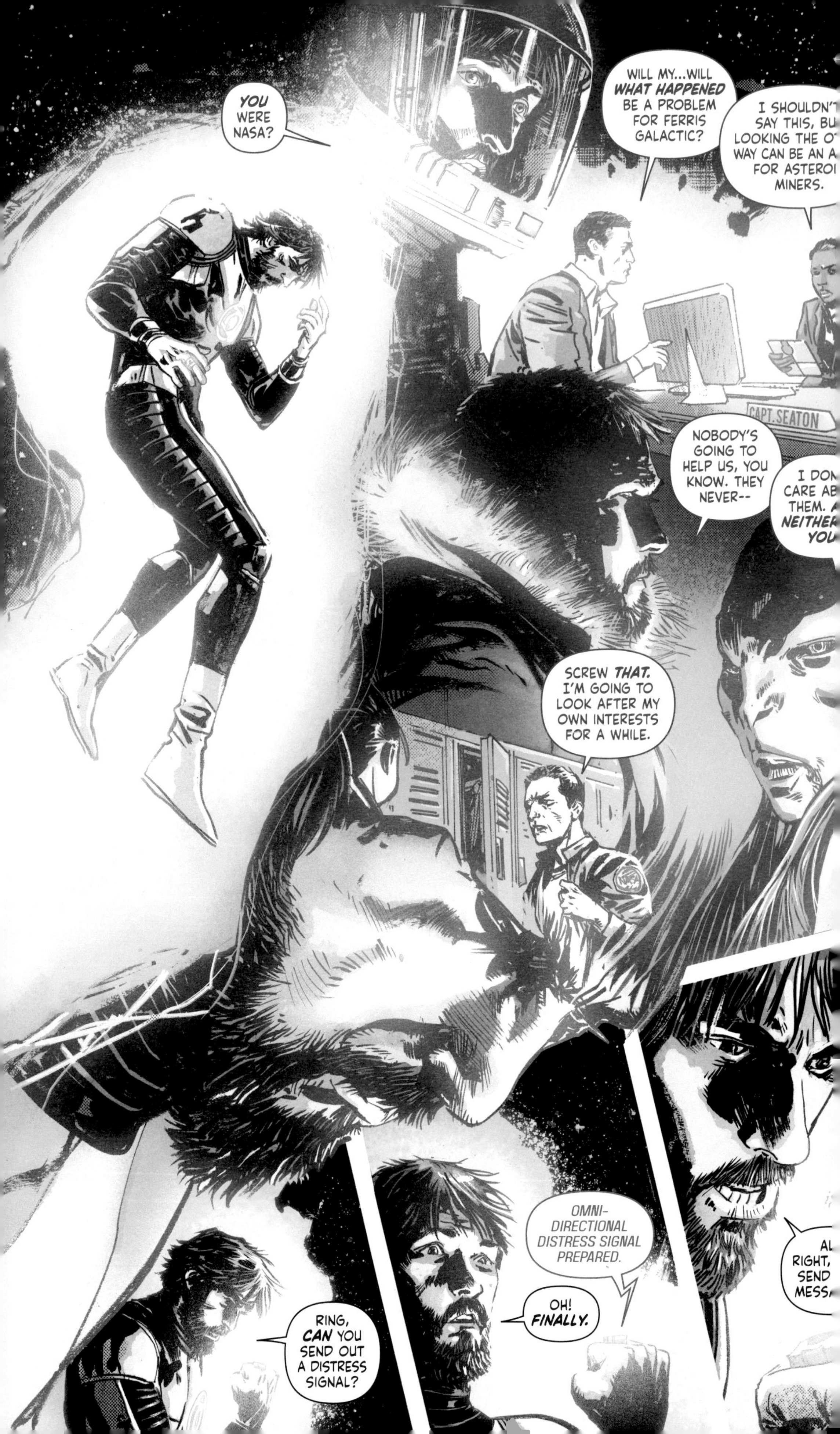
YOU WERE NASA?
WILL MY...WILL WHAT HAPPENED BE A PROBLEM FOR FERRIS GALACTIC?
I SHOULDN'T SAY THIS, BU LOOKING THE OT WAY CAN BE AN A FOR ASTEROI MINERS.
CAPT. SEATON
NOBODY'S GOING TO HELP US, YOU KNOW. THEY NEVER--
I DON CARE AB THEM. A NEITHER YOU
SCREW THAT. I'M GOING TO LOOK AFTER MY OWN INTERESTS FOR A WHILE.
RING, CAN YOU SEND OUT A DISTRESS SIGNAL?
OMNI-DIRECTIONAL DISTRESS SIGNAL PREPARED.
OH! FINALLY.
AL RIGHT, SEND MESS

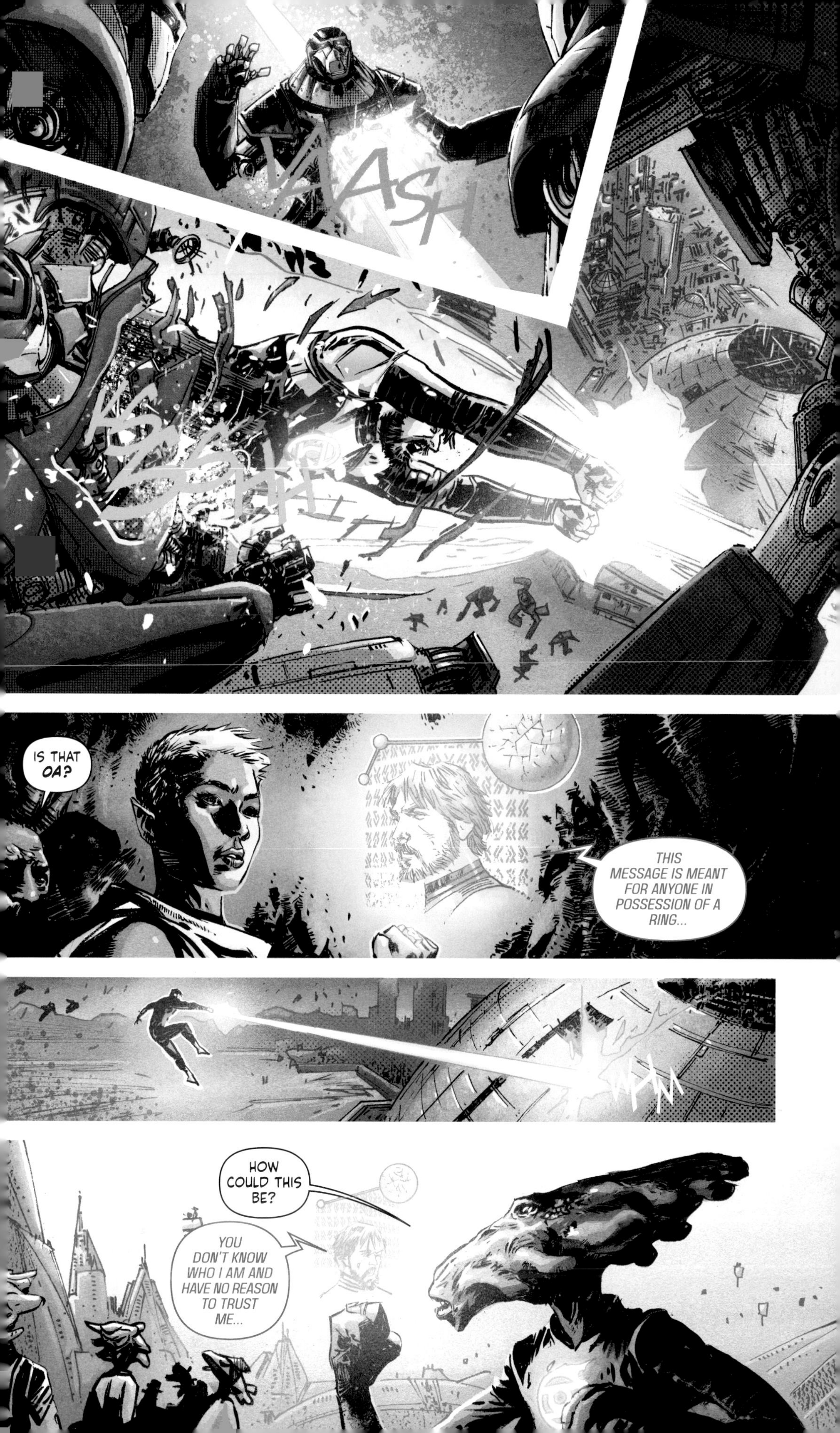
IS THAT OA?
THIS MESSAGE IS MEANT FOR ANYONE IN POSSESSION OF A RING...
HOW COULD THIS BE?
YOU DON'T KNOW WHO I AM AND HAVE NO REASON TO TRUST ME...

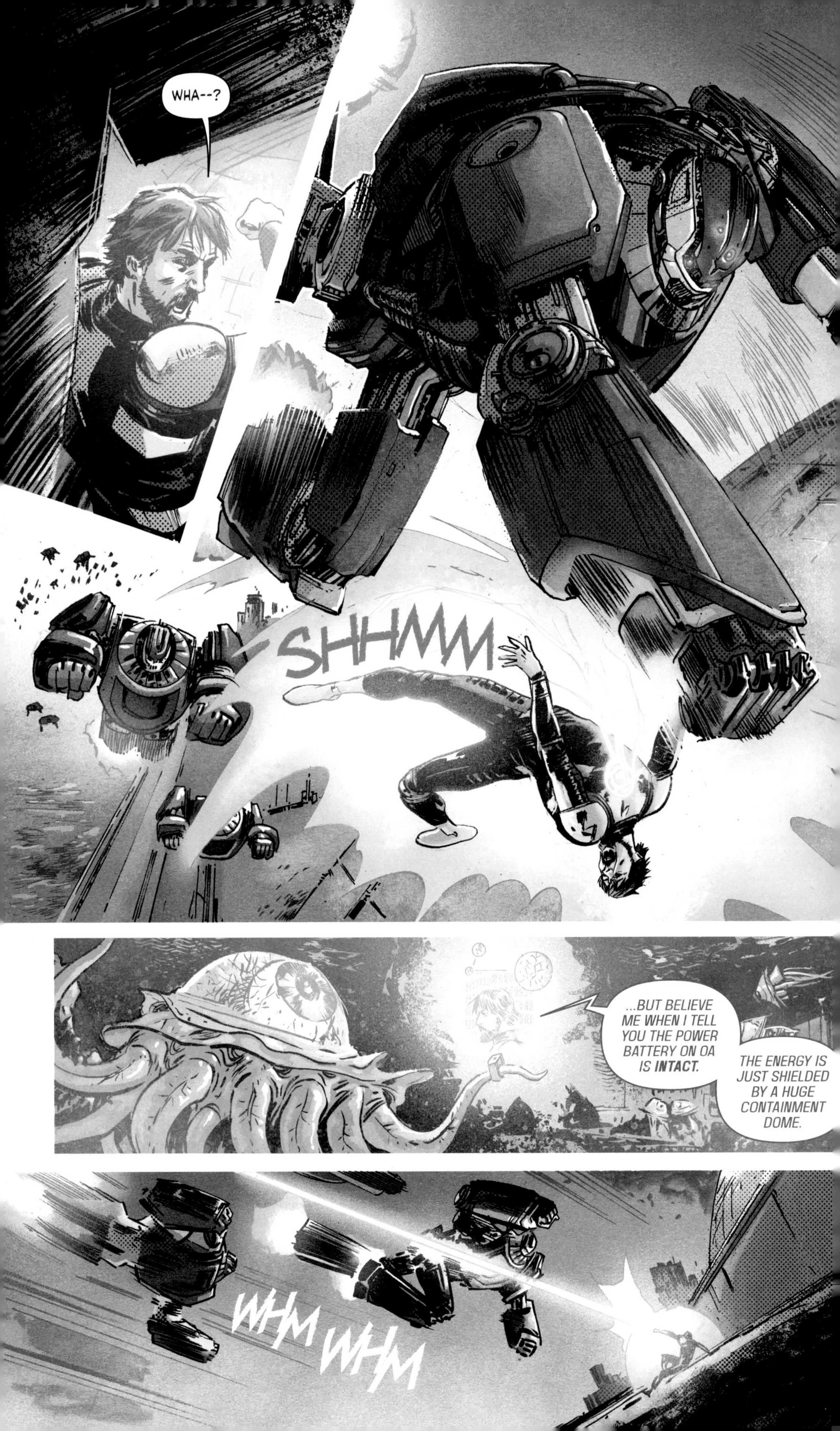
WHA--?
SHHMM
...BUT BELIEVE ME WHEN I TELL YOU THE POWER BATTERY ON OA IS **INTACT**.
THE ENERGY IS JUST SHIELDED BY A HUGE CONTAINMENT DOME.
WHM WHM

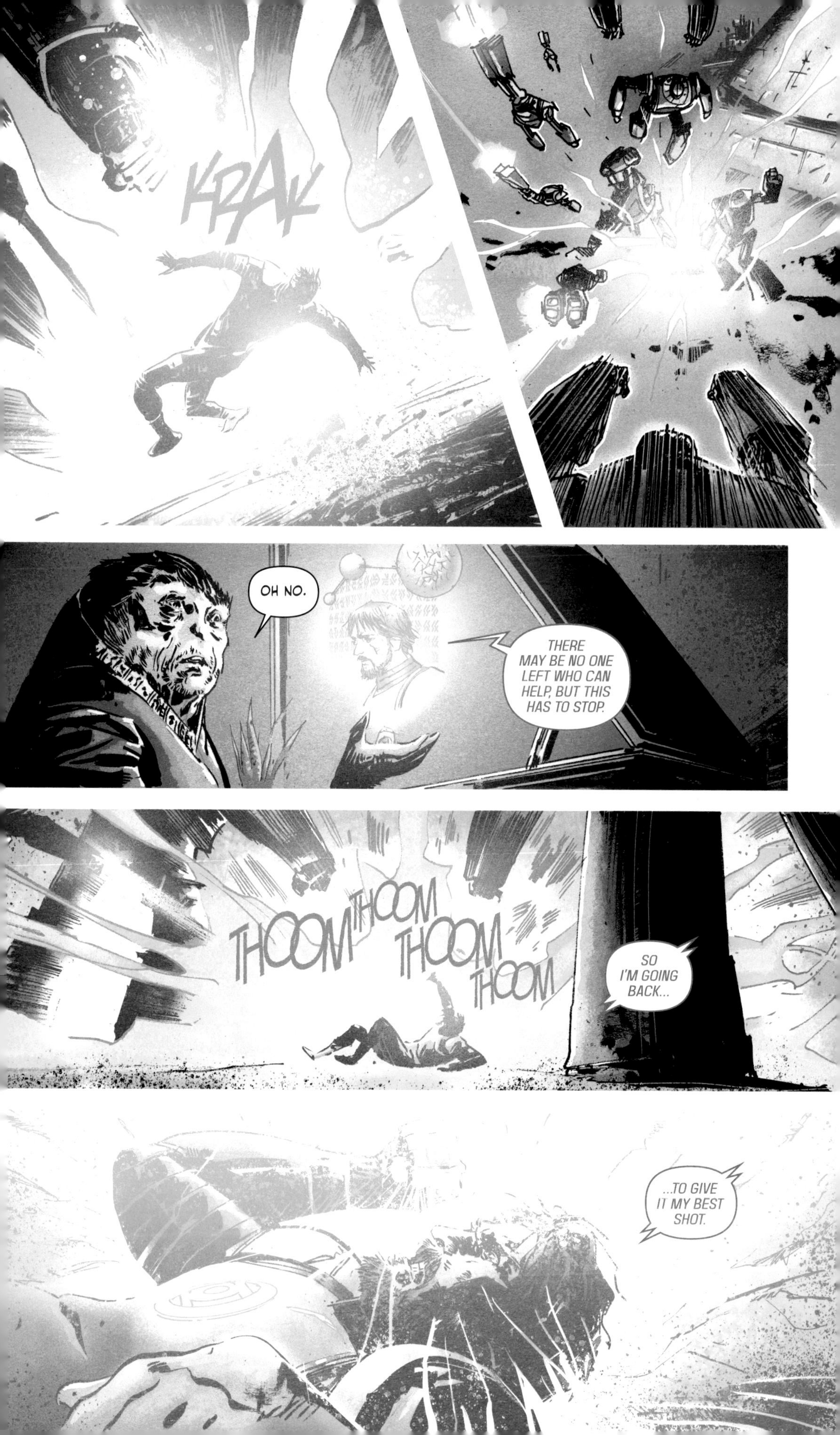
KRAK
OH NO.
THERE MAY BE NO ONE LEFT WHO CAN HELP, BUT THIS HAS TO STOP.
THOOM THOOM THOOM THOOM
SO I'M GOING BACK...
...TO GIVE IT MY BEST SHOT.

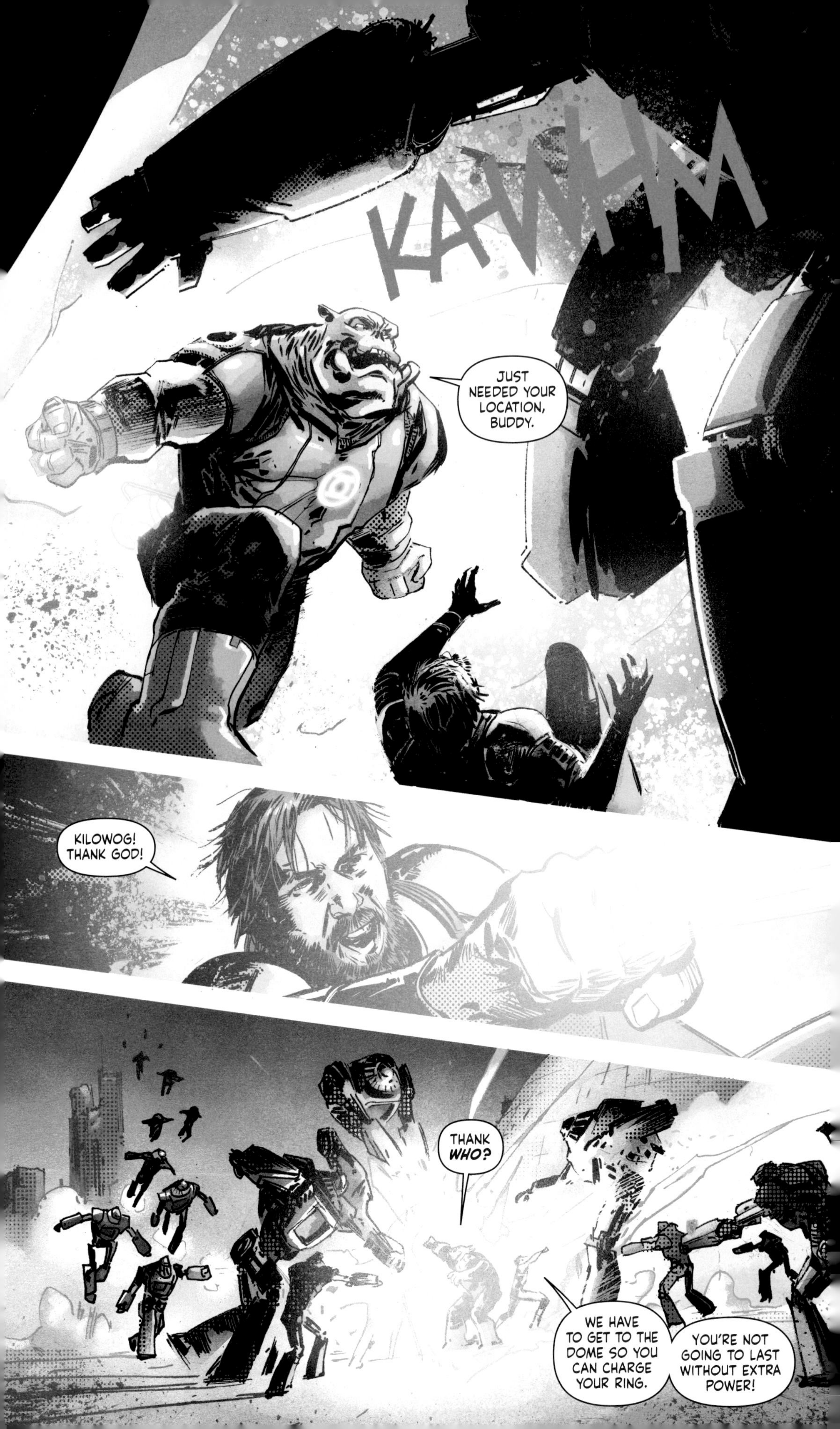
KAWHM
JUST NEEDED YOUR LOCATION, BUDDY.
KILOWOG! THANK GOD!
THANK WHO?
WE HAVE TO GET TO THE DOME SO YOU CAN CHARGE YOUR RING.
YOU'RE NOT GOING TO LAST WITHOUT EXTRA POWER!

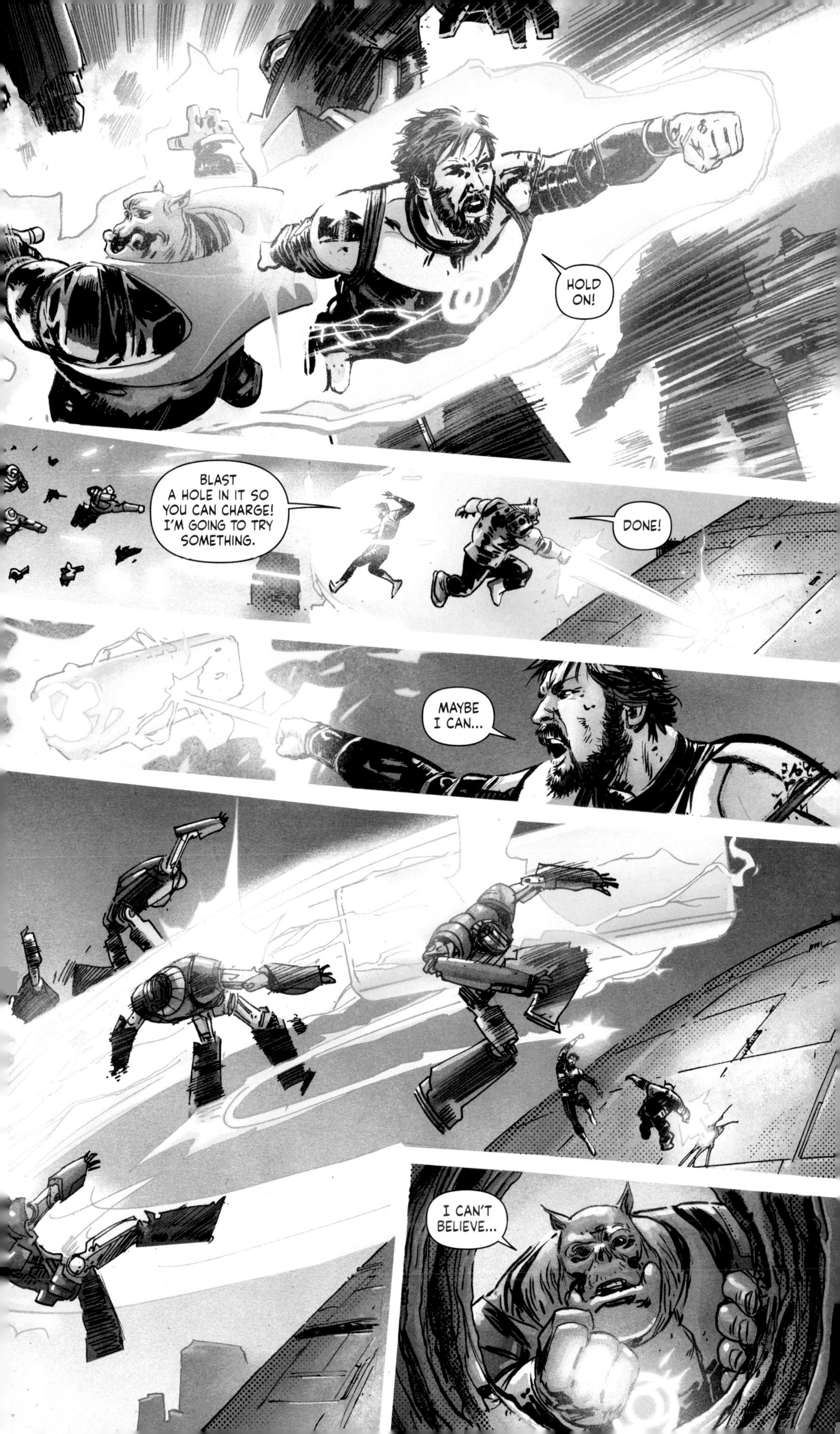
HOLD ON!
BLAST A HOLE IN IT SO YOU CAN CHARGE! I'M GOING TO TRY SOMETHING.
DONE!
MAYBE I CAN...
I CAN'T BELIEVE...

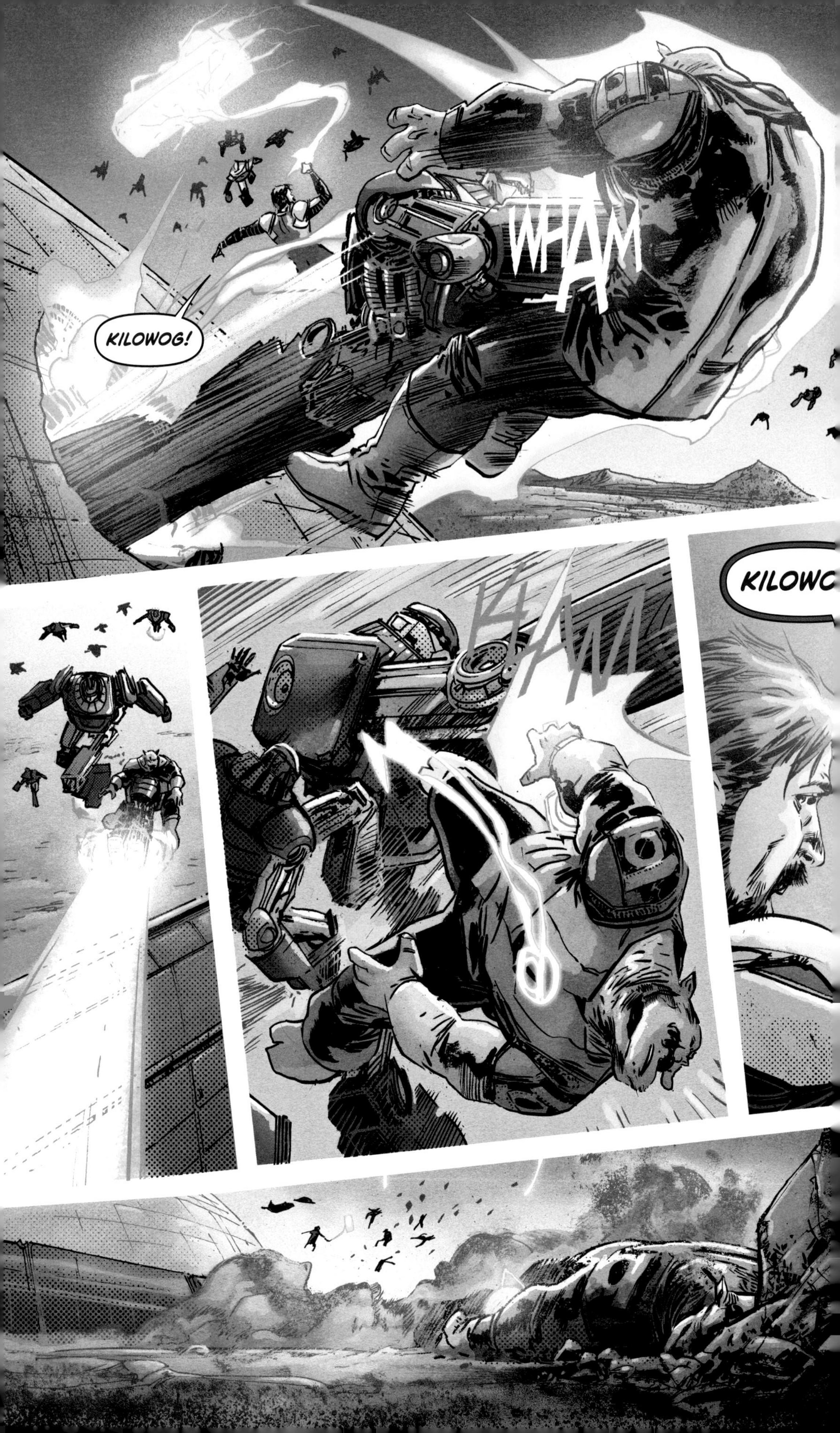
KILOWOG!
WHAM
KILOWO

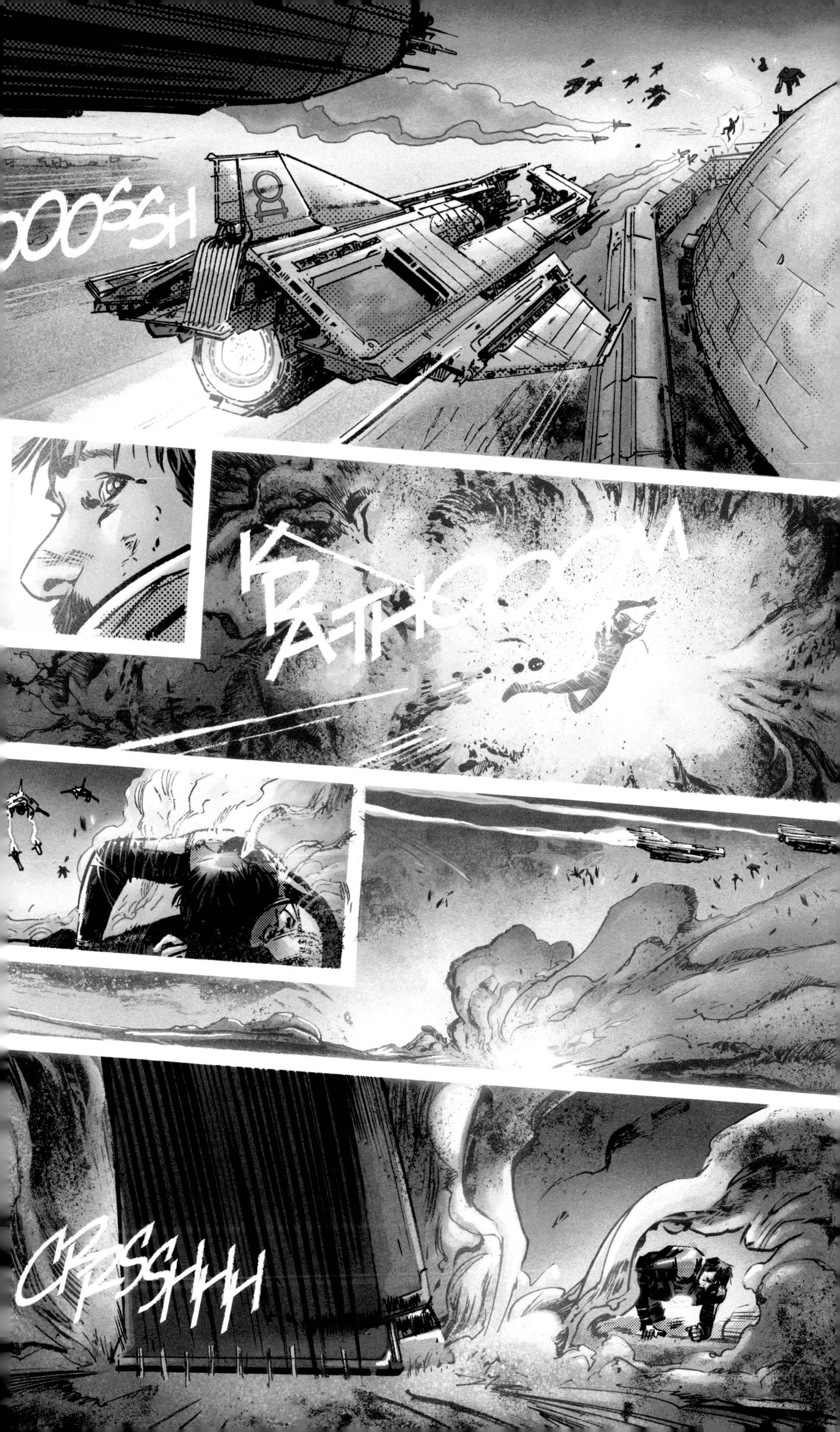
OOOSSH
KRATHOOOOM
CRSSHHH

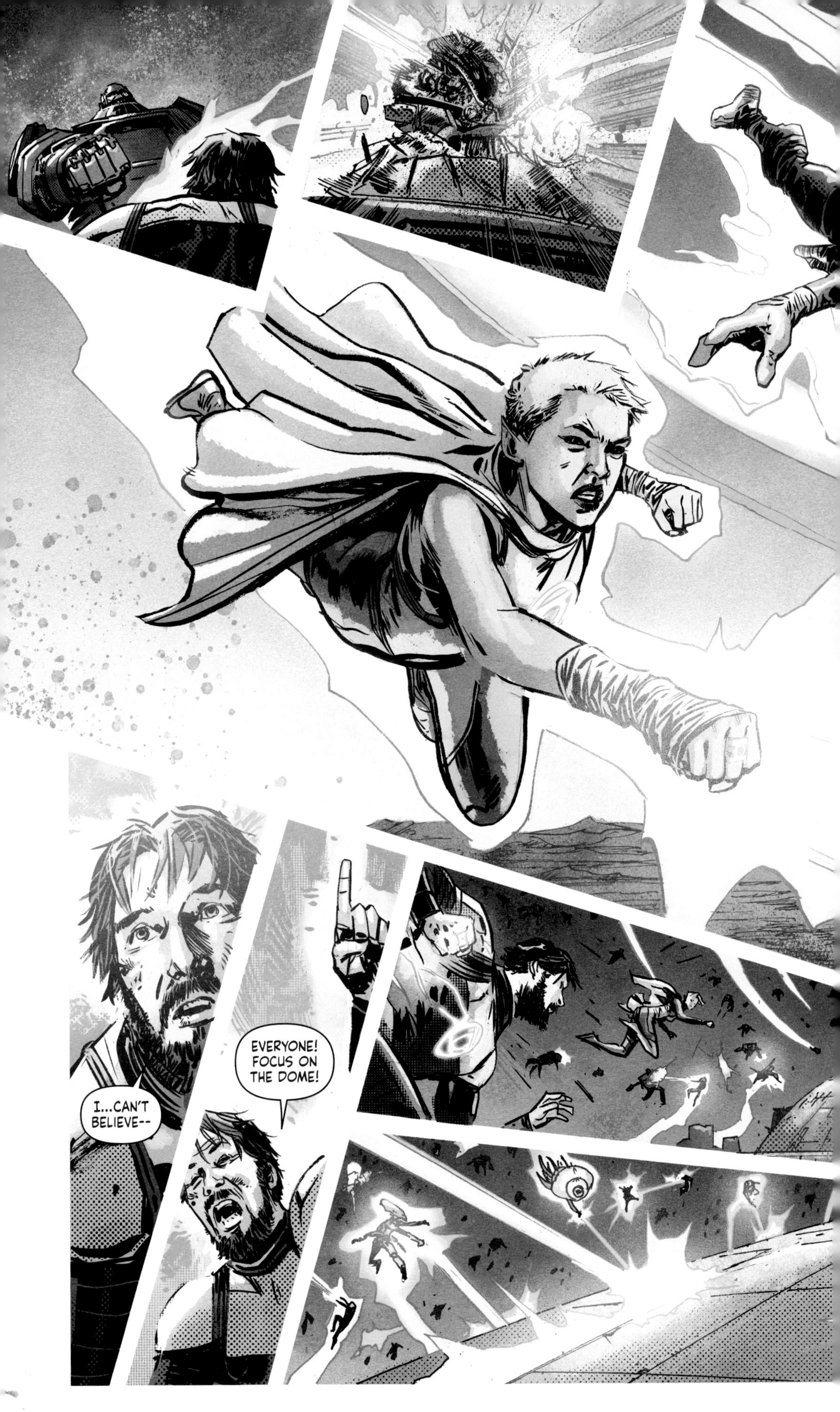
I...CAN'T BELIEVE--
EVERYONE! FOCUS ON THE DOME!

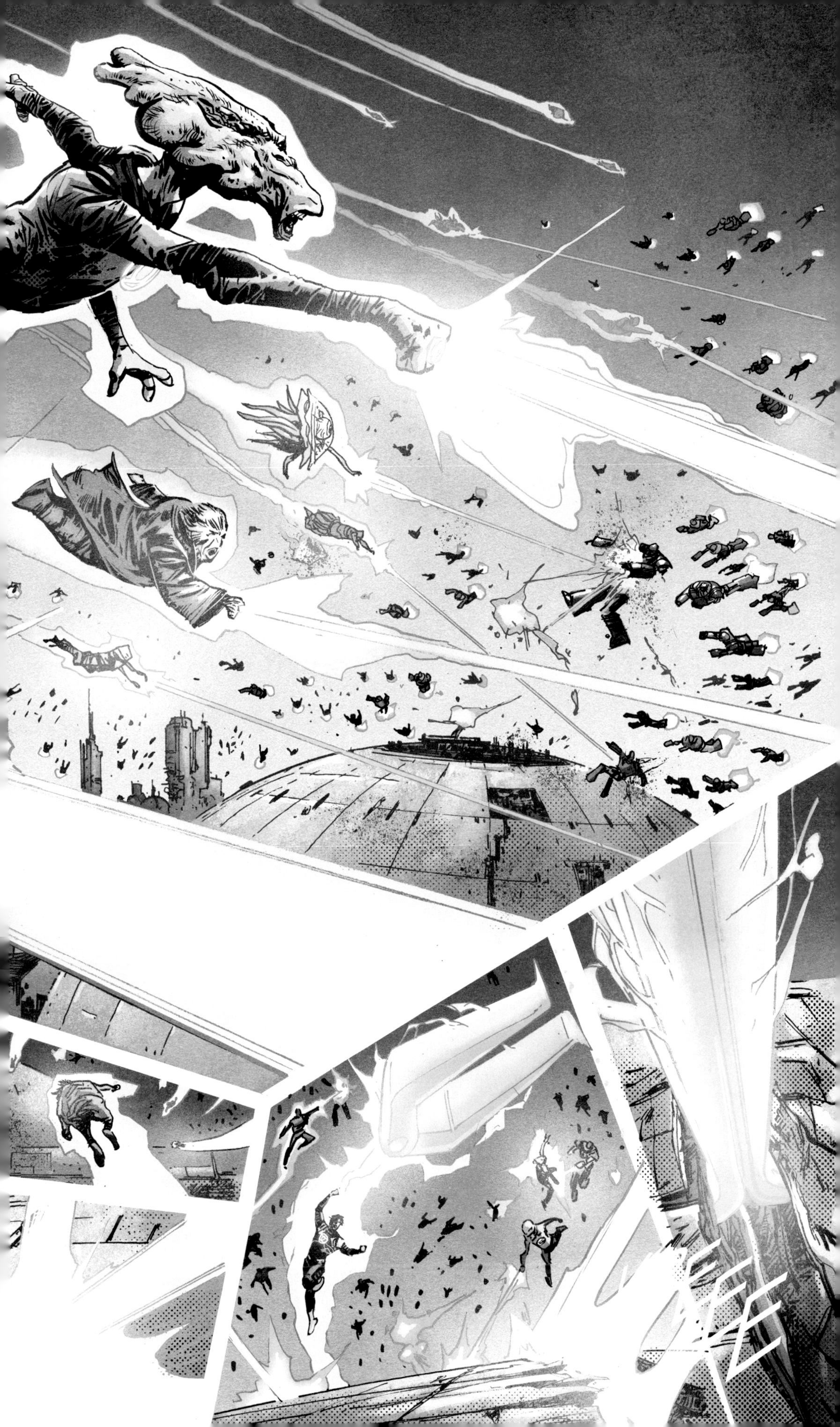

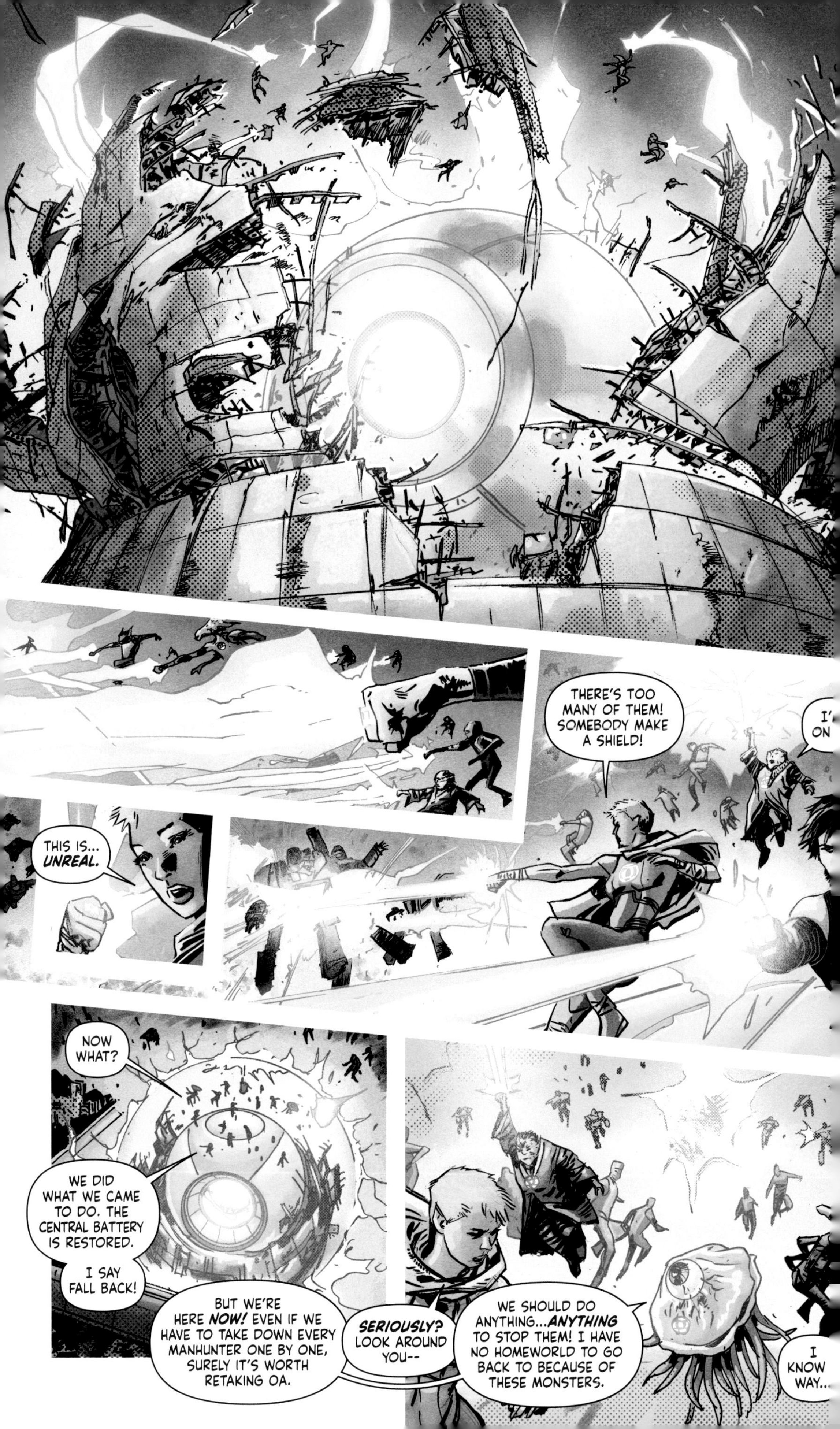
THERE'S TOO MANY OF THEM! SOMEBODY MAKE A SHIELD!
I'
ON
THIS IS... ***UNREAL.***
NOW WHAT?
WE DID WHAT WE CAME TO DO. THE CENTRAL BATTERY IS RESTORED.
I SAY FALL BACK!
BUT WE'RE HERE ***NOW!*** EVEN IF WE HAVE TO TAKE DOWN EVERY MANHUNTER ONE BY ONE, SURELY IT'S WORTH RETAKING OA.
SERIOUSLY? LOOK AROUND YOU--
WE SHOULD DO ANYTHING...***ANYTHING*** TO STOP THEM! I HAVE NO HOMEWORLD TO GO BACK TO BECAUSE OF THESE MONSTERS.
I KNOW WAY...

BUT IT'S... WELL...

IF WE USE THE RINGS TO CHANNEL AS MUCH ENERGY AS POSSIBLE BACK INTO THE BATTERY, IT WILL CREATE A LOOP.

THE BATTERY WON'T BE HARMED, BUT THE BLAST IT CREATES SHOULD BE BIG ENOUGH TO... WELL, TO *DESTROY* OA.

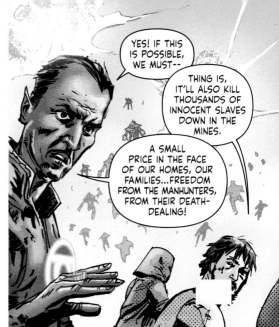

YES! IF THIS IS POSSIBLE, WE MUST--

THING IS, IT'LL ALSO KILL THOUSANDS OF INNOCENT SLAVES DOWN IN THE MINES.

A SMALL PRICE IN THE FACE OF OUR HOMES, OUR FAMILIES...FREEDOM FROM THE MANHUNTERS, FROM THEIR DEATH-DEALING!

OKAY, GANG, WE'RE OUT OF TIME!

WAIT!

IF WHAT THIS SCRUFFY LANTERN SAYS IS TRUE, THERE'S STILL ANOTHER WAY!

I'M A PHYSICIST AND... WELL...I DON'T THINK WE NEED A LOOP THAT BIG. WE COULD CHANNEL--

GET TO THE POINT!

WE HAVE *TOOLS* TO CONTROL THE POWER NOW.

I THINK I KNOW HOW TO WIPE OUT EVERY MANHUNTER ON THE SURFACE WITHOUT DESTROYING OA OR KILLING THE SLAVES.

OKAY, 'NOUGH OF THIS! 'RE GOING WITH HE PHYSICIST'S PLAN!

RIGHT?

RIGHT.

HOW DO WE DO IT?

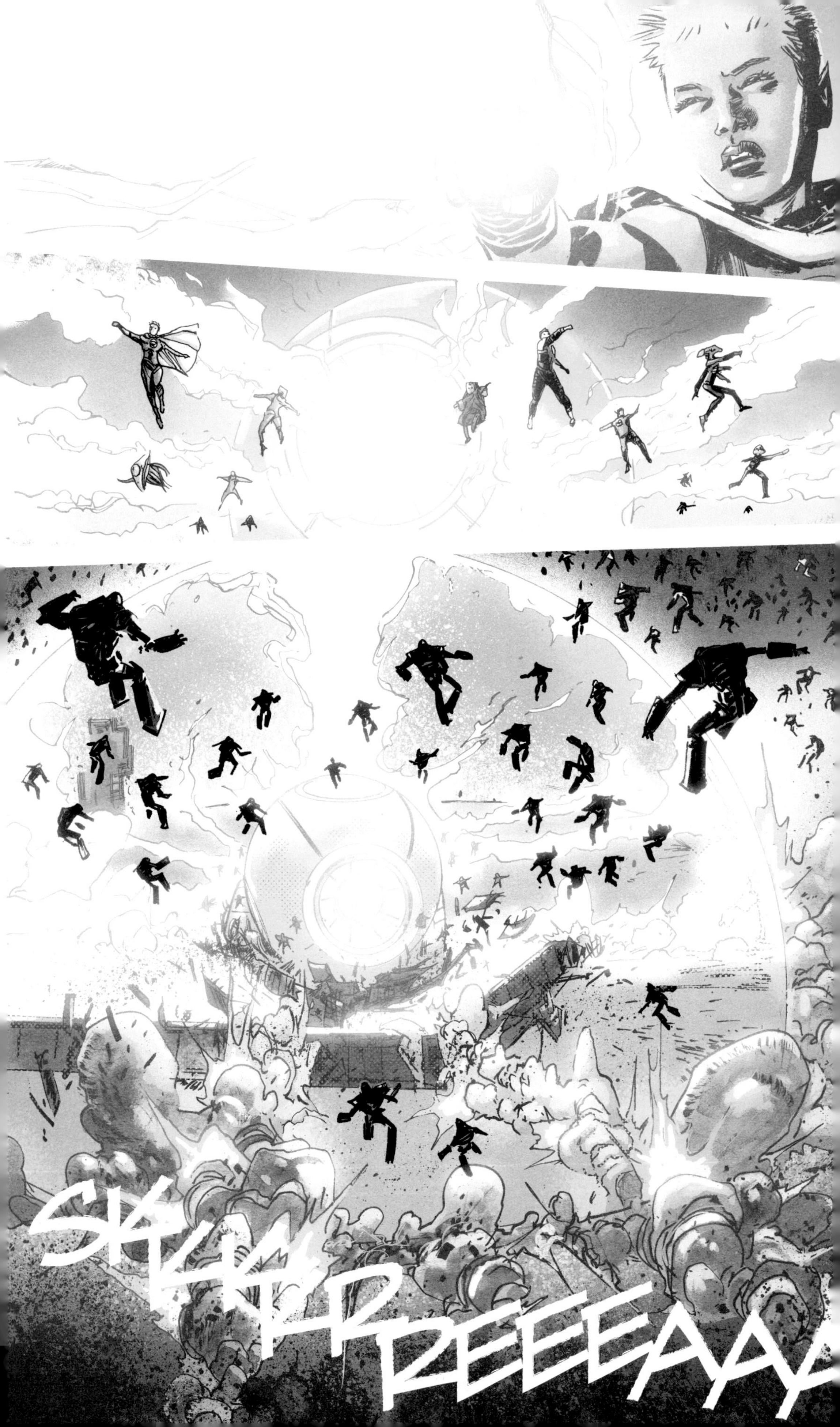
SKKKRREEEEAAY

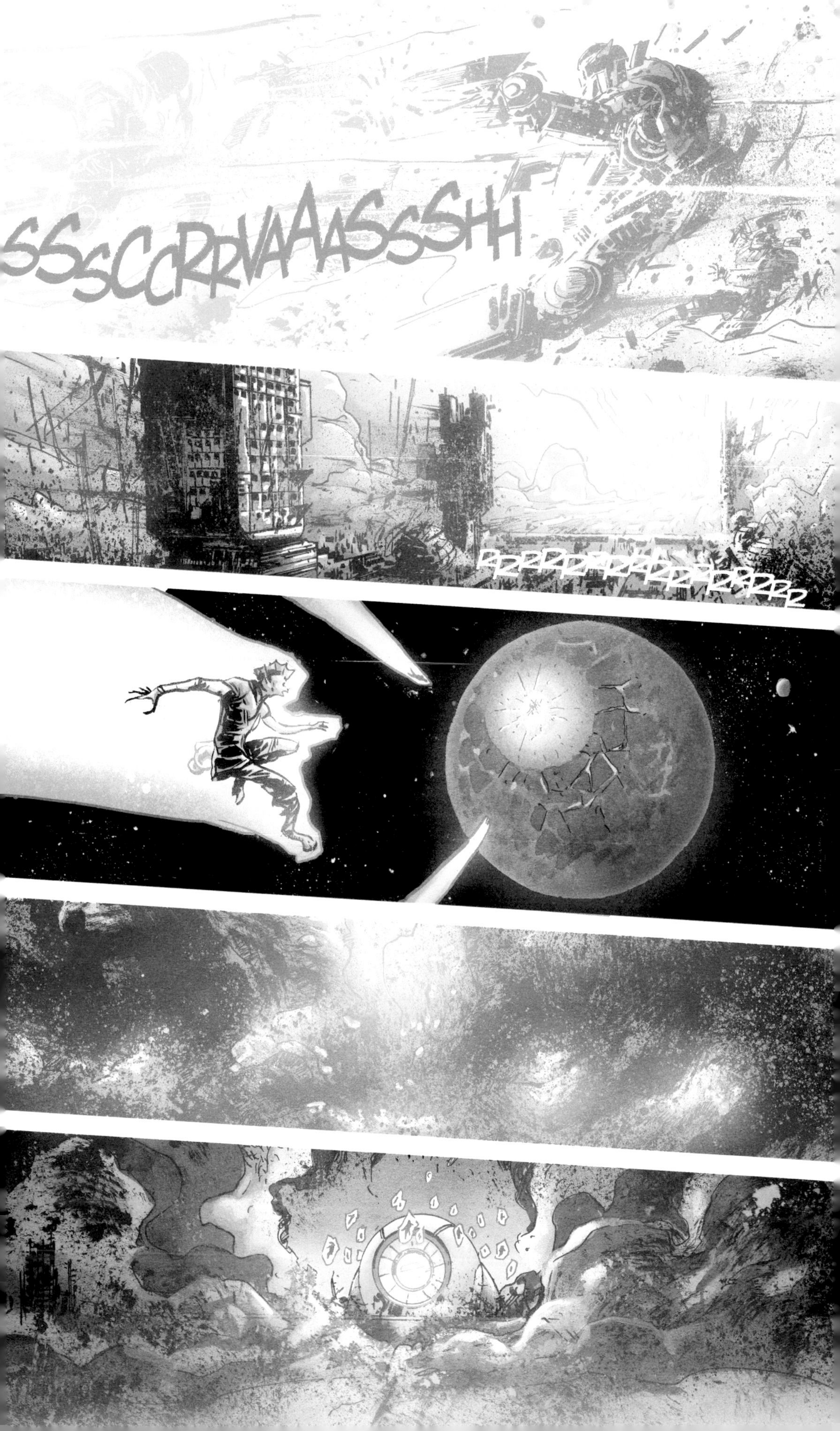
SSSCCRRVAAASSSSHH
RRRRRRRRRRRRRRRRRRRR

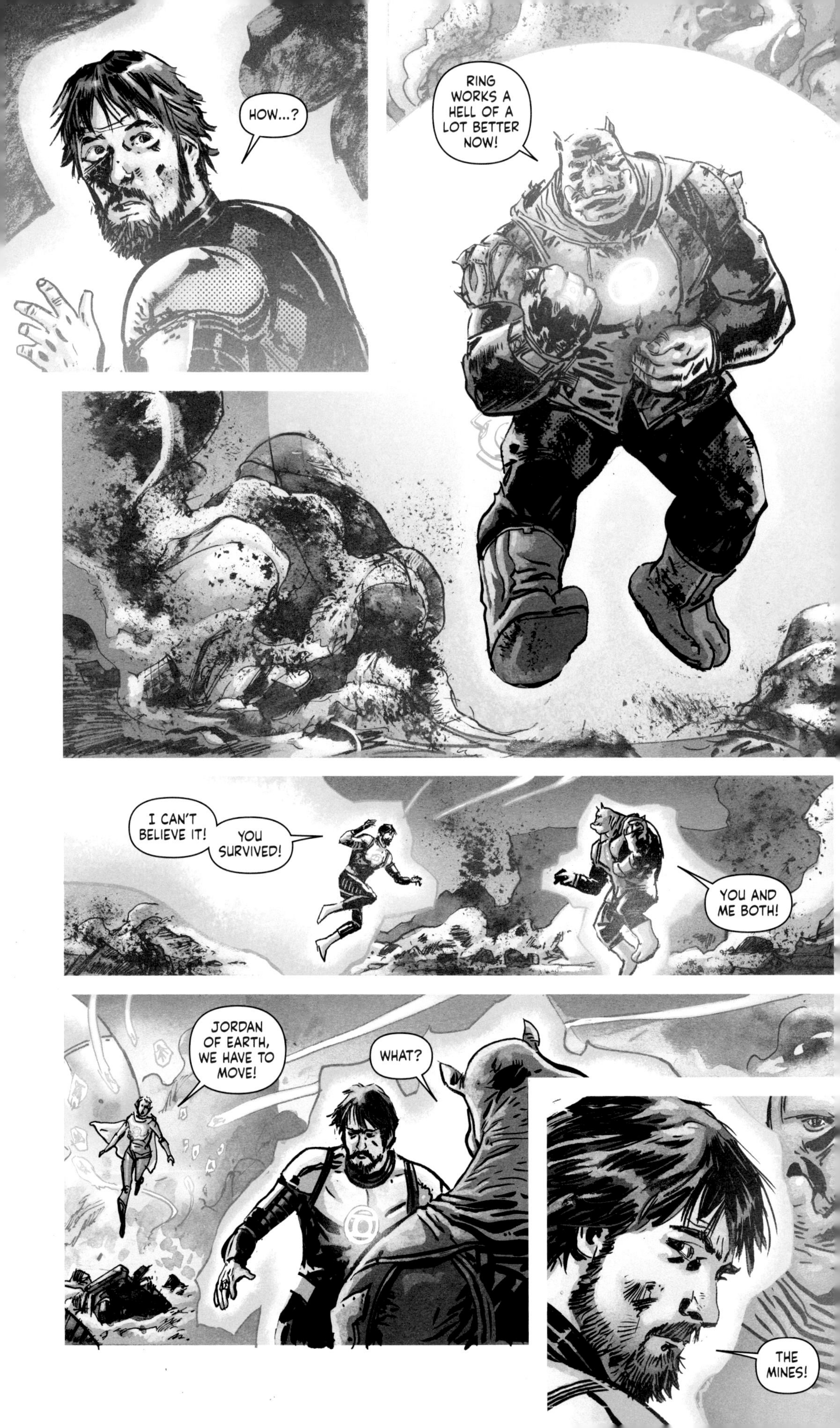
HOW...?
RING WORKS A HELL OF A LOT BETTER NOW!
I CAN'T BELIEVE IT!
YOU SURVIVED!
YOU AND ME BOTH!
JORDAN OF EARTH, WE HAVE TO MOVE!
WHAT?
THE MINES!

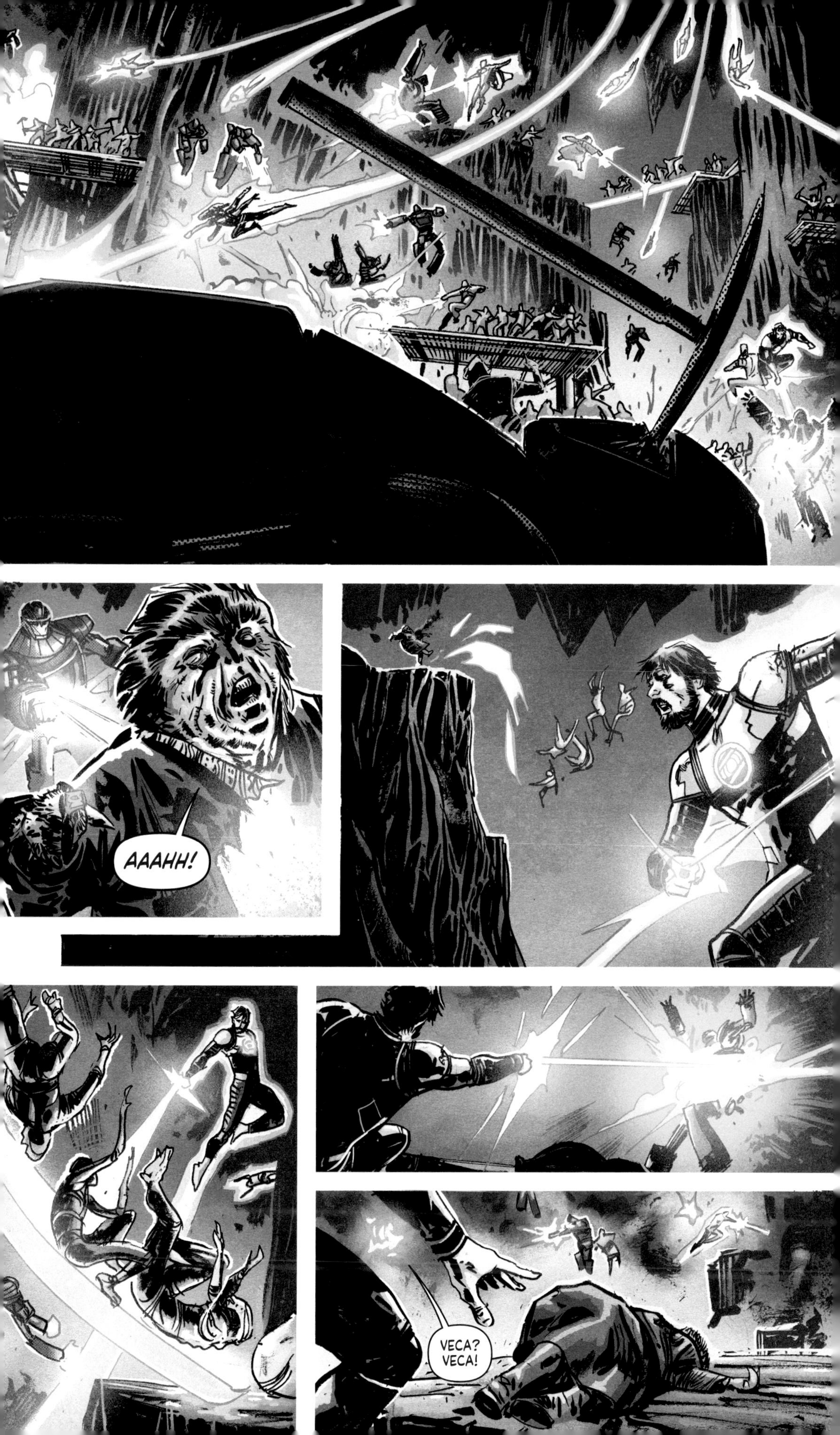
AAAHH!
VECA? VECA!

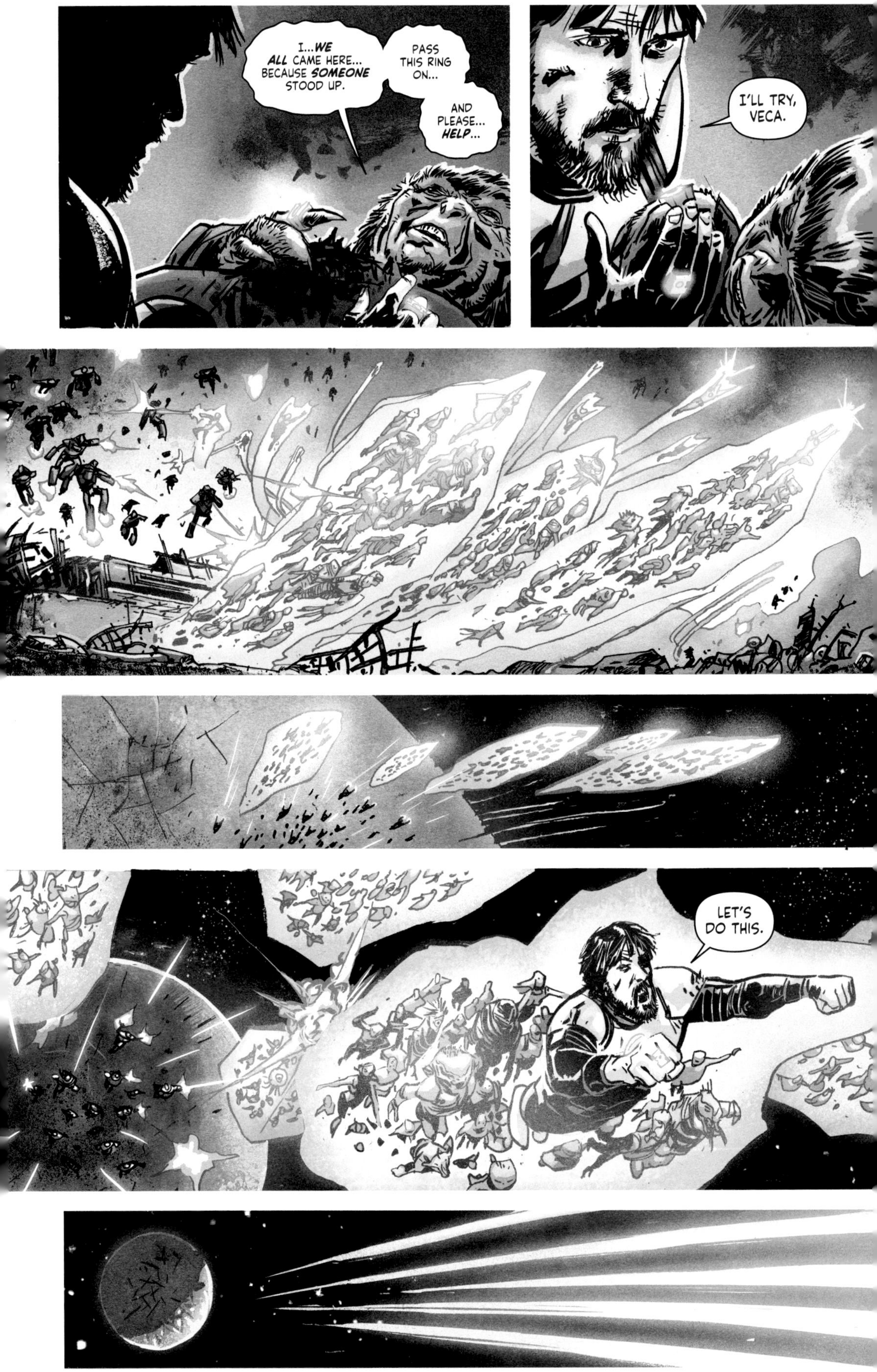
I...WE ALL CAME HERE... BECAUSE SOMEONE STOOD UP.
PASS THIS RING ON...
AND PLEASE... HELP...
I'LL TRY, VECA.
LET'S DO THIS.

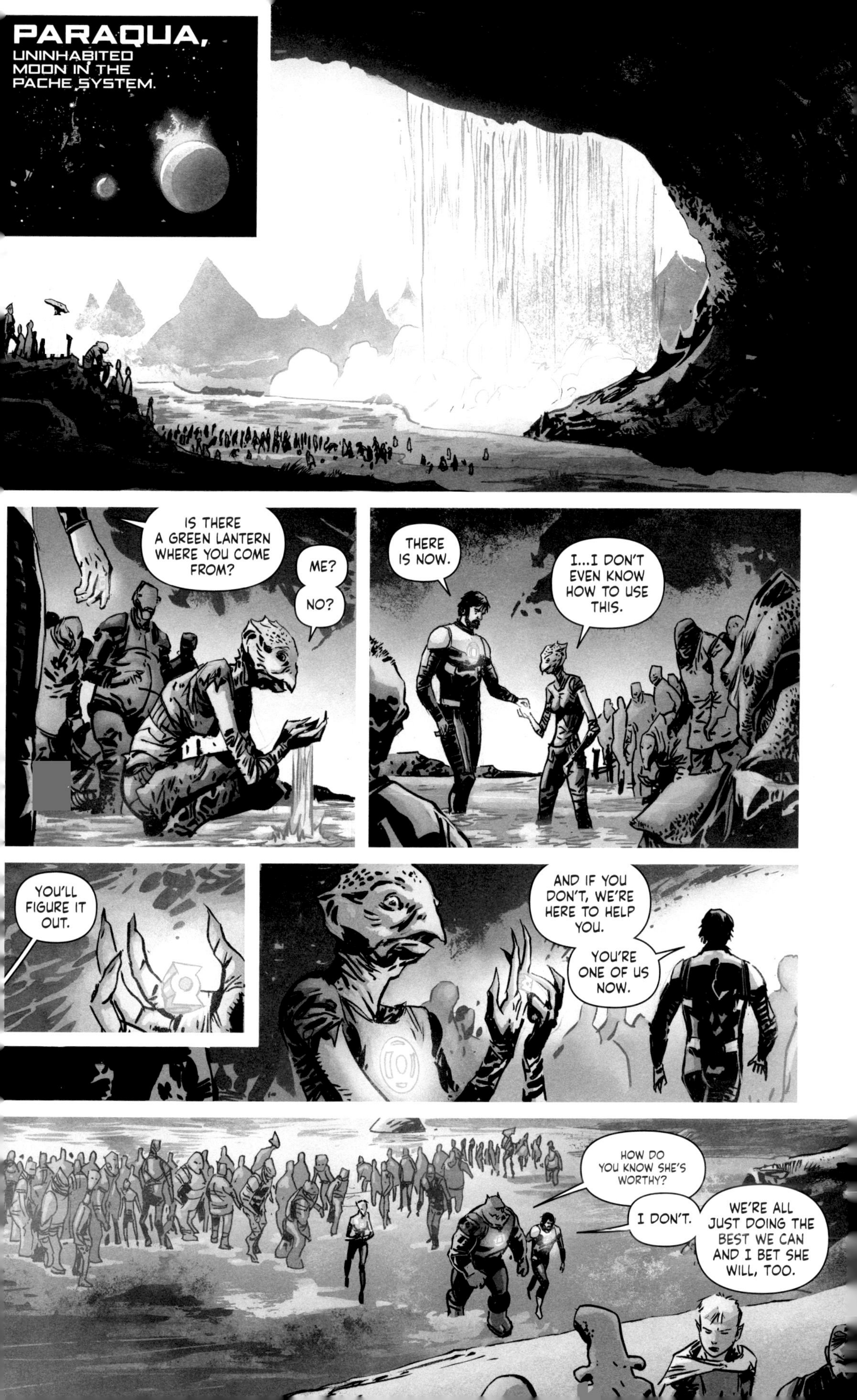
PARAQUA,
UNINHABITED MOON IN THE PACHE SYSTEM.
IS THERE A GREEN LANTERN WHERE YOU COME FROM?
ME?
NO?
THERE IS NOW.
I...I DON'T EVEN KNOW HOW TO USE THIS.
YOU'LL FIGURE IT OUT.
AND IF YOU DON'T, WE'RE HERE TO HELP YOU.
YOU'RE ONE OF US NOW.
HOW DO YOU KNOW SHE'S WORTHY?
I DON'T.
WE'RE ALL JUST DOING THE BEST WE CAN AND I BET SHE WILL, TOO.

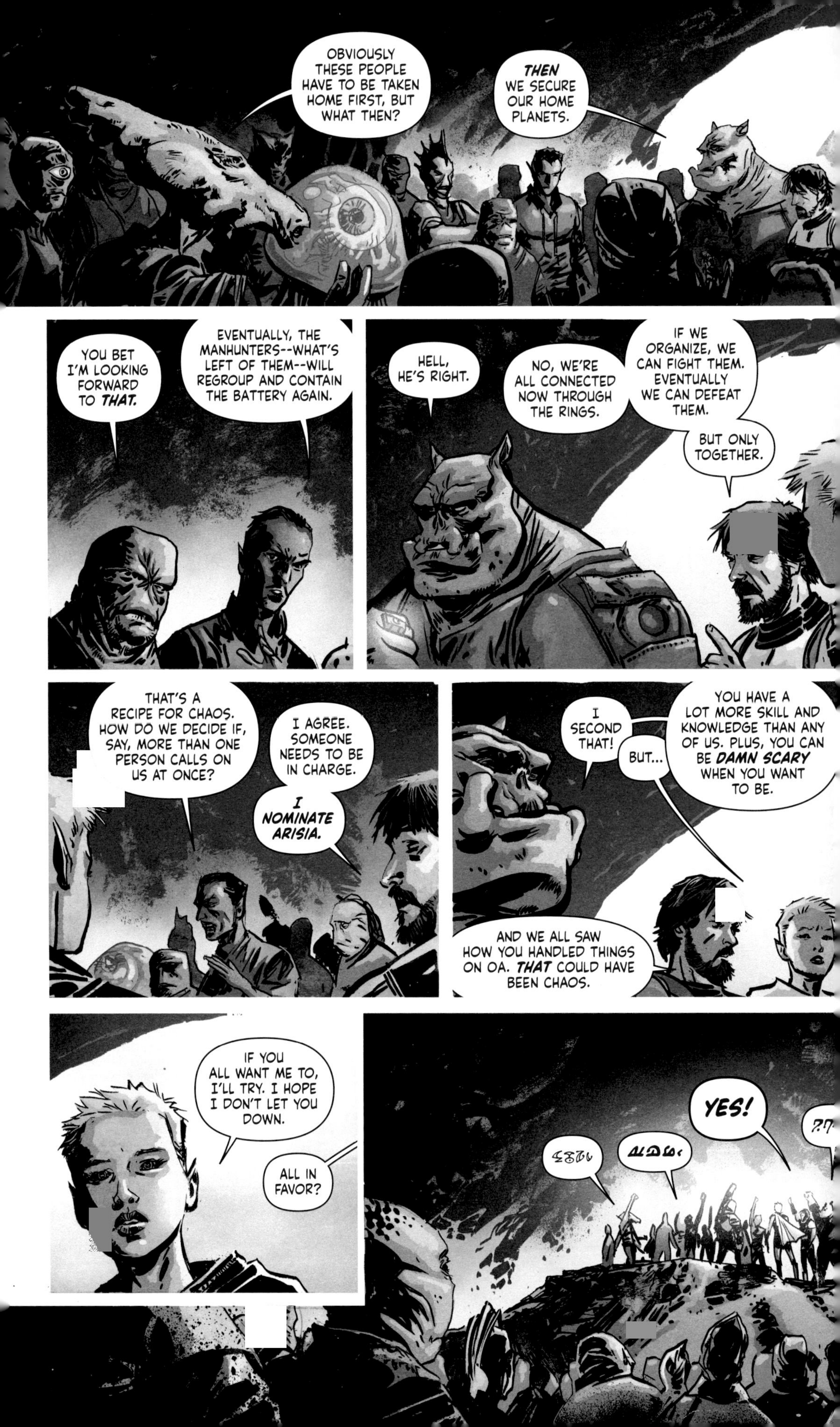
OBVIOUSLY THESE PEOPLE HAVE TO BE TAKEN HOME FIRST, BUT WHAT THEN?
THEN WE SECURE OUR HOME PLANETS.
YOU BET I'M LOOKING FORWARD TO THAT.
EVENTUALLY, THE MANHUNTERS--WHAT'S LEFT OF THEM--WILL REGROUP AND CONTAIN THE BATTERY AGAIN.
HELL, HE'S RIGHT.
NO, WE'RE ALL CONNECTED NOW THROUGH THE RINGS.
IF WE ORGANIZE, WE CAN FIGHT THEM. EVENTUALLY WE CAN DEFEAT THEM.
BUT ONLY TOGETHER.
THAT'S A RECIPE FOR CHAOS. HOW DO WE DECIDE IF, SAY, MORE THAN ONE PERSON CALLS ON US AT ONCE?
I AGREE. SOMEONE NEEDS TO BE IN CHARGE.
I NOMINATE ARISIA.
I SECOND THAT!
BUT...
YOU HAVE A LOT MORE SKILL AND KNOWLEDGE THAN ANY OF US. PLUS, YOU CAN BE DAMN SCARY WHEN YOU WANT TO BE.
AND WE ALL SAW HOW YOU HANDLED THINGS ON OA. THAT COULD HAVE BEEN CHAOS.
IF YOU ALL WANT ME TO, I'LL TRY. I HOPE I DON'T LET YOU DOWN.
ALL IN FAVOR?
YES!

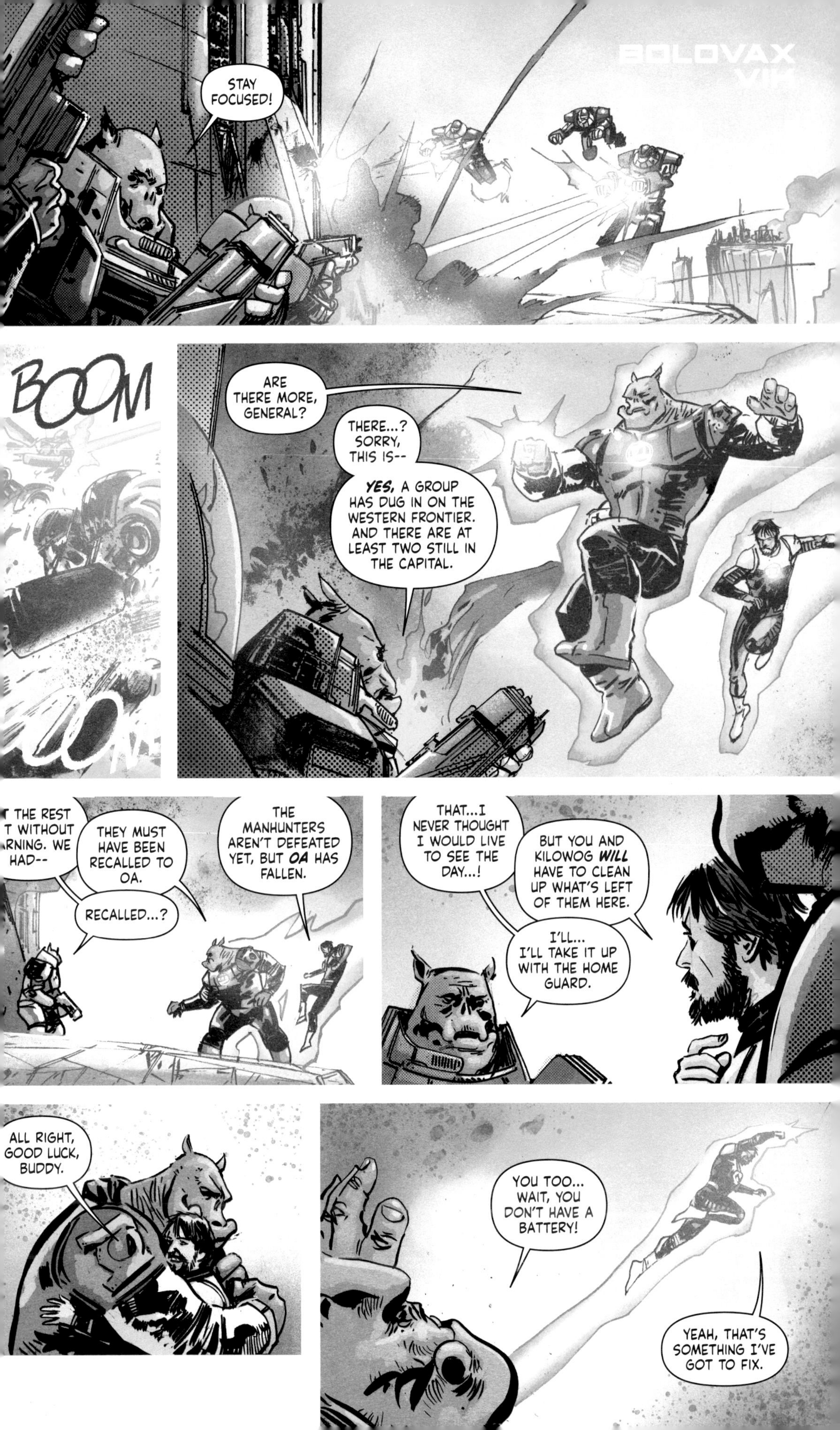
BOLOVAX VIK
STAY FOCUSED!
BOOM
ARE THERE MORE, GENERAL?
THERE...? SORRY, THIS IS--
YES, A GROUP HAS DUG IN ON THE WESTERN FRONTIER. AND THERE ARE AT LEAST TWO STILL IN THE CAPITAL.
T THE REST T WITHOUT RNING. WE HAD--
THEY MUST HAVE BEEN RECALLED TO OA.
RECALLED...?
THE MANHUNTERS AREN'T DEFEATED YET, BUT *OA* HAS FALLEN.
THAT...I NEVER THOUGHT I WOULD LIVE TO SEE THE DAY...!
BUT YOU AND KILOWOG *WILL* HAVE TO CLEAN UP WHAT'S LEFT OF THEM HERE.
I'LL... I'LL TAKE IT UP WITH THE HOME GUARD.
ALL RIGHT, GOOD LUCK, BUDDY.
YOU TOO... WAIT, YOU DON'T HAVE A BATTERY!
YEAH, THAT'S SOMETHING I'VE GOT TO FIX.

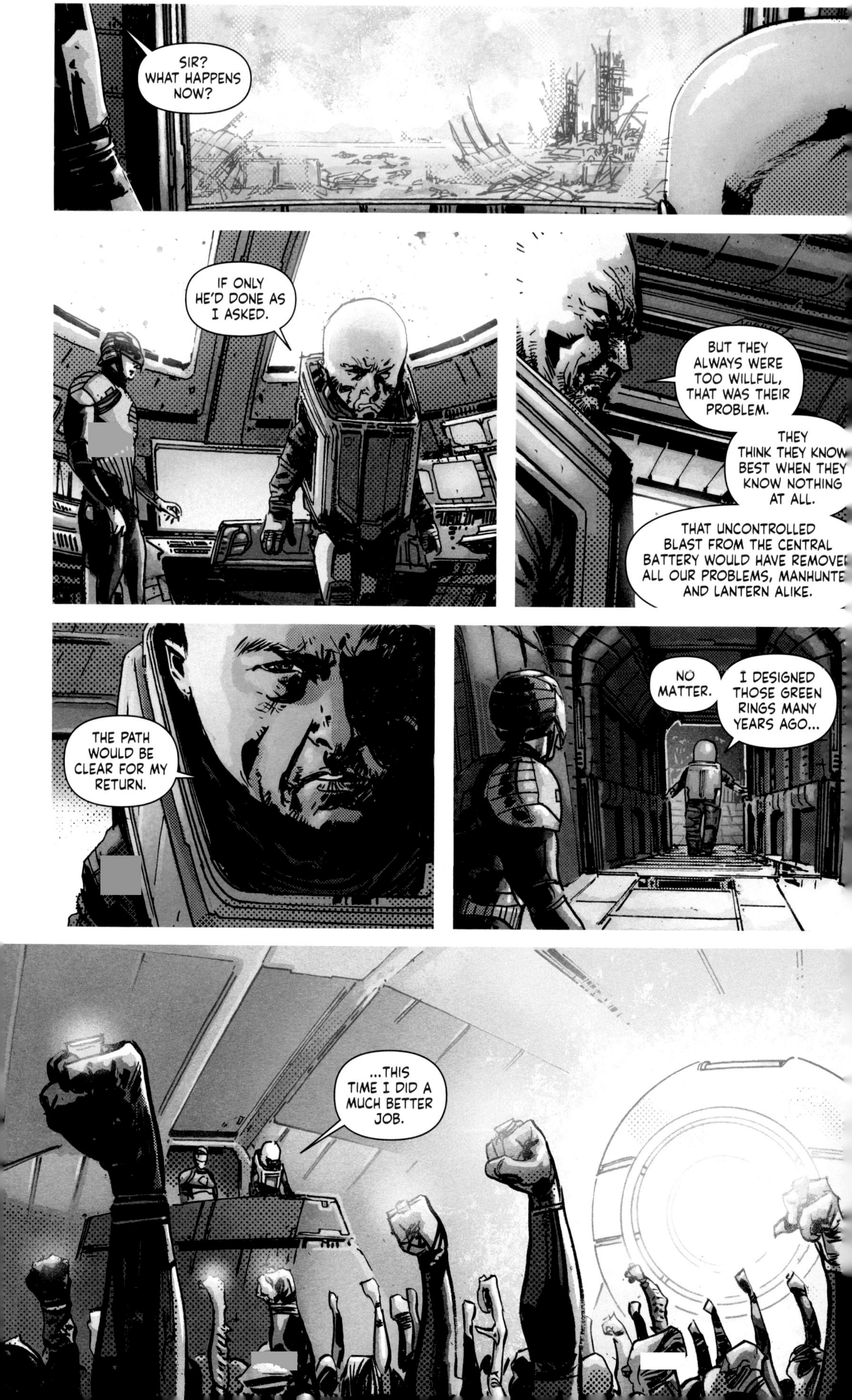
SIR? WHAT HAPPENS NOW?
IF ONLY HE'D DONE AS I ASKED.
BUT THEY ALWAYS WERE TOO WILLFUL, THAT WAS THEIR PROBLEM.
THEY THINK THEY KNOW BEST WHEN THEY KNOW NOTHING AT ALL.
THAT UNCONTROLLED BLAST FROM THE CENTRAL BATTERY WOULD HAVE REMOVE ALL OUR PROBLEMS, MANHUNTE AND LANTERN ALIKE.
THE PATH WOULD BE CLEAR FOR MY RETURN.
NO MATTER.
I DESIGNED THOSE GREEN RINGS MANY YEARS AGO...
...THIS TIME I DID A MUCH BETTER JOB.

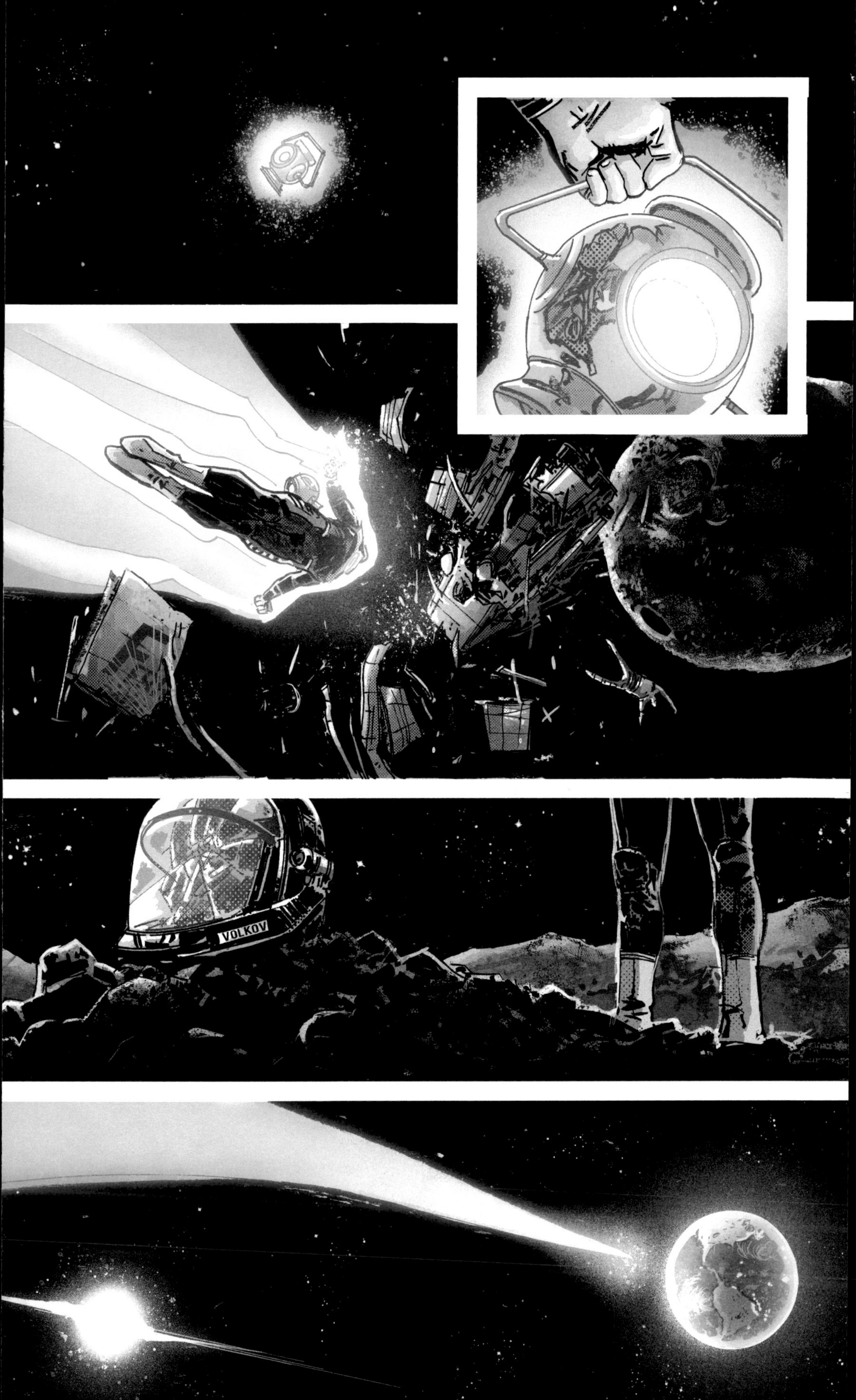
VOLKOV

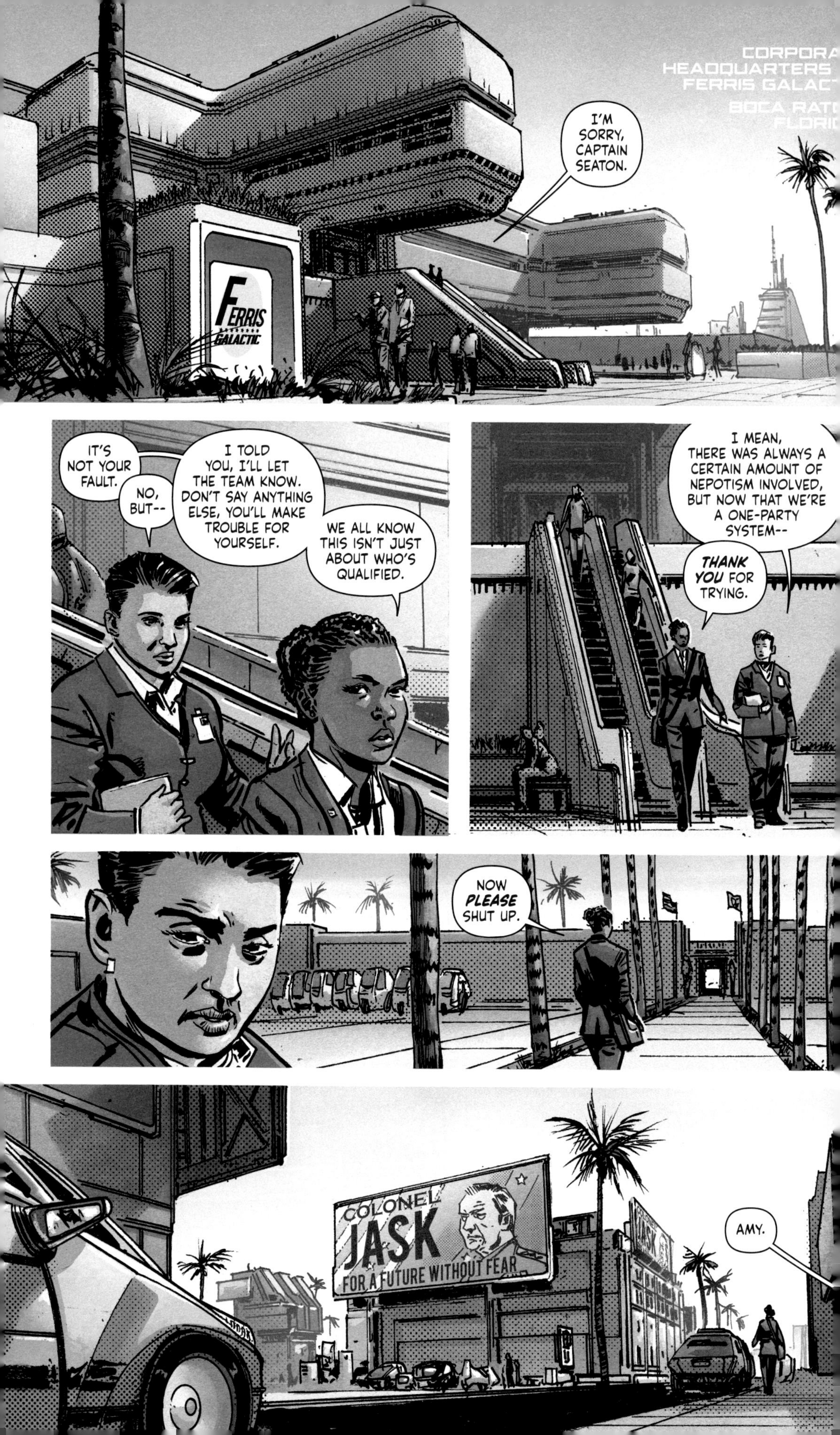
CORPORA
HEADQUARTERS
FERRIS GALAC
BOCA RAT
FLORI
I'M SORRY, CAPTAIN SEATON.
FERRIS GALACTIC
IT'S NOT YOUR FAULT.
NO, BUT--
I TOLD YOU, I'LL LET THE TEAM KNOW. DON'T SAY ANYTHING ELSE, YOU'LL MAKE TROUBLE FOR YOURSELF.
WE ALL KNOW THIS ISN'T JUST ABOUT WHO'S QUALIFIED.
I MEAN, THERE WAS ALWAYS A CERTAIN AMOUNT OF NEPOTISM INVOLVED, BUT NOW THAT WE'RE A ONE-PARTY SYSTEM--
THANK YOU FOR TRYING.
NOW *PLEASE* SHUT UP.
COLONEL JASK
FOR A FUTURE WITHOUT FEAR
JASK
AMY.

JORDAN! IS THAT REALLY YOU?

WHERE... HOW DID YOU--

IT'S... A STORY.

AMY, THERE'S MORE OUT THERE THAN WE *EVER* IMAGINED.

WELL, YOU PICKED A HELL OF A TIME TO COME BACK. OUR WHOLE TEAM IS GROUNDED. THEY ACTUALLY THREATENED TO ARREST ME!

COLONEL
JASK
FOR FUTURE WITHOUT

I'M NOT SURPRISED. LOOKS LIKE WE HAVE A LOT OF WORK TO DO HERE AT HOME.

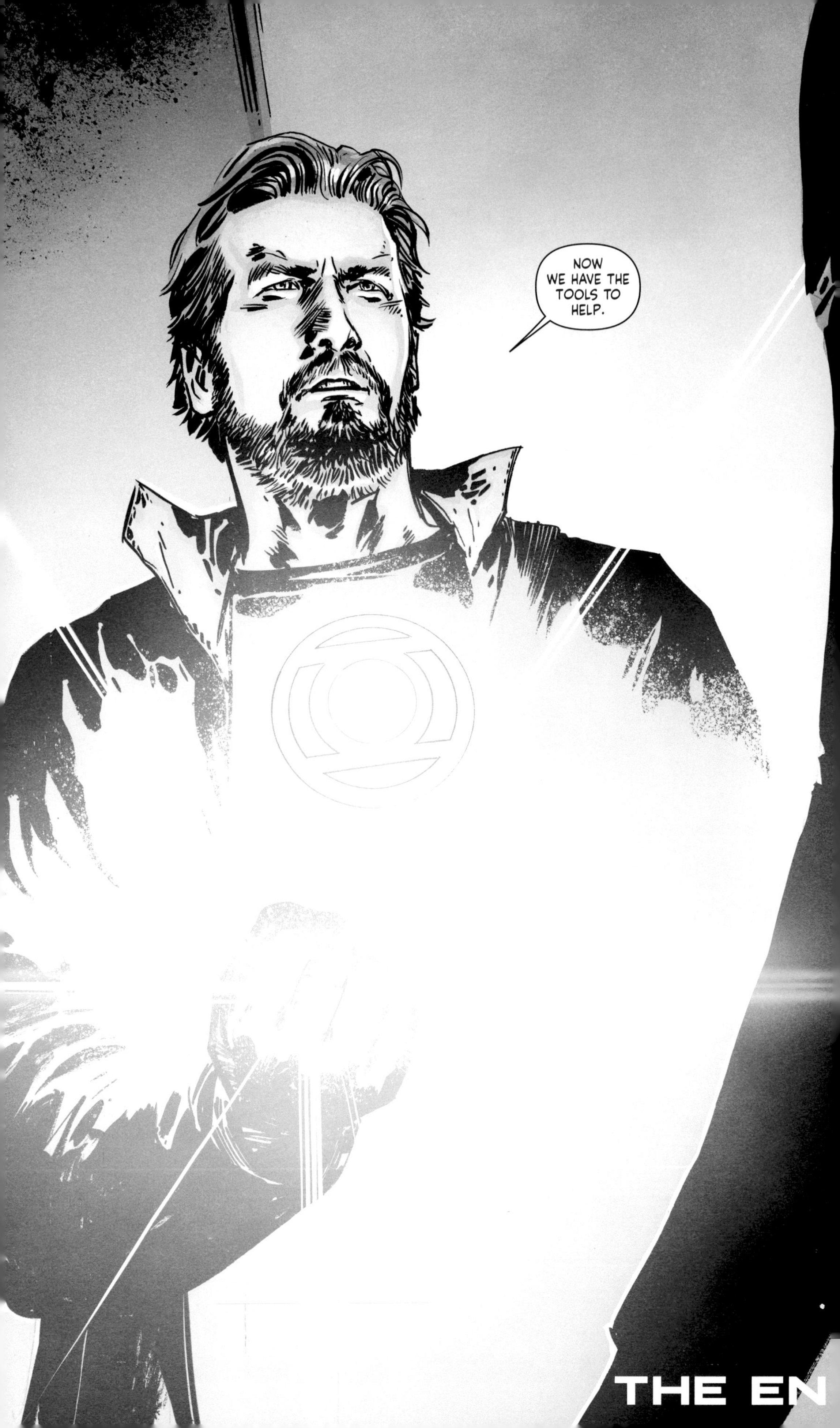
NOW WE HAVE THE TOOLS TO HELP.
THE EN

Earth One Sketchbook

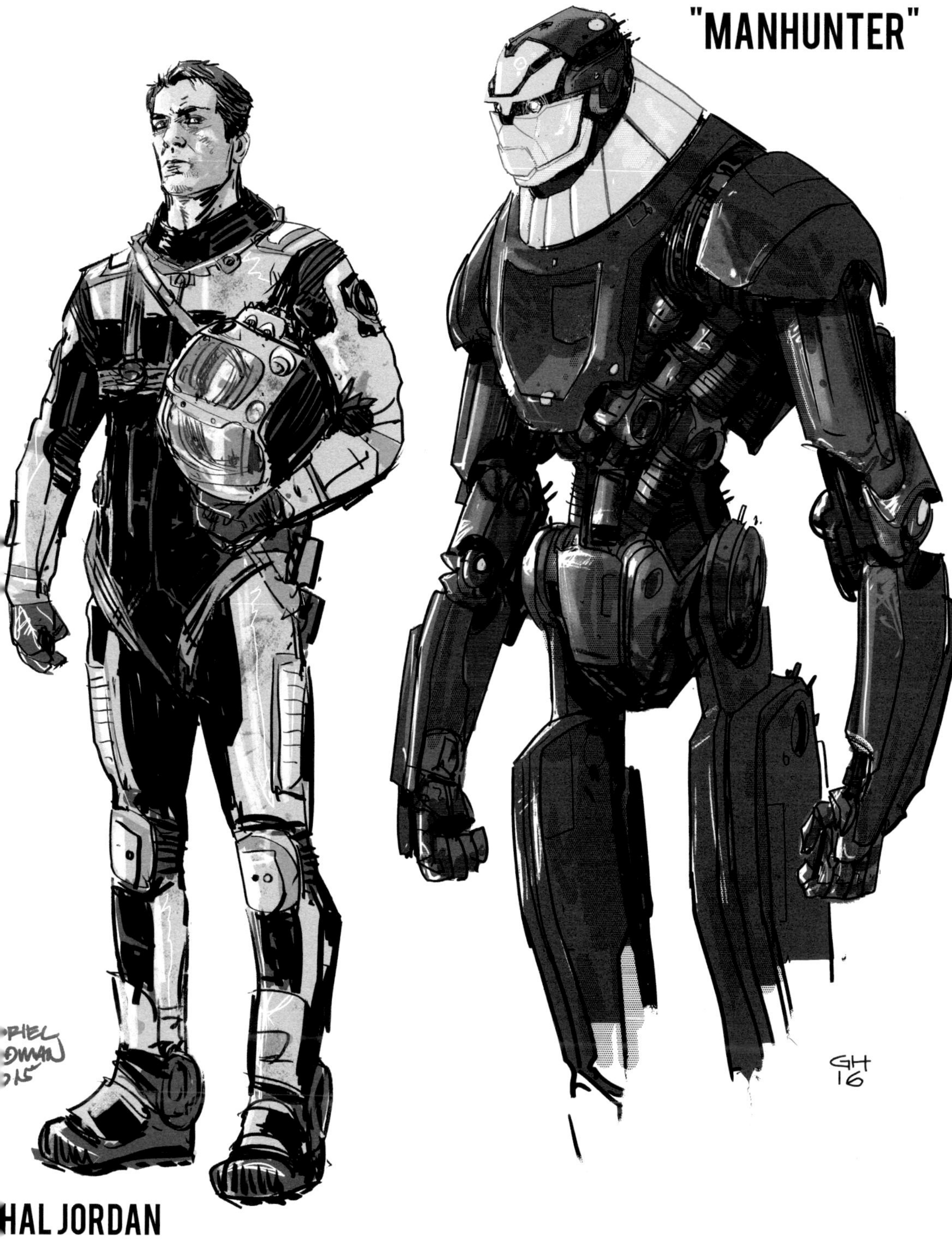
"MANHUNTER"
HAL JORDAN
GH 16

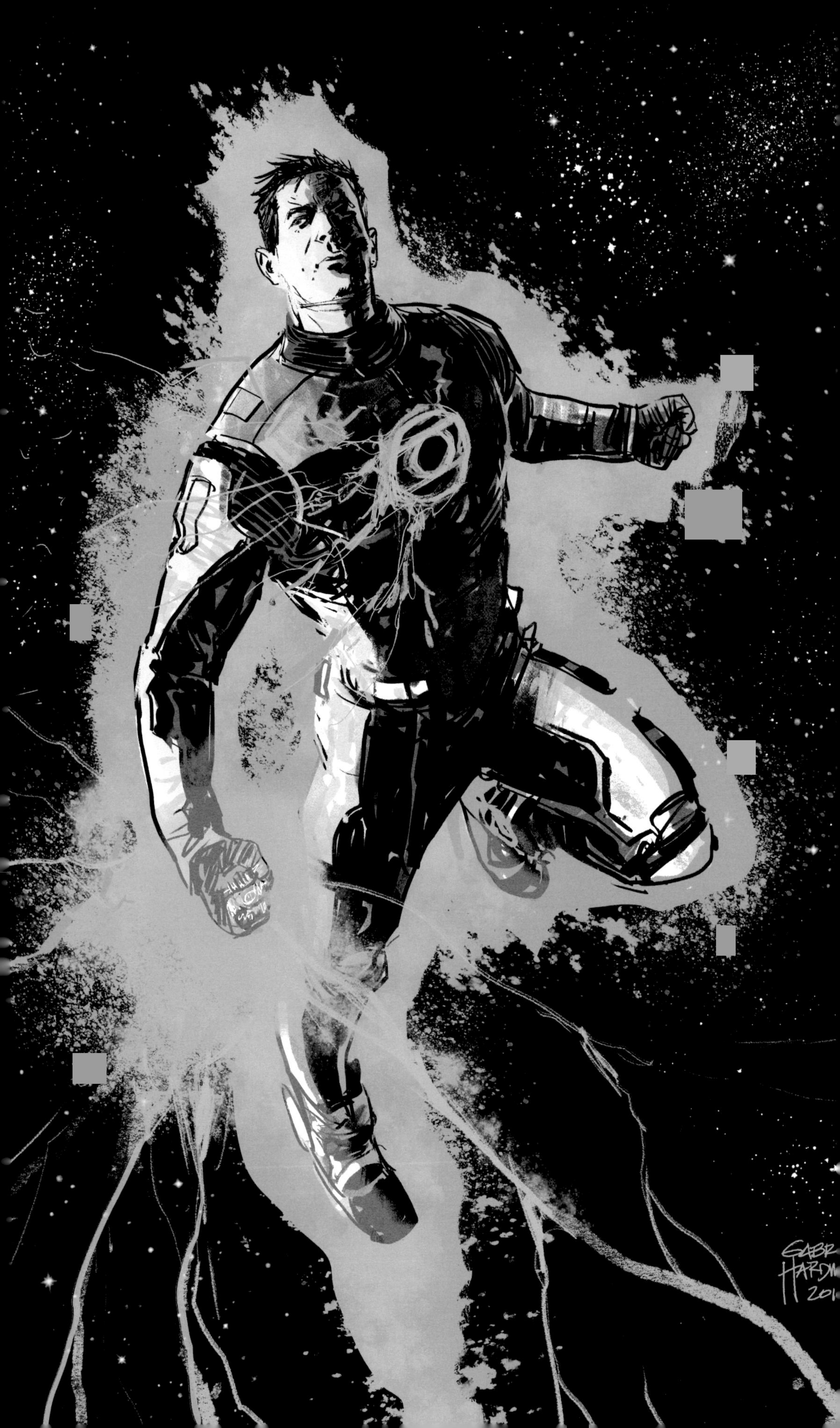

GREEN LANTERN: EARTH ONE
By Gabriel Hardman and Corinna Bechko

There is no GREEN LANTERN CORPS. Not anymore. Not since the MANHUNTERS rose up, killed their former masters, and occupied Oa 350 years ago. And this HAL JORDAN isn't chosen. He's a nobody from a remote world called Earth who finds a RING and realizes he must reinstate the Corps to live up to his, and its, potential.

Trained as an astronaut, Hal yearned for the thrill of discovery. But space exploration is now solely privately funded, so Hal took an unfulfilling job prospecting asteroids for mineral resources with FERRIS GALACTIC. At least he's not on Earth, where a state of technological and cultural stagnation holds sway – more GRAVITY than STAR TREK.

During a survey, Hal and his colleague VOLKOV find the crashed remains of Green Lantern ABIN SUR's ship. Sur's body is desiccating inside, green ring on his finger. In the corner: a DEAD MANHUNTER. Volkov confiscates the Lantern battery and ring for Ferris Galactic, accidentally ignites the ring, and rips their lander open. Hal is protected from the implosion when he ends up with the ring at the last second. But there's no instruction manual. Hal struggles to control the ring, nearly dying in space when…The MANHUNTER, recharged by exposure to sunlight, attacks! It must fulfill its original mission: kill the Green Lantern of this sector, now Hal Jordan.

Sur sacrificed himself to stop this Manhunter and Hal has undone that. Hal barely holds his own during the epic fight. They end up far beyond the Kuiper belt, Hal having defeated the malfunctioning android but exhausted, lost, and alone.

He's saved by KILOWOG, one of the few remaining Green Lanterns – his ring passed down through generations. We assume he'll be Hal's mentor now, teaching him the ways of the Corps. But Kilowog barely knows more than Hal. He just does the best he can to protect his corner of the galaxy from the brutal rule of the Manhunters.

The galaxy isn't what Hal expected. There's wonder out here, but horror and oppression too. Could there also be more LANTERNS? More depowered rings, never recharged because in occupying Oa, the Manhunters built a containment structure around the CENTRAL POWER BATTERY?

Hal convinces a small group of Lanterns to leave their home planets unguarded in a bid to destroy the structure on Oa so rings throughout the galaxy can be restored.

Battling their way across Oa to the battery, KILOWOG is KILLED just as they accomplish their task. The Manhunters are not defeated yet, but now the Corps has a small foothold. Kilowog's ring is passed on to a new bearer to defend his home planet.

Hal fulfills his own duty to the reborn Corps by returning to Earth. He will defend it from the Manhunters, who are now keenly aware of its existence, while serving as an aspirational example that the galaxy is vast and Earth must meet its challenges head on.

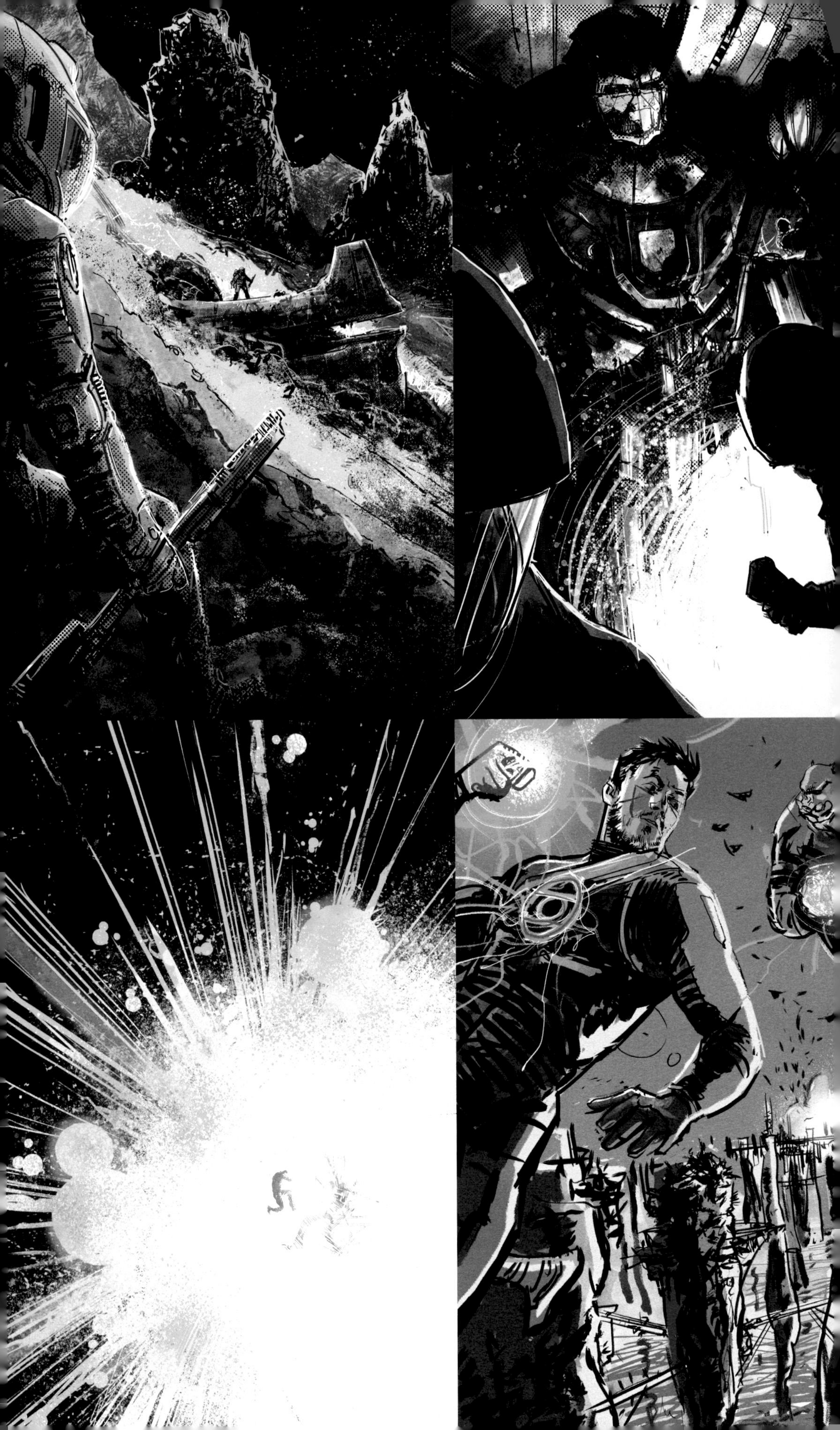

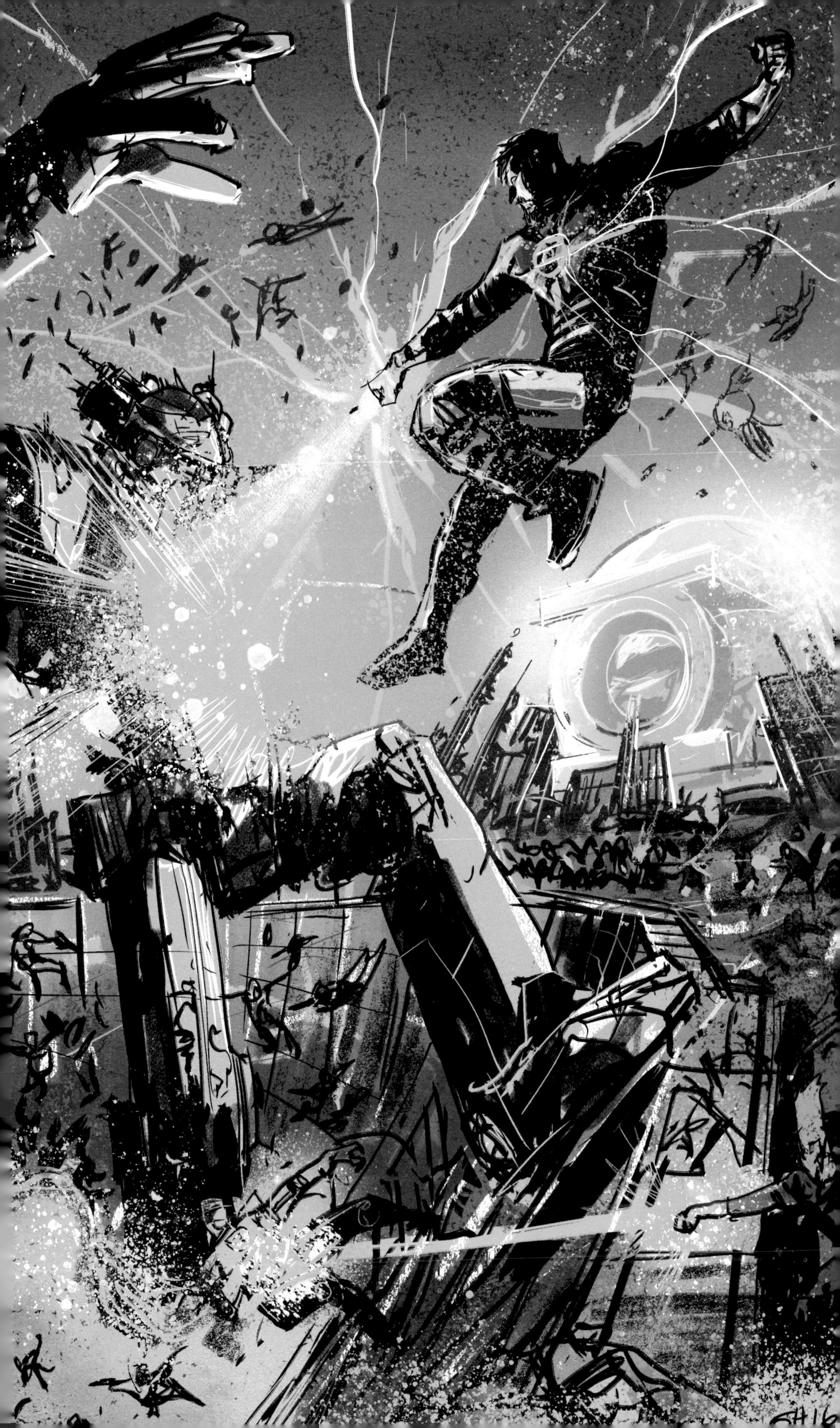

CORINNA BECHKO is a *New York Times* best-selling author who has been writing both comics and prose since her horror graphic novel *Heathentown* was published by Image/Shadowline in 2009. She has worked for numerous publishers including Marvel, DC, Dynamite, Dark Horse and Sideshow on titles such as *Star Wars: Legacy, Savage Hulk, Angel, Once Upon a Time, Court of the Dead: The Chronicle of the Underworld* and the Hugo-nominated series *Invisible Republic*, which she co-writes with Gabriel Hardman. Her background is in zoology and it usually shows. She lives in Los Angeles with her husband Gabriel Hardman and a small menagerie. She prepares fossils in her spare time.

GABRIEL HARDMAN is the co-writer and artist of the Hugo-nominated sci-fi series *Invisible Republic* as well as writer/artist of *Kinski* and *The Belfry*, published by Image Comics. He also co-wrote *Star Wars: Legacy, Planet of the Apes, Savage Hulk* and SENSATION COMICS FEATURING WONDER WOMAN with Corinna Bechko. He has drawn *Hulk, Secret Avengers* and *Agents of Atlas*, as well as the OGN *Heathentown*. Hardman is an accomplished storyboard artist, having worked on movies such as *Logan, Interstellar, Inception* and *Tropic Thunder*. He lives with his wife, writer Corinna Bechko, in Los Angeles.

JORDAN BOYD, despite nearly flunking kindergarten for his exclusive use of black crayons, has moved on to become a prolific comic book colorist. Some of his recent projects include SAVAGE THINGS (Vertigo), *Evolution* (Skybound) and *Deadly Class* (Image)